The Gardener's Guide to Growing
IRISES

The Gardener's Guide to Growing
IRISES

Geoff Stebbings

DAVID & CHARLES
Newton Abbot

TIMBER PRESS
Portland, Oregon

To my parents, Len and Pearl

ACKNOWLEDGEMENTS

I wish to thank all my friends who have helped me grow iris in the past, and especially those who have supplied photographic material for this book: Pauline Brown of V.H. Humphrey, Christine Barker of Myddleton House and Richard Brook of Zephyrwude Nursery. I would also like to thank Bob and Eileen Wise for their special help throughout the years, Jennifer Hewitt and other members of the British Iris Society.

NOTE Throughout the book the time of year is given as a season to make the reference applicable to readers all over the world. In the northern hemisphere the seasons may be translated into months as follows:

Early winter	December	*Early spring*	March	*Early summer*	June	*Early autumn*	September
Midwinter	January	*Mid-spring*	April	*Midsummer*	July	*Mid-autumn*	October
Late winter	February	*Late spring*	May	*Late summer*	August	*Late autumn*	November

Illustrations on pages 10, 12 and 14 by Coral Mula

Copyright © Geoff Stebbings 1997
First published 1997

Geoff Stebbings has asserted his right to be identified as author of this work in accordance with the Copyright, Designs and Patents Acts 1988.

First published in the UK in 1997 by David & Charles Publishers,
Brunel House, Newton Abbot, Devon
ISBN 0 7153 0229 9

First published in North America in 1997 by Timber Press Inc.,
133 SW Second Avenue, Suite 450, Portland, Oregon 97204, USA
ISBN 0-88192-388-5
Cataloguing-in-Publication Data is on file with the Library of Congress

Printed in Italy by Lego SpA

Photographs: page 1 *Iris* 'Sultan's Sash'; page 2 *Iris* 'Protégé'; page 3 *Iris* 'Harpswell Happiness'

CONTENTS

INTRODUCTION

There is no other familiar garden plant that can match the poise, form and colouring of the iris, and for centuries these plants have been cultivated, used for perfume and for their symbolic and decorative value. They are exclusively plants from the northern hemisphere, where they are found wild in most temperate countries. They grow in almost every habitat from the edge of streams, or even in water in the case of *I. pseudacorus*, to the driest deserts of the Middle East. The flowers may be small, white and held aloft in clouds on tall leafy stems, as in *I. confusa*, which would not even be recognized as a member of the genus by most gardeners, or be the typical iris of the herbaceous border. Throughout its geographical range the plant body has adapted to its environment, being sometimes bulbous or rhizomatous, at other times fleshy. Some species survive below ground for the more difficult months of the year, while others are evergreen.

To refer to iris as though they had a single form is an oversimplification that many gardeners seem to make. Reasons such as 'They have such a short season', 'I would love to grow them but I haven't got a pond' or 'I don't like purple flowers, they remind me of funerals' are offered for rejecting one of the most diverse and beautiful groups of plants we can grow in our gardens.

Iris are also in a state of flux, with new hybrids continually being introduced. Earlier plants are soon superseded, and in this book I have tended to recommend either those older hybrids that are likely to remain with us for some time to come or newer plants that show significant improvements. Otherwise I have

concentrated on colour patterns and general descriptions, leaving the reader to choose from the most recent catalogues. In common with any plant group, the newest cultivars are available from specialist nurseries that should be supported for their hard work at hybridizing and for their introductions of new cultivars from around the world. These nurseries also support iris societies through which much of the most important work in promoting and improving the iris has taken place.

THE EARLY HISTORY OF THE IRIS

The iris has a long and noble history. The name itself is derived from the ancient Greek name for the messenger of the god Hera. Iris brought messages from Hera to earth via the rainbow, and the flowers in this genus do indeed encompass all the colours of the rainbow.

The earliest iris to have been cultivated may have been Oncocyclus species, such as *I. susiana*, as long ago as 7000BC. Later the Persian Empire, in what is now Iraq, Israel, Jordan and Syria, had a culture based on agriculture and the local iris species may have been collected. Certainly an iris is illustrated in a hieroglyph carved in 1500BC, during the reign of Thotmes III, listing medicinal plants. This was without doubt one of the Oncocyclus iris, characterized by their extraordinary, beautiful flowers, which are so difficult to grow in Britain. The Palace of Knossos on Crete contains a painting of similar date that shows a prince wandering through a field of waist-high iris, possibly *I. xiphium*.

The Greek philosopher Theophrastus described an iris that is probably *I. pallida*, and commented on its use in perfume, an early reference to orris root, derived from the rhizomes of some bearded iris species and still in use today. Hundreds of years later, Dioscorides gave a more

Spuria iris like 'Russian White' are the giants of the iris world, with flowers on chest-high stalks.

full description of the iris' virtues in his *Vienna Codex*. These included the removal of freckles, the healing of ulcers and the promotion of sleep.

The symbolic representation of the iris is firmly linked with France. The fleur-de-lis or fleur-de-lys is as French as the tricolor (the iris also has a trinity of parts). It is likely that 'lis' does not refer to lily, but to Lys (a river), Louis (a king), or *luce* (meaning light, in reference either to its shining flower, or a torch or symbol held high). The fleur-de-lis is a stylized flower of *I. pseudacorus*, the yellow iris that is common in damp ground throughout Europe.

Several legends attempt to explain its association with France. One is that in the twelfth century Louis VII was attempting to escape his enemies and, searching for a place to cross the River Lys in Flanders, noticed a deer cross where there were clumps of *I. pseudacorus*. Knowing that the water there must be shallow, he and his army escaped and he picked the flower and held it aloft as a symbol. Therefore the 'lys' could either be from 'Louis' or the river itself. An alternative tale is that as he was setting out for the Crusades he awoke one morning to find his white banner decorated with three purple fleur-de-lys. Considering this a good omen, he took it as his emblem and his men called it the fleur-de-Louis. It even appeared on English coats of arms, being adopted by Edward III after his French conquests and only disappearing in 1801.

In Britain, *I. pseudacorus* was much used in herbalism and the Elizabethan herbalist John Gerard knew that there were many other species: 'Some have tuberous or knobbly roots, others bulbous or Onion roots; some have leaves like flags, others like grass or rushes.' In *A Modern Herbal*, Mrs M. Grieve writes that 'The acrid juice snuffed up the nostrils excites violent sneezing' and it was much used to clear head complaints, but the juice of the rhizome is acrid and is not a safe home remedy. The sombre colouring of the other British native, *I. foetidissima*, led to association with evil creatures but it was also used for dye, the flowers providing a yellow colour and the iron sulphate in the roots giving black.

Orris root from *I. pallida* (and to a lesser extent *I. florentina* and *I. germanica*) has been widely used as a fragrance, and also as a powder for the skin and for wigs. In Japan the rhizomes of *I. tectorum* produced a similar powder used to whiten the face, and when land was in short supply and the cultivation of ornamental plants

was forbidden it was planted on roofs, hence its name 'roof iris'. Small chips of orris root were chewed to freshen the breath, and were also used to keep wounds open so that they would heal slowly. The Romans flavoured their wines with orris and threw it on fires to create a pleasant aroma. Rosaries often carried beads carved out of orris root which were used either on their own or to accompany beads made out of rose petals, from which the word rosary derives.

The Native Americans used fibres from the leaves of *I. tenax* to make ropes, a function fulfilled by *I. spuria* in Europe, and *I. versicolor*, the New World equivalent of *I. pseudacorus*, was used for the iridin in the rhizome, which is diuretic and causes nausea as well as being a remedy for skin infections and syphilis.

Because of the architectural shape of the iris flower, it has long been used in art and as an inspiration for decorative motifs. Perhaps the earliest depiction is in *Adorrazione* by Hugo van der Goes (1435–1482), which shows a collection of *I. florentina* and *I. germanica* with a lily. Later, Leonardo da Vinci included iris in *The Madonna of the Rocks*. From ancient Japanese and Persian art through painters-turned-gardeners such as William Caparne to William Morris, and generations of fabric and wallpaper designers after him, the iris flower has provided the inspiration for some impressive works of art. In India, the Taj Mahal has iris (*I. susiana*) carved into its stone and at Scotland's Glasgow Garden Festival in 1988 three giant steel iris appeared as street architecture, confirming the plant's popularity as a recurring motif.

THE IRIS TODAY

The number of iris species in general cultivation today is surprisingly small and many are known only by photographs or herbarium specimens. It would be wrong to ignore these, because in a decade they may be relatively common, but it would be misleading to treat them as though they could be bought at any local nursery. For details of the rarest iris, I refer the reader to Brian Mathew's excellent monograph *The Iris* (Batsford, 1989). No book can possibly be comprehensive and this one is intended to be accessible to beginners and useful to more experienced growers. It touches on most aspects of the genus *Iris* and it is my wish that it will encourage more gardeners to grow more of these beautiful flowers.

PLATE I

I. 'Honeycomb'
Intermediate Bearded

I. 'Superstition'
Tall Bearded

I. 'Cardinal'
Tall Bearded

I. 'Meter White'
Tall Bearded

I. 'Argus Pheasant'
Tall Bearded

I. 'Brown Lasso'
Border Bearded

I. 'Arctic Fancy'
Intermediate Bearded

All plants shown at approximately ⅓ size

1

CLASSIFICATION & BOTANY

Even in a book intended for practical gardeners a certain amount of technical explanation is required for the reader to understand and appreciate the different plants in a genus such as *Iris*. To some extent this is the most important chapter in this book because it puts the plants described in other chapters into context and where plants have botanical affinities other, often cultural, similarities can be assumed.

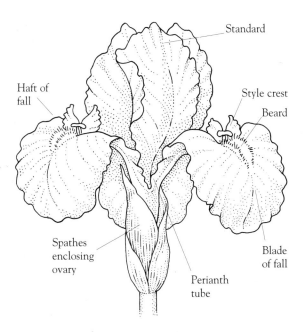

Fig 1 The flower of the bearded species shows most of the iris characteristics quite clearly and has an extra one – the beard on the falls.

Standard

Haft of
fall

Style crest

Beard

Spathes
enclosing
ovary

Blade
of fall

Perianth
tube

Iris is a genus within the plant family *Iridaceae*. This family of 92 genera contains 1800 species (of which *Iris* contains about 200, all from the northern hemisphere) and is characterized by the structure of the flowers.

FLOWER STRUCTURE

The flowers have three outer petals, three inner petals and three stamens (the male, pollen-bearing organs). Because the outer petals protect the inner petals when the flower is in bud, as sepals do in other flowers, but are highly colourful, they are commonly referred to as 'tepals', a word used to refer to both the inner and outer petals of many flowers, particularly in the lily, iris and daffodil families.

The ovary, which will become the seed pod, is positioned outside the flower and can be seen even when the flower is closed, unlike a lily or tulip where the ovary is inside the flower. The style (connecting the ovary to the receptive stigma) is three-lobed, and often enlarged or even petaloid (resembling petals). This basic flower structure occurs in all the flowers in cultivation in the *Iridaceae*, albeit twisted and pulled into a variety of shapes in their efforts to adapt to different pollinators.

The flower sits above the ovary, which is usually divided into three cavities. The six tepals are often fused together at the base into a tube separating the ovary from the rest of the flower. In some iris, for example *I. unguicularis* and the bearded *I. pumila*, this perianth tube acts as the 'stem' which holds the flower above ground. The three outer tepals, which are partially visible when the flower is in bud, are usually the largest, and bend back on themselves so that they often hang downwards. These are called 'falls'. They nearly always have a distinctive marking in their centre, which can be a splash of colour, a furry beard or ridges, all of which help to direct insects to the pollen.

The three inner tepals, called the standards, usually stand erect in the centre of the flower. They can be horizontal (*I. tectorum*), drooping (*I. bucharica*) or even reduced to tiny spikes (*I. danfordiae*). What makes the genus so distinctive are the other three 'petals', often unnoticed because they are almost hidden within the centre of the flower, which spring from the inside of the flower and spread out over the top of the falls. In fact these are not really tepals at all; they originate on the top of the ovary and are modified styles, in this case called style arms. In some species and hybrids they form an important and colourful part of the flower, especially if the two upper lobes that stand upright above the fall are enlarged and colourful. At the base of these, in just the right place to catch the pollen from the back of a pollinating insect as it crawls into the depth of the flower, is the stigma lip, which folds back as the insect explores to reveal its receptive surface. The pollen is held on an anther under each style arm, and is deposited as the insect reverses out. The stigma lip is pushed closed by such action, helping to prevent self-pollination.

In most common garden iris it is the falls that show the most variation and modification, and among the bearded iris they are most important because of their size and beauty. The lower part of the fall (that nearest the centre of the flower) is often a different colour from the rest, and frequently striped. These markings on the 'haft' can add to the beauty of the flower, or, as is more common in modern hybrids, they are seen as a defect. The falls may be enlarged, very droopy, or almost horizontal. They may be the same colour as the standards, a contrast or a blend, and may be ruffled or edged with small prickles (called lace). The beard itself can be of contrasting colour or even modified into spiky or rounded petals (horns and spoons).

BRACTS AND PODS

The flowerbuds are protected by bracts, from which the flowers emerge. These may be leaf-like, or quite dry and papery. They are sometimes important in distinguishing between species but are rarely large or showy enough to affect garden display.

The dwarf bulbous iris 'Cantab', raised by E. A. Bowles, is named after the Cambridge blue of its flower.

Once the flower has been pollinated and the potential seeds fertilized, the seed pod develops. These vary in shape, and are roughly oval in bearded iris, and rounded in cross section. They are long and narrow in Dutch iris, and may have a pronounced 'beak' at the end as in the spuria iris. The seeds themselves may be quite flat, where they are packed in three series in the pod, or rounded. Some have a fleshy appendage (aril) that attracts ants which carry the seeds away (Oncocyclus and Regelia sections). *I. foetidissima* is the one species to have brightly coloured seeds.

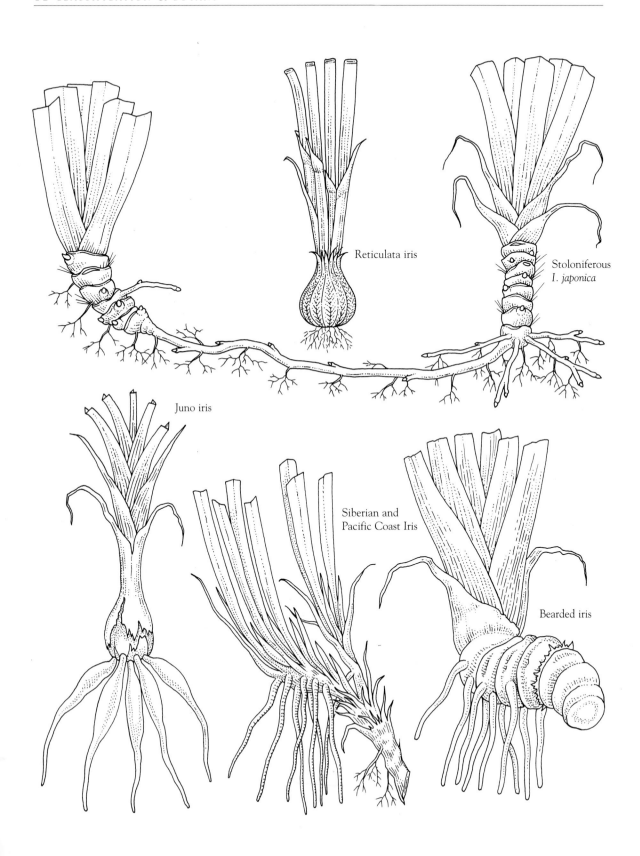

Reticulata iris

Stoloniferous
I. *japonica*

Juno iris

Siberian and
Pacific Coast Iris

Bearded iris

THE PLANT BODY

Iris plants are very varied but the hybrid bearded iris, which is most familiar, will serve as the norm. This type of iris has a creeping stem (rhizome) that forms roots on its underside. The leaves are produced alternately, facing upwards, and the flowers are held on a vertical stem at the end of each rhizome that reaches anything from a few centimetres to over a metre (3¼ft) in height. Once the stem has flowered the rhizome ceases to grow but two growth buds in the leaf axils, just behind the flower stem, become active and replace the one original stem.

Thus the horizontal stems (rhizomes) of traditional bearded iris are really quite long, while bulbous species such as *I. reticulata* have only a tiny piece of stem (rhizome) beneath the bulb – although the flower stems of Dutch iris may be 50cm (20in) or more in height. Other iris have short creeping stems but as these are under the ground and not fleshy they are less obvious. A few unusual iris do have tall vertical growth stems that are above soil level. *I. confusa*, the best known of these, produces fans of leaves on tall growth stems as well as basal fans on a well-grown plant. Often these leaf fans become too heavy, flop over and produce roots, and this may be an effective method of spread in the wild.

The roots of iris also vary considerably, but are usually unseen. Those of Pacific Coast Iris (*I. innominata* and related species) are thin and wiry, while those of the Junos (*I. bucharica*, for example) are thick and fleshy. Bulbs, which are modified leaves rather than roots, are underground organs which store food for the plant in times when conditions for growth are not suitable, and those iris from climates where there is frequently a dry summer period have bulbs, thick rhizomes or modified roots. Those from more equable climates have thinner roots and rhizomes, though the leaves may disappear below ground in winter to escape cold damage.

LEAVES

Iris leaves show almost as much variation as the flowers. All are generally 'grassy' – long and narrow – but they may be flat in cross-section (bearded iris), square (*I. reticulata*), or channelled and curved, clasping the

Fig 2 The iris plant itself can be a small bulb, a thick horizontal rhizome, a thin tough wiry stem, or almost anything in between.

flower scape (*I. bucharica*). They are in many shades of green and may be stiffly upright or spreading, in some cases enhancing the flowers. In general, iris foliage is not as important as the flowers from a gardener's point of view, but it contributes much more to the look of a border than that of other garden plants such as alliums, dahlias and colchicums. However, bulbous species may present a minor problem in the border when they die down in late spring, as the foliage of *I. reticulata* and its relatives can be less appealing than the flowers for the several months needed to nourish the bulbs for next year's display.

CLASSIFICATION

Any classification system is open to question and to change because it is an artificial structure imposed on a naturally evolving set of plants. However, the present system of classification for all plants, first proposed by the Swedish botanist Carl von Linné (Linnaeus) in 1753 and broadly based upon floral characteristics, works well, although reclassification is constantly underway; for example, newly obtained genetic data ('fingerprinting') can reinforce, or alter, long-established relationships.

Problems of classification are particularly acute at species level. All individuals of a species should have a large number of characteristics in common and should be able to breed with one another. However, if a species has a very wide distribution and is found right across a continent, examples from opposite ends of its geographic range may not look very similar, even though it is clear from the variants taken at, say, 100km (62 mile) distances that a progression of minor changes links them all. It is sometimes impossible to say just when a plant does become a new species. In addition, new species are constantly being found as geographical areas are reopened for exploration. However, because this is a practical guide and not a botanical work, many of the more contentious issues are not relevant here and rare species that are unlikely to be available except through specialist seedlists are not covered.

THE GENUS *IRIS*

Working on the basis of Brian Mathew's ideas, *Iris* is divided into six subgenera. One of these contains only one or two rather anomalous species from the Himalayas, but the other five all include some plants

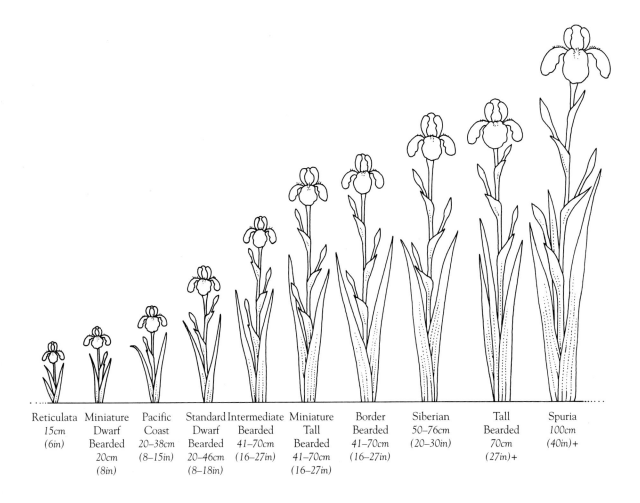

Reticulata	Miniature Dwarf Bearded	Pacific Coast	Standard Dwarf Bearded	Intermediate Bearded	Miniature Tall Bearded	Border Bearded	Siberian	Tall Bearded	Spuria
15cm (6in)	20cm (8in)	20–38cm (8–15in)	20–46cm (8–18in)	41–70cm (16–27in)	41–70cm (16–27in)	41–70cm (16–27in)	50–76cm (20–30in)	70cm (27in)+	100cm (40in)+

Fig 3 Diagrammatic representation to show the approximate height range of the groups of iris most commonly grown as garden plants.

that can be grown in the open in most temperate zones. The subgenera are:

    Iris subgenus Iris
    Iris subgenus Limniris
    Iris subgenus Nepalensis
    Iris subgenus Xiphium
    Iris subgenus Scorpiris
    Iris subgenus Hermodactyloides

The divisions of subgenera, sections and series usefully categorize the species into groups that have many characters in common, and often plants in the same series (or section or subgenus) require similar conditions.

SUBGENUS IRIS

This group includes some of the most familiar of all iris as well as some of the most exotic. It is further subdivided into six sections.

Section Iris

These are the bearded (or pogon) iris, and a few species, including *I. pallida* and *I. variegata*, have been used to create the myriad hybrids known today. All species have thick rhizomes and fans of leaves. The flowers are (usually) held on branched stems, and the three falls have pronounced furry beards. Unlike the rest of the subgenus, the seeds do not have a fleshy aril.

In general, these are sun-loving plants requiring a well-drained soil, all but the commonly available hybrids and species needing extra grit added to most soils. All prefer alkaline soil (though it is not essential, especially in the case of the hybrids) and most come from southern and eastern Europe.

In the last 100 years, thousands of hybrids have been raised and named and the flower size, shape, colour range and flowering period have all been improved. To divide these into categories, both for exhibition purposes and to help gardeners identify the type of plant they want, a classification system loosely based on height has been devised. As a general rule the shorter plants flower first, in mid-spring, and the groups are listed here in approximate height order (that is to say the height of the flowering stem), starting with the shortest.

Miniature Dwarf Bearded (MDB) These grow up to 20cm (8in), with unbranched flower stems. They generally flower in mid-spring.

Standard Dwarf Bearded (SDB) These grow 20–38cm (8–15in) tall and flower well in areas of weak sunshine, like all the shorter hybrids. Most make good clumps and are easy and reliable garden plants. They flower in late spring.

Intermediate Bearded (IB) These reach 41–70cm (16–27in) and are midway in height, flower size and flowering period between the SDBs and the Tall Bearded cultivars, blooming at the very end of spring.

Border Bearded (BB) This useful category includes plants that flower with the Tall Bearded iris in early summer and have similar sized flowers but on shorter stems, 41–70cm (16–27in) high. Many are superb garden plants, especially for windy sites and small gardens.

Miniature Tall Bearded (MTB) These are the same height as Border Bearded cultivars and flower with them, but are more graceful, with smaller flowers. They are sometimes called Table Iris and are more useful as cut flowers than the other categories.

Tall Bearded (TB) These can reach 1m (40in) or more and flower from very early summer in most years. Many people know iris only through the 'purple flag' or *I. germanica*, an almost indestructible old hybrid. Generations of plant breeders have transformed the TB into a thing of great beauty.

The main species in this section that make good garden plants or are historically interesting include:

I. albicans
I. amoena
I. aphylla

I. attica
I. flavescens
I. florentina
I. germanica
I. imbricata
I. kashmiriana
I. kochii
I. × lurida
I. lutescens
I. pallida
I. plicata
I. pseudopumila
I. pumila
I. reichenbachii
I. suaveolens
I. subbiflora
I. variegata

Iris japonica is not hardy in all zones but is nevertheless popular for its sprays of white flowers splashed with blue and egg-yolk yellow.

Section Psammiris

A small group of plants from Russia and north-west China that are extremely rare in cultivation. They are short-growing, rhizomatous iris that flower in late spring. The two most frequently grown species are *I. bloudowii* and *I. humilis*, both of which have yellow flowers.

Section Oncocyclus

These beautiful plants hail from arid areas of Turkey, east to the Caucasus and Iran, and south to the Sinai peninsula. With a natural climate of scorching hot dry summers and cold but dry winters they are understandably unhappy when grown outside in temperate zones. Although they are cold-tolerant when dormant, if winter rains stimulate early growth this will be frosted and the plants fatally weakened. Most need to be grown in a bulb frame in order to control watering in colder areas.

The flower stems bear only one bloom, but these are some of the most striking iris of all. However, they are very prone to virus diseases and are not readily available from nurseries. Species include:

> *I. acutiloba*
> *I. barnumae*
> *I. gatesii*
> *I. lortetii*
> *I. paradoxa*
> *I. sari*
> *I. susiana*

Some of these species have been crossed with the bearded iris, resulting in plants with unusual coloration and markings. These 'arilbred' or 'oncobred' iris are more tolerant of normal garden conditions.

Section Regelia

These are found further east than the Oncocyclus iris and are slightly better able to cope with temperate climates, though all are rare, and most are difficult to grow in the open garden. Each stem carries two flowers. Three of the most beautiful and most amenable to cultivation are *I. hoogiana*, *I. korolkowii* and *I. stolonifera*.

Section Hexapogon

These iris have beards on both the falls and standards but are extremely rare in cultivation. Because they are natives of desert areas of central Asia, Iran and parts of Afghanistan, they are not suited to temperate climates. *I. falcifolia*, a dwarf plant with small lilac flowers that appear in spring, is occasionally grown with difficulty.

Section Pseudoregelia

The species in this group have spotted or blotched flowers and are rarely grown because they are difficult. Most are from mountain areas of eastern Asia. The most frequently seen are *I. kemaonensis*, which has lilac-purple tepals, and the mauve *I. tigridia* from Mongolia.

SUBGENUS LIMNIRIS

This group, the beardless iris, is split into two sections: the Lophiris (commonly called the Evansias) and the Limniris, which is further subdivided into 16 series, all quite distinct.

Section Lophiris

The Evansias are beautiful and most are easy to grow, though some are tender. They are also called crested iris because instead of a beard the falls have a series of ridges or crests, often of a different colour from the rest of the tepal, and the standards are flaring or horizontal to give a flattish flower shape. They come from North America and east Asia and most are content in the equable temperate climates. The best-known are:

> *I. confusa*
> *I. cristata*
> *I. gracilipes*
> *I. japonica*
> *I. lacustris*
> *I. milesii*
> *I. tectorum*
> *I. wattii*

Section Limniris

The section Limniris is divided into 16 series. These are as follows:

Californicae These iris from well-drained soil on the west coast of the USA are fairly dwarf, pretty plants, mostly blooming in early summer. Each species is variable in colour, and they hybridize among themselves and with some of the Sibiricae series. As a group they are popularly called Pacific Coast Iris (PCI). Although the species are not as popular as the hybrids the following are often cultivated in gardens:

I. bracteata

I. chrysophylla

I. douglasiana

I. fernaldii

I. hartwegii

I. innominata

I. macrosiphon

I. munzii

I. purdyi

I. tenax

I. tenuissima

Chinenses These are rarely cultivated species from east Asia with flattish flowers. Only *I. minutoaurea* has been grown in Britain.

Ensatae This group does not contain *I. ensata* (due to a historical mix-up) but one species from central Asia, *I. lactea*. This is a tough, drought-tolerant plant flowering as tardily as late summer in the wild, but it is not showy and is rarely grown.

Foetidissimae This contains one evergreen species, *I. foetidissima*, which is distinct for its bright red seeds that follow the flowers in early summer. It is native to the UK.

Hexagona These are water-loving iris from the southeastern USA and are called Louisiana Iris. They are not commonly grown in the UK, and though some are very attractive when in flower in early summer they often do not flower freely. The most interesting and attractive species are:

I. brevicaulis

I. fulva

I. giganticaerulea

I. hexagonae

I. nelsonii

Laevigatae These moisture-loving plants come from Europe, Asia and North America. They need quite a rich soil and most are strong, robust plants blooming in early and midsummer. This group includes the native yellow *I. pseudacorus*, seen in the wild throughout the UK, and the Japanese clematis iris, *I. ensata* (syn. *I. kaempferi*). All are water iris and the most important to gardeners are:

I. ensata

I. laevigata

I. pseudacorus

I. versicolor

I. virginica

In damp soil, *Iris versicolor* var. *kermesina* from North America is a strong-growing iris.

Longipetalae This series contains just two species, *I. longipetala* and *I. missouriensis*, often called Rocky Mountain Iris. They come from Washington State, Oregon and California. They require moisture in spring and dry summers but are rarely grown, perhaps because they dislike root disturbance.

Prismaticae This contains just one North American species, *I. prismatica*, which is not difficult to grow in moist soil with light shade, but the pale lavender flowers in early summer are overshadowed by the wealth of other iris in bloom at that time.

Ruthenicae Includes *I. ruthenica* from Eastern Europe to China and Korea. It is a small iris requiring moist soil.

Sibiricae This Asiatic group contains familiar garden plants that usually flower in early and midsummer. Most are easy to grow in temperate zones, including:

I. *bulleyana*
I. *chrysographes*
I. *clarkei*
I. *delavayi*
I. *dykesii*
I. *forrestii*
I. *sanguinea*
I. *sibirica*
I. *typhifolia*
I. *wilsonii*

Spuriae This group contains many robust garden-worthy plants from which dozens of hybrids have been created. In the wild, in Europe, Russia and Asia, many grow in damp soils and even in salt marshes, but they make good garden plants for all but the driest situations. The most obvious characteristic of the group is the presence of three nectar drops on the flower where the petals join the perianth tube. Most species flower in midsummer. Interesting species include:

I. *crocea*
I. *graminea*
I. *kerneriana*
I. *orientalis* (syn. I. *ochroleuca*)
I. *polysticta*
I. *pontica*
I. *sintenisii*
I. *spuria*

Syriacae These are unusual species with swollen leaf bases and spiny bristles. All are very rare in cultivation and are generally little known. The four species are:

I. *aschersonii*
I. *grant-duffi*
I. *masia*
I. *melanosticta*

Tenuifoliae These are mostly semi-desert plants from central Asia and are very rare in cultivation. The species are:

I. *bungei*
I. *cathayensis*
I. *kobayashii*
I. *loczyi*
I. *songarica*
I. *tenuifolia*
I. *ventricosa*

Tripetalae The series name refers to the fact that these species have small standards and the violet-blue flowers appear at first glance to have three petals. Only one

species, I. *setosa*, is generally in cultivation and it is very variable, coming from east Asia, Japan, Alaska and eastern Canada. It is a delightful plant and easy to grow.

Unguiculares The two species in this series are united by their flowering in winter but have different cultivation requirements. Both are valuable and beautiful garden plants. I. *unguicularis*, from Algeria, Tunisia and the Mediterranean, needs very dry sunny conditions, while I. *lazica*, a plant from the Black Sea coast, prefers slightly shaded, moist soil.

Vernae One species (I. *verna*) from the eastern USA completes this series. It has lilac flowers in spring and grows in humus-rich soil.

SUBGENUS NEPALENSIS

This contains three species, of which just one is occasionally grown. I. *decora* is mauve-flowered and can be raised from seed but is short-lived in cultivation. The other species are I. *colletti* and I. *staintonii*.

SUBGENUS XIPHIUM

These bulbous plants from Western Europe and North Africa have led to the development of the hybrids that are popularly known as English, Spanish and Dutch iris, from I. *latifolia*, I. *xiphium* and I. *tingitana* × I. *xiphium* respectively. They flower naturally in early to midsummer and each unbranched stem produces from one to three flowers. The species are:

I. *boissieri*
I. *filifolia*
I. *juncea*
I. *latifolia* (syn. I. *xiphioides*)
I. *serotina*
I. *tingitana*
I. *xiphium*

SUBGENUS SCORPIRIS

The Juno iris are easily distinguished and among the most beautiful plants in the genus. They are bulbous plants with fleshy roots and tend to be rather leafy, with a leek-like appearance. In many species the flowers are produced at ground level before the foliage develops fully, while in others they are produced in great numbers on leafy plants. The flowering season varies from early to late spring. The flowers are interesting because

Iris kerneriana has the distinctive slender flower shape of most spurias but on a graceful and delicate plant. However, its constitution is surprisingly strong.

the standards are narrow and horizontal or slightly pendulous. Most of these plants are difficult to grow in the garden in temperate zones and need specialist care and cultivation in a bulb frame. They come mainly from Turkey, the Caucasus, as far south as Israel and east to Pakistan, where summers are hot and dry and winters are cold and dry. There are 50 species in this group but only those likely to be available are listed here:

I. *aitchisonii*
I. *albo-marginata*
I. *aucheri* (syn. I. *sindjarensis*)
I. *baldshuanica*
I. *bucharica*
I. *caucasica*
I. *cycloglossa*
I. *galatica*
I. *graeberiana*
I. *magnifica*
I. *nicolai*
I. *palaestina*
I. *persica*
I. *planifolia*
I. *vicaria*
I. *warleyensis*
I. *willmottiana*

Some primary hybrids between two species, such as 'Warlsind' and 'Sindpur', are occasionally offered by nurseries.

SUBGENUS HERMADACTYLOIDES

This is the group of dwarf bulbous iris that brighten rock gardens in spring. They have netted (reticulate) skins on the bulbs and just one or two long leaves that are usually square in cross-section. They grow wild in Turkey, the Caucasus, south to Israel and east to Iran and central Asia. They require a sunny, well-drained soil and deep planting at 15cm (6in) to maintain flowering-size bulbs. The brightly coloured flowers

Iris danfordiae (grown here with *Cyclamen hederifolium*) is easy to grow – at least in the first year – and inexpensive to buy, making it ideal where quick colour is required in early spring.

appear in spring, often with snowdrops. Many of the species are best grown in a bulb frame. The species are less often grown than the cultivars of *I. reticulata*, but include:

I. bakeriana
I. danfordiae
I. histrio
I. histrioides
I. kolpakowskiana
I. pamphylica
I. reticulata
I. winogradowii

POPULAR PLANTS

The parts of the genus that have most attracted the attention of gardeners and plant hybridists in the past have been the bearded or pogon iris in section Iris, the Sibiricae, Laevigatae, Californicae and Spuriae series in section Limniris and the Xiphium and Hermadactyloides subgenera, and it is these that form the basis of this book, along with others that are obtainable and of easy cultivation in the UK and similar climates.

On account of the fact that they are so resistant to drying out and amenable to being moved, the bearded iris have formed the basis of most commercial iris sales, although specialists have always supplied a greater range to gardeners who plan their orders in advance. However, in the last 15 years, owing to the demand from gardeners for a wider range of plants, even the range of iris available from garden centres is improving.

In addition to the true iris there are similar plants that are sometimes called iris, the most important being *Hermodactylus tuberosus* from the Mediterranean. It has tuberous roots and an ovary with one chamber, but would be recognized as an iris by most gardeners.

2

THE BEARDED IRIS
Section Iris

Most gardeners view iris as flowers of summer, and their perception is based upon the tall bearded iris – *I. germanica* (flag irises or just flags). Their flowering is generally considered a pretty, but fleeting, show – certainly no more than a plant with such boring leaves could be expected to produce.

The bearded iris are so universally known that many books and articles on the genus do not seem to acknowledge the existence of any other type of iris at all. There are probably about 30 species in the section, but this is a very confused group because there are a large number of hybrids which have been given species names. This plethora of hybrids offering a huge range of different characteristics gives this section its popularity but also makes it muddled, which is typical of many plants that have been grown and loved by gardeners over a long period.

These iris are mainly native to southern Europe and east to Turkey with some from the Caucasus and western Asia, and some species have been in cultivation for centuries. Gardeners always prize mutations and forms that would be eliminated through natural selection, and in many cases it is difficult to trace the ancestry or origin of domesticated plants. So it is with *I. germanica*, which is almost certainly a hybrid that originated in the Mediterranean area.

PLANT STRUCTURE

All the bearded iris are recognizable by their stout, horizontal rhizomes that root from the lower side. The leaves are often greyish-green and are arranged in fans at the ends of the rhizomes. Some remain evergreen and a few are truly deciduous, but most retain small leaf fans in winter. When the fan produces a flower stalk, the tip of the rhizome that produced it dies and axillary buds in the leaf axils of the rhizome produce new shoots which extend the length and width of the clump. Typically, the original shoot is replaced by two new shoots, doubling the number of flowers and fans each year. Some vigorous modern cultivars produce a great number of sideshoots, often with unsatisfactory results if they are congested and have insufficient room to mature and reach flowering size. Other cultivars have a habit of flowering out (flowering themselves to death by producing flower stems at the expense of vegetative growth) and such undesirable characteristics are often ignored in the rush for new flower sizes and colours. Plants with these sorts of weaknesses would doubtless not survive in the wild, and the species and primary hybrids (crosses between two species) do not exhibit such traits.

The leaves are usually broad compared with most other iris – the classic 'sword-shaped' – and the flower stems bear two or more flowers. The stems are usually branched, although those of dwarf species and hybrids may not be. The flowers have recognizable standards and falls and on the falls there is a beard, a fluffy line of short hairs that may be a contrasting colour or tipped with yellow or gold. In wild species the beard almost certainly acts as a guide to pollinators, or as a pollen trap to help self-pollination should cross-pollination not occur, but in recent years hybridizers have concentrated much effort on enhancing the colour, size and shape of the beard to make it a considerably more important part of the flower.

Most of the species can be grown outside in temperate climates if given a well-drained soil in full sun. Very light, sandy soils may not give rise to the rot that causes the death of the more difficult small species, but they will not encourage vigour either; the ideal is a rich, slightly alkaline soil in a raised bed or rock garden.

For general garden use, the following species can be recommended: *I. albicans*, *I. flavescens*, *I. florentina*, *I. germanica*, *I. imbricata*, *I. kashmiriana*, *I. kochii*, *I. × lurida*, *I. pallida*, *I. plicata* and *I. variegata*. None of the species can compare with the large-flowered hybrids for diversity of colour or sheer size of bloom, but in the general garden border they have their uses.

LARGER SPECIES

All the larger-growing species produce their flowers in late spring or early summer.

IRIS ALBICANS

This iris is often confused with *I. florentina*, but differs from it in having largely unbranched flower stems and (typically) pure white flowers with a yellow beard from green or purple-tinted bracts. The flowers are sweetly scented and only three or four are carried on each stem, up to 60cm (2ft) high. The leaves are a beautiful grey-green, rather wide and short, and often have a gentle twist that gives a young clump of plants an attractive appearance that is less obvious in congested groups. This species is native to Arabia but was first named in 1860 from a plant found growing in Almeria, Spain. It is now widespread throughout the Mediterranean area because it spread with the Ottoman Empire from the thirteenth century and was commonly planted on Muslim graves. It was also carried by the Spanish to Mexico, and in every warm, dry country where it has been planted it has escaped. Gertrude Jekyll aided its spread, bringing plants back to England from Turkey.

In dry, sunny gardens this is an attractive plant, but it does not appreciate winter wet. This is a classic plant for the herb garden where it would look perfect with rosemary, which should still be in flower, or with thymes and artemisias at its feet and a pillar of deep green bay behind. There is a blue variant, called 'Madonna'.

IRIS FLAVESCENS

I. flavescens is not the prettiest of iris species according to most experts, in fact it is not even a good species (in the botanical sense, meaning that it is simply a variant of another plant). However, it is a 'good doer' in almost any situation. Some authorities believe it to be a form of *I. variegata*, the whole flower being the same pale yellow found in that species, while others consider it to be a hybrid of *I. pallida* and *I. variegata*, though there is less visual similarity to *I. pallida*, the supposed female parent.

The leaves are greener than *I. pallida*, which characteristically has steely grey leaves, and the branched stems reach about 60cm (2ft) with many medium-sized, primrose-yellow flowers marked with brown on the haft, which gives a rather dirty effect. It is extremely vigorous and flowers in early summer, sometimes slightly before the Tall Bearded cultivars. It prefers full sun, but also succeeds in light shade if the soil is well drained. This is the sort of iris that is stout enough to survive as an edging to the cottage path, fighting it out with *Nepeta* (catmint), *Alchemilla*, *Saxifraga* × *urbium* (London pride) and *Cheiranthus* (wallflowers) in a riot of colour, but it must be given a reasonable chance to breathe after they have flowered and been cut back or removed – none of the bearded iris will tolerate vegetation keeping moisture around their rhizomes for long.

IRIS FLORENTINA

If species are being collected for their historical or cultural interest the first to be sought must be *I. florentina*, one of the sources of orris root.

Orris is obtained from the dried rhizome of the plant, and, rather curiously, smells of violets. It has been used for a variety of household purposes for centuries and today is still an important ingredient of many perfumes, soaps and even sweets, as well as being added to maturing Chianti. When fresh the root is bitter, but with age (up to three years) the sweet fragrance develops. Traditionally it is grown in commercial quantities in Tuscany and other upland areas of Italy but the roots can be prepared domestically, though it requires a wait of several years before the rhizomes are mature and hard and two more years before they are fully dried and cured.

As a garden plant *I. florentina* is possibly superior to *I. albicans* because the flower stems carry more flowers, on two or three branches. However, they are not quite pure white, having a blue tint, particularly when in bud. This is another very easy plant to grow, and is readily propagated by dividing the rhizomes after flowering. It is reported that it does not set seed, and this could be because of a lack of suitable insects or because it is a hybrid; modern thinking now places this as a white variant of *I. germanica*, which is probably a hybrid and also has scented rhizomes.

IRIS GERMANICA

I. germanica is often quoted as the parent species from which the modern Tall Bearded iris are derived, but this theory has now been revised and this plant itself is considered to be an ancient hybrid. I am not certain if there is any connection, other than by name, with Germany, but plants are often named after the country that supplied them to the taxonomist, not the true country of origin. This is considered a native of the Mediterranean region and is a very tough and resilient plant, surviving well in neglected gardens and as escapes. When in flower it can reach up to 1.2m (4ft), though it may grow to just half this height. The grey-green leaves are usually half the height of the flower stems. The flowers are variously coloured purple, with the standards usually paler than the falls, and the beard is yellow to orange. Most gardeners are given this plant rather than making a conscious effort to buy it, and as they discover more exciting iris they reduce the size of their clumps to make room but, treated kindly, it will make a grand display, showing well against the bright yellow foliage of golden privet or conifers. Indeed, it will grow at the base of golden conifers, where little else will, largely because it will be effectively dormant from early summer when the soil will be parched and impoverished.

Other species, such as *I. florentina*, *I. kochii* and *I. trojana*, are frequently reduced to mere varieties of *I. germanica* and there are other strains that are now considered cultivars such as 'Amas', 'Kharput', and 'Nepalensis', named after the parts of the world where they were collected. Despite all this apparent variety, a bed of all the different kinds of *I. germanica* would not be very exciting, except to a botanist, as the flowers would all be in shades of purple, and despite the common usage of the name as a catch-all for Tall Bearded iris, the beautiful ones are probably hybrids of *I. pallida* and *I. variegata*, with the influences of other species in some cases. Where *I. pallida* and *I. variegata* meet in the wild hybrids that resemble *I. germanica* occur, which gives credence to the view of that species being of hybrid origin.

IRIS IMBRICATA

I. imbricata comes from damp mountain meadows of Armenia, Iran and Transcaucasia and seems to be a wild species. It is another pale yellow species but has larger flowers than *I. flavescens*, up to 10 cm (4in) across, held on stout stems that may be as short as 30cm (1ft) but are usually rather taller. The stems are branched, which gives a good visual spread of flowers, and often several open at once, providing a colourful display. However, it is the bracts from which they emerge, which are inflated and almost transparent yet fleshy, that make this such a distinctive plant. (In *I. flavescens* the bracts are papery when the flowers open.) The leaves are a rather yellowy green and match the pale buff yellow flower colour to provide a handsome garden plant that would look good planted either with sympathetic colours such as *Stachys byzantina* 'Primrose Heron' at its feet and shrubby potentillas as a background, or with a contrast of dark purple foliage provided by small hebes like 'Mrs Winder' or purple-leaved cotinus and *Physocarpus opulifolius* 'Diabolo'.

Despite its preference for moist soils in the wild this is a plant for well-drained soil and sun. It is not too big for a large planting pocket in the rock garden, where it will make an imposing show.

IRIS KASHMIRIANA

A less common, and by all accounts less amenable, species is *I. kashmiriana*, which is tall and white-flowered, with a pleasant perfume. It can be distinguished from *I. albicans* by the flowers being held on comparatively long side branches (they are almost sessile in *I. albicans*) and it differs from *I. florentina* in its narrow green bracts that can reach 10cm (4in) long. The leaves are as long as the flower stems and reach 60cm (2ft). In its native Kashmir, India and Nepal it is planted on Muslim graves, as is *I. albicans* further west. It is also reported growing on roofs in India, where it is presumably planted like the Japanese plant *I. tectorum* and Europeans grow *Sempervivum* (houseleeks).

IRIS KOCHII

This species is sometimes lumped with *I. germanica*, but it is shorter and the wide falls and standards are a deep, smooth purple. Although not strikingly beautiful, it is a solid and reliable plant with a bit more finesse than *I. germanica*.

PLATE II

I. 'Velvet Bouquet'
Miniature Tall Bearded

I. 'Chian Wine'
Miniature Tall Bearded

I. 'Offenham'
Tall Bearded

I. 'Trevaunance Cove'
Tall Bearded

I. 'Quiet Though
Tall Bearde

All plants shown at approximately ⅓ size

I. 'Morwenna'
Tall Bearded

I. 'Loveday'
Tall Bearded

I. 'Champagne Elegance'
Tall Bearded

I. 'Carolyn Rose'
Miniature Tall
Bearded

IRIS × LURIDA

This is almost certainly a hybrid or group of hybrids between *I. pallida* and *I. variegata* which includes the hybrid *I. × sambucina* from Italy, Spain and the Balkans and *I. × neglecta*. It has violet falls and paler standards and this colouring is to be found in the Neglecta group of iris hybrids.

IRIS SQUALENS

This ancient hybrid is rather dull, and the worst you might expect from crossing a pale yellow iris and a blue iris (*I. pallida* or *I. germanica* and *I. variegata*).

IRIS PALLIDA

The leaves of this species are a beautiful grey-green, and appear clean and even silvery. In late spring tall, elegant flower stems carry up to six blue flowers, each up to 10cm (4in) across, with contrasting yellow beards. Both the falls and standards are a clear soft blue with a hint of lavender and they have a glorious, sweet scent. The name refers to the pale colour of the flowers when compared to *I. germanica*, against which everything was once judged, perhaps because of its widespread distribution.

There are a few wild variants that are worthy of note: the flowers of ssp. *pallida* emerge from silvery, papery bracts, while ssp. *cengialtii* has slightly deeper-coloured flowers with an orange-tipped beard that spring from brownish, papery bracts. *I. pallida* var. *dalmatica* is, to most eyes, no different from ssp. *pallida* and may be nothing more than a regional collection. Whichever form is grown this is an iris that will delight, with its well-formed, showy but weatherproof flowers, its perfume and its healthy, attractive, evergreen leaves. Because the flower stems are not well branched the flowers tend to be held at the top third of the stem, perhaps above neighbouring plants, but this is hardly a criticism. It flowers with, and slightly before, most Tall Bearded iris and is a classic partner for *Aquilegia*, especially the lilac, mauve and purple shades of the European *A. vulgaris*, which does not have the fussy flower outlines of the long-spurred hybrids with their American influence and yellow colouring. The soft yellow background of *Philadelphus coronarius* 'Aureus' leaves or, alternatively, the silver of artemisias at its feet are also interesting combinations that can be extended to suit any scale of planting.

Even more exciting effects can be achieved with *I. pallida* 'Variegata', undoubtedly the most versatile and attractive variegated iris, if not the best of all variegated plants. The leaves are clearly striped with primrose yellow, of an intensity that matches the flowers, and are most beautiful in early summer and after flowering when new growth brings a greater intensity to their colouring. For white gardens, the other variegated kind, 'Argentea Variegata', with white-striped leaves, may be chosen. It is almost as lovely, and although the flowers are not quite as good, in my experience, that should not deter anyone from planting it.

A strange hybrid called 'Paltec' or *I. × paltec* should be mentioned. This is a cross between *I. pallida* and the distantly related *I. tectorum*, a crested iris with deep lavender blue flowers with floppy standards to give an almost flat flower. The result is a flower that looks very like *I. pallida* but with heavier veining, and a look about it that is not quite right. It is not an improvement on either species, and the standards seem to want to be upright, but do not have the strength and usually flop helplessly. It is at its most pathetic in windy weather, but I confess to a soft spot for it and it is effective in the garden, growing and flowering well.

IRIS PLICATA

Another of the best in this group of iris is *I. plicata*. It is an important plant because it has given the picotee pattern of deep colour around the edges of white standards and falls to a whole class of plicata cultivars, led for a long time by the successful 'Stepping Out'. This plant is a delight, with rather small flowers emerging from silvery bracts (rather like those of *I. pallida*) on tall stems. They are beautifully sculpted with arched falls (which unfortunately curl forward a little at the base) and incurved standards; they have exceptional grace and poise. The basic flower colour is a crisp white with short deep lilac lines around the edge of the petals to give the effect of a pale lilac/purple border. *I. plicata* is probably the same plant that was named after the botanist Swert (*I. sweertii*). The name *I. plicata* was first coined in 1789 by the French botanist Lamarck, who is best remembered for his own (now largely discredited) theory of evolution. Most gardeners will prefer the large hybrids, but I commend the plant that is being grown as *I. plicata* or *I. sweertii* to anyone who likes their iris small but classy.

Iris pallida 'Argentea Variegata' is strikingly variegated and a beautiful companion for silver-leaved plants.

IRIS VARIEGATA

The last of the common Tall Bearded iris but – since it is one of the parents of the modern hybrids – not the least is *I. variegata*. This must not be confused with iris that have variegated leaves – this name refers to the different colours in the flowers. Once again the flower pattern of the species has led to a series of hybrids that exhibit the same markings and in this case the flowers have pale yellow standards and yellow falls heavily veined in maroon/purple, sometimes so thickly that the lower part of the fall is completely purple. This is a slender species that reaches about 45cm (18in) when in flower and the scentless flowers are not over large, with a diameter of about 7cm (3in), carried well above green leaves with prominent longitudinal veins. *I. flavescens* is considered by some to be a plain yellow form of this species, and it certainly has the same ground colour to the petals and similar leaves, but *I. variegata* could not be confused with any other.

This is a central European species and is easy to grow in well-drained soil in sun. It is one of the most striking of all the colour combinations in iris species and the variegata pattern is popular with gardeners. One of the stock-in-trade iris, grown by the thousands, is the bold 'Staten Island' but this has long been superseded by brighter and bolder coloured cultivars such as the delightful Miniature Tall Bearded 'Bumblebee Deelite'. It was also a pattern that attracted the earliest hybridizers and 'Gracchus' from 1884 is still a worthy garden plant, though its small flowers cannot compare with the brilliance of today's creations.

A particularly lovely variant of the species, often separated and called *I. reginae*, has a ground colour of white overlaid with purple or violet. It is just as robust as the species and looks good with pink and blue hardy geraniums, such as *Geranium sylvaticum* and *G. × magnificum*, in front of *Rosa glauca*. A violet-veined white variant has been recorded as *I. amoena*, and this has given its name to all the large hybrids that possess white standards and lilac or mauve falls.

HYBRID BEARDED IRIS

These species are the building blocks of the bearded iris of today, and with such diverse and promising materials it is not surprising that we have such fine plants in our gardens. However, the development of the modern iris was not an easy or straightforward series of events – as with most plants, breeding progressed as a series of problems and solutions.

Hybrid bearded iris did arise spontaneously in the wild. John Gerard, who wrote the most famous of the 'Herbals', grew 16 different iris, according to his own records, of which some must have been bearded, and in 1601 Charles de l'Ecluse (better known as Clusius) wrote that he had experience of growing iris from seed and observed the great variation exhibited in the seedlings. (If the many 'species' are natural hybrids, it would be expected that their seedlings would show considerable variation.)

Just the action of bringing the different species into contact would permit interbreeding and hybrids, but it was probably in Paris in 1822 that the first named hybrid (a plicata) was introduced, modestly named 'Buriensis' after its raiser, the amateur breeder de Bure.

'W. R. Dykes' is an ancient yellow hybrid that would not arouse attention if raised today but it was an important milestone in the breeding of modern yellows.

The term 'breeder' is probably something of an exaggeration because there was little understanding of plant reproduction in those days and most of the ensuing introductions, until the end of the nineteenth century, were seedlings raised from bee pods (accidental crosses made by insects). However, 'Buriensis' set into motion a spate of French interest that led to the introduction of 100 cultivars by Monsieur Lémon in his catalogue. Not all were of his raising but he did at least recognize a commercial demand for iris and made them more generally available to an interested gardening public. He did not bother to make controlled crosses because he was quite satisfied with what nature produced unaided, and it is interesting that 'Jacquesiana', an uncontrolled cross raised by Jacques, a head gardener near Paris, which was listed in Lémon's catalogue in 1840, was given a Highly Commended award by the Royal Horticultural Society in 1916.

Lémon's 'Madame Chereau', a mauve and white plicata named for the wife of the then President of the National Horticultural Society of France, was introduced in 1844 and is still grown in collections of historic iris. (I believe this to have been the small plicata iris that I grew as *I. plicata* for many years.) Few of today's introductions will have such staying power, though they do have rather more competition.

Other French growers followed Lémon's example and the firm of Vilmorin-Andrieux et Cie introduced iris that were highly regarded at the time. These included 'Ambassadeur', a reddish brown, and 'Dejazet', but none was more important than 'Alcazar' (1910), a large purple that we would now consider dull in colour. These and others were offered to the public by Verdiers of Paris, Van Houtte (of *Spiraea* fame) in Holland and John Salter in London. The latter wrote in 1842 that *I. pallida, I. sweertii, I.* 'Buriensis', *I. germanica* and *I. plicata* were being used through 'artificial impregnation', as he called it, to produce new colours.

Ferdinand Cayeux raised iris at the beginning of the twentieth century, before his retirement in 1938, and his 'Deputé Nomblot', a medium mauve-pink, is still grown today, though probably most often under the misnomer of *I. germanica*. His 'Pluie d'Or' is now implicated in the development of the plicata pattern, especially in yellow and brown iris.

It is particularly appropriate that much of the early work on iris was performed in France, as the fleur-de-lis is so closely associated with that country, but British gardeners were not slow to follow. In 1885 Thomas Ware of Tottenham introduced the pretty 'Gracchus' but the most famous nineteenth century stockist of iris was Peter Barr of Tooting, who helped William Caparne start his programme of breeding Intermediate iris. Michael Foster was also instrumental in steering Caperne's work and was the British grower who had the most influence on the development of the modern Tall Bearded iris. His influence is commemorated in the Foster Memorial Plaque which is awarded by the British Iris Society to those who have performed outstanding work for the genus *Iris*.

Foster began his garden in Cambridge in 1872 and through his network of gardening friends collected a huge range of wild species and hybrid iris. Among these were four 'wild' iris (*I. amas, I. trojana, I. cypriana* and *I. mesopotamica*), which were tetraploid. *I. pallida* in its natural state with two sets of chromosomes has a count of 24, but these four species had double that number. Tetraploids have larger flowers, greater thickness to the petals and often deeper, richer colours, and Michael Foster recognized the potential of his new plants. He crossed these vigorous, tall plants with existing cultivars, and with *I. pallida*, and raised many hybrids that were, in great part, the ancestors of today's cultivars.

One of the finest, according to his friends, was 'Caterina', a pale lavender, raised from *I. cypriana* and *I. pallida*. Others were 'Kashmir White' and 'Lady Foster'. The crossing of these tetraploids with diploid *I. pallida* is more important than this simple explanation may suggest, since the usual product of such a cross is a triploid which is sterile. This is then no use to further breeding, but in the case of these iris, fertile tetraploids were the result and so the breeding could continue.

MODERN BEARDED IRIS

An even bigger name in the development of the iris, also influenced by Foster, was W. R. Dykes, who died in a motor accident in 1925. He wrote *The Genus Iris*, the classic work on the genus (though now out of date taxonomically), and *A Handbook of Garden Irises*. He also raised many hybrids at his gardens at Godalming in Surrey, including thousands of TBs, and about 50 were named. Of these, the most famous was 'W. R. Dykes', a large (tetraploid) yellow, huge for its time, which was named for him by his widow shortly after his death. The colour is a pale creamy yellow and it often shows soft mauve stippling or even streaking (a trait that seems to have developed through time and was not present at all in its early days). Such was its novelty value at the time that it commanded a price of £20 a rhizome when first introduced. It was eagerly sought and used extensively for hybridizing. Mrs Dykes continued her husband's work and introduced 'Gudrun', of her own raising, which was a benchmark large clean white.

By now there was much transatlantic trade in the genus and Peter Barr supplied iris to many American iris growers. The first grower to work extensively with them was Bertrand Farr, who imported all of Barr's cultivars (more than 100). Until then he ran a music business in Pennsylvania, but was so taken with the iris that he changed career and began a nursery in Wyoming. Like Michael Foster, he used the tetraploid

The 'hang-dog' ears of 'Alcazar' were not considered a fault in 1910 – the bright colouring and large flower size were what drew attention.

'species' and his many successful cultivars were sold for 50 to 75 cents each, prices that were deemed outrageous at the beginning of the 1900s (but were modest when compared with the introduction of 'Dominion' in Britain 10 years later). In 1920 he listed 250 Tall Bearded cultivars and many others. 'Quaker Lady' was one of his most popular seedlings and was imported to Britain and used as a parent. Other notable American hybridizers were Grace Sturtevant, who introduced the whites 'Taj Mahal' and 'Snow White', Bruce Williamson, Paul Cook, Hans and Jacob Sass, William Mohr and Sydney Mitchell.

At his nursery in Enfield, Middlesex, British grower Amos Perry was an enthusiastic and active hybridizer, not only of iris but also of *Hemerocallis*, while iris-grower Olive Murrell registered 92 seedlings, the most acclaimed of which was 'White City', the Dykes Medal winner of 1940.

Dykes' name is not only remembered in the medal awarded for the best iris each year by both the British and American Iris Societies; he also influenced many people, as Michael Foster had done before him. Among these was A. J. Bliss, a civil servant, who was encouraged by Dykes to experiment with crossing wild-collected *I. pallida* from Italy and *I. variegata* from Hungary in an attempt to prove or disprove the hybrid origin of *I. amoena*, *I. neglecta* and others. The work produced hundreds of seedlings, many of which were indistinguishable from the 'species' in question, but some were so good that they were named and introduced. Alas, like so many of the older hybrids they are no longer grown, but one of his seedlings was to have a profound effect on gardeners. It was called 'Dominion', and its progeny (the Dominion race), which included 'Cardinal' and 'Bruno' were declared by the Vilmorin et Cie company to be the finest iris in all the world.

'Dominion', which has lustrous purple petals and falls with a velvety sheen, was a hybrid of Foster's *I. amas* (syn. 'Amas') and an *I. pallida* × *I. variegata* seedling. Bliss, recognizing that it was special, sent it to the Royal Horticultural Society's garden at Wisley, Surrey, where

'Bewick Swan', raised by Bryan Dodsworth in Britain, won the British Dykes Medal in 1984.

in its fourth year of growth it was discovered by Robert Wallace, the proprietor of the Wallace nursery firm in Colchester, Essex (now merged with the Barr company and trading as Wallace and Barr). Marketing and commercial enterprise are often thought to be modern considerations in the plant-growing business, with Plant Breeder's rights and copyrighting of cultivars only evolving in the 1970s and 1980s, but Wallace was an astute businessman and after an immediate visit to Bliss in Devon he bought the entire stock of 'Dominion'.

The demand for new iris was not great during the First World War so Wallace took the decision to bulk up stock and in 1917 'Dominion' was introduced in his catalogue with a photograph, a tempting description and, most importantly, a price of £5. Gardeners are vulnerable to the lure of the latest and best cultivars, and anything that cost that much . . . well, it must be good. Fortunately it was good, and so were its descendants.

One of the first American nurserymen to acquire 'Dominion' was Frank Schreiner of Minnesota. All hybridizers know the importance of starting work with the latest cultivars in their attempt to stay ahead of rivals. Older hybrids and species are useful in bringing new genes into the mix, but in the quest for the brightest yellow, for example, it is usually best to start with the best contemporary efforts. Schreiner also bought the fiendishly expensive 'W. R. Dykes' and offered it in his annual list of 100 iris. His sons began a phenomenal breeding programme and in 1947 moved the business to Oregon, where they continue to introduce the latest cultivars.

TALL BEARDED IRIS

The Tall Bearded iris (TBs) are, by definition, taller than 70cm (27in) from the soil to the top of the flower spike, and the last of the bearded iris to flower, sometimes continuing into midsummer. Whatever its function in the wild species, in the hybrids the beard has often been developed in size and colour to augment the colour of the falls. As the range of flower colours has been increased by hybridizers the breeding goals have become more detailed and contrasting beard colour is an important and often elusive one.

This may sound insignificant, but it truly can make or break a flower. The 1984 Dykes Medal winner

'Bewick Swan' is a beautiful ruffled white of great substance, but it is made a breathtaking iris by its large bright tangerine beard, which, if nothing else, helps to make the white petals even more pristine. Surprisingly, the truly blue iris is a fairly rare flower and a modern development, and hybridizers are now making blue flowers with red (or deep orange) beards. 'Skyblaze' is one example.

IMPORTANT QUALITIES IN CULTIVARS

Just as rose breeders are criticized for creating roses that have little scent, some iris hybridizers may have concentrated too much on novelty of flower type and colour and neglected the rest of the plant. A good iris should, above all, have strong, healthy foliage and a stout constitution. Each fan should produce offsets sufficient to form a good clump. Unfortunately some put all their efforts into flowering and while this is gratifying for a year or so, they may well flower themselves to death and produce no fans to overwinter.

Another failing is producing too many offsets. There is a bud at the base of every leaf and once the flower stem has bloomed the action on the rhizome is the same as pinching the tip out of any shoot – the lower buds surge into growth. In some cultivars most of the buds on the previous year's rhizome will grow, and if left unthinned there will be little chance of them having room to reach flowering size. The result is a clump that misses flowering for at least one year unless the plant is divided yearly. While this is acceptable to the dedicated iris enthusiast it is not for the average gardener who is just starting to become interested in iris.

All the established commonly available iris in general nursery lists can be guaranteed at least to be easy to grow and not to 'bloom out' – die after flowering without making increases.

Apart from vigour, other qualities can make a particular cultivar better than the next. The number of flowers on each stem is important, because each one will last about three days, and it follows that the more buds on the stem, the better or longer the display will be. Most cultivars will have a socket (the name for a bud position, within the bracts) at the top of the stem with two buds and two branches lower down the main stem, which will hold two buds. This is the minimum, and three branches are to be preferred. The upper branch may be only a few centimetres long

The American-bred 'Edith Wolford' combines heavy ruffling and unusual colouring which won it the American Dykes Medal in 1993.

but the lower branches will be longer, with the lowest being the longest.

Because the flowers are quite large it is important that their spacing is sufficient to allow each to open properly. Often the top branch is so close to the top bud that if both open at once the individual flower shape is lost in a colourful, but congested, mass of petals. This problem has increased with the bigger size of modern cultivars and their flaring, ruffled falls and standards. The placement of branches is also important, because a few branches towards the top of the stem will give less vertical depth of flower display than the same number of branches placed lower down.

Where exhibition is concerned, well-placed branches on an elegantly curved main stem and three or four immaculate flowers are needed. In the garden simultaneous flowering is less important, and indeed it may result in a shorter, though spectacular, flowering period.

In addition to the branching and placement of the stems the overall plant habit is important, because, leaving aside those extremes that make very few or too many offsets, a cultivar that makes four shoots from every fan of leaves but has poorly branched stems may be a better garden plant for display than one that has half as many shoots but well-branched stems (it may also be better as a cut flower). The other disadvantage of sturdy, heavily branched stems with large flowers is

'Zua' is an old Intermediate iris, but shows 'lacing' on its small, milk-white petals.

that, especially in their first year after replanting, they are likely to be blown over in the average summer. I discovered this for myself the first year the National Collection began to bloom in earnest and I vowed that if I ever did any serious hybridizing it would be to introduce hybrids with decent roots! It is worth noting that 'Alcazar', 'Deputé Nomblot', 'Gracchus' and all the others that are often dismissed as unworthy of garden space today stood up like flagpoles.

GOOD FLOWER SHAPE

While the basic flower shape has been and continues to be manipulated, there are basic concepts as to what is a good iris. An iris flower should be well-proportioned, and the standards will not be larger than the falls. Early hybrids such as 'Dominion' or 'Wabash', good though they are, have petals of a rather thin substance. This would not allow the width of petal favoured today as it is simply not strong enough, so modern developments have created stiffer, thicker petals. They are also wider so that at the haft (the top of the falls where they flow down into the 'throat' of the flower) they almost touch, or even overlap. The falls themselves are not floppy as they are in old cultivars, and their greater substance can hold the falls horizontal in some cases. It is a matter of personal taste whether such 'flaring' falls are really an improvement. They do not reveal such a large surface area to the viewer in the garden as looser falls do until they are seen from directly above, but as in all aspects of

gardening, the plants should be judged as a whole rather than on just one aspect.

It is a fault of some that as the flowers age over the three days the falls in particular continue to grow so that by the third day the balance of the flower is destroyed. In old cultivars, the standards suffered from the same defects as the falls and often flopped as the flowers aged.

The standards have been enlarged, stiffened and improved in line with the falls and most now have the strength to stand upright. Again, taste will decide what is preferable but the traditional domed standards where the petals were curved along their length and touched at the top, sometimes even curled around each other, is now joined by other shapes. Now standards can be straight along their central axis, so that they stand out at an oblique angle, leaving an open centre to the flower. Personally I feel that if this is taken too far, in combination with very flaring falls, a flat 'clematis' flowered iris could be produced, which would be rather a shame (but you may think otherwise, in which case you might care to grow 'Paltec'). However, this shape can be extraordinarily attractive. Less extreme examples with curved and cup-shaped open standards are among my favourite cultivars, including the superlative 'Edith Wolford'.

One reason why the flaring falls and standards have become so popular is that breeders have been adding other qualities to the flowers that just would not fit on to traditional, tightly structured flowers. The most attractive, in my opinion, is ruffling. This is caused by extra growth at the edge of the petals so that pleating is caused. In some flowers such as 'Bryngwyn' and the older 'Cliffs of Dover' this ruffling is quite gentle and does not obscure the general classic flower shape, while in others like 'Titan's Glory' the ruffling almost obscures (but does not detract from the beauty of) the flower shape. In 'Autumn Leaves' the falls are even lightly serrated, but fortunately they are not too wide and the flowers are not over-large so the overall effect is very pleasant.

Ruffling, whether heavy or light, gives interest and beauty to flaring flowers, but the next development is less common and less pleasing, to my eyes. This is lace, which looks as though the petals are made of plastic and someone has pushed a pin into and almost through them, stretching the petals into small peaks. It

'Lurid' is an exciting space-age iris with orange and white fuzzy horns that lift off the falls.

is usually associated with extreme ruffling at the petal edges and it gives a very frilly edge to the standards and falls by obscuring the line of the petal edge, though it is often most pronounced on the standards. Examples include 'Lace Jabot' and 'Chartreuse Ruffles'. Although it is an Intermediate rather than a Tall Bearded, it is worth mentioning that the old cultivar 'Zua', registered in 1914, has a type of lace on its pale blue or white petals, giving the impression that the petals have been partly melted over a hairbrush.

Fortunately, flowers with no standards and extra falls have not been popular, and to my knowledge there are none in commerce. However, in 50 years they may be common in the same way as that flower shape is in cultivated forms of I. ensata. Multi-petalled iris that

regularly produce more than three standards and falls should not be confused with the habit that some iris have of producing flowers with four or even five standards and falls on terminal flowers, those buds at the top of the spike. Some cultivars seem more prone than others, 'Sherbourne' being one of them.

SPACE-AGE IRIS

The most controversial developments have been in pursuit of the 'space-age' iris. This loose term refers to a number of additions (or outgrowths) from the fall that cause some iris lovers to throw up their arms in horror. In my experience they do not detract from the beauty of the flower, in fact they do not even appear in some seasons, but I confess that I would not want them on a flower with ruffles and lace!

The most basic of these developments, which all sprout from the base of the beard, is the horn. Usually

The blooms of 'Arcady' are gently waved rather than ruffled and most elegant in pale blue.

this is quite short but it lifts away from the petal surface so that if the fall drops away from the horizontal, the horn stands out proud. Horn is an apposite term because it usually ends in quite a sharp-looking point, though it is of course soft. Sometimes the horn may be furry along some of its length and it may be of a contrasting colour to the fall and the beard, 'sometimes' referring not just to the cultivar but also the season, the country it is grown in, and even the flower on the spike. This variability is one of the reasons that some growers are so against 'space-agers'. While I have no

desire to see all iris with horns, I believe that they add a bit of fun and extra interest if the basic flower and plant is gardenworthy in the first place – novelties on bad irises are fine for breeding but not to name and sell. 'Sky Hooks' was one of the first relatively stable introductions and has been widely used to further this race. My favourite is the striking 'Thornbird', in sombre shades which are described by the raiser, Monty Byers of California, as 'ecru'. The dull purple horn is often jagged, like a lick of flame, and is always present, in my experience.

Next on the scale of oddity is the spoon, which is like a larger horn with a tiny petal on the end, and depending on the season there may be flounces, a number of petaloid structures emanating from the end of the beard. The good thing is that those iris that should produce them will usually make the effort of producing a horn or two if nothing else. At the moment these iris are not common, but they have their devotees. In their favour, many are strong growers and make a good splash of colour in the garden, though currently their flowers are less refined than others.

FLOWER COLOUR

The Tall Bearded iris have the widest colour range of all, but there is still, despite the effort breeders have expended in the process, no true blue or scarlet. There is no truly black or green iris either, but colours get as close as most people would truly want, and there is every combination of colours imaginable . . . or there will be before long, I suspect.

There are many colour patterns and, though the less common ones may be more rapturously received, none are generally thought of as better than others, although haft markings, the tiger stripes at the top of the falls, are thought to be a defect except where they are an obvious and integral part of the colour pattern of the flower. Personally, I find they detract from the beauty of most iris, though they do not affect the garden display value of plants.

The other flower parts that are increasingly important are the style arms, and particularly the two crests on each above the stigmatic flap, which form a 'roof' for the top of the beard and serve to fill the void between the base of the standards. Usually the colouring matches the standards but it can be completely different and suffused with other shades to create a beautiful feature in itself.

In 'self' colours the whole flower is one colour, although there may be a little variation around the beard (called either a blaze or flare) which is often paler.

BLUE

Blue is the colour most often associated with iris and some of the classic hybrids are blue. Some of the best are 'Jane Phillips' (1946), a Dykes Medal winner with mid-blue flowers and a very pale, almost white beard; 'Arcady' (1959), a distinct waved rather than ruffled pale blue, flaring but with rather narrow petals; 'Babbling Brook' (1965), a lovely ruffled mid-blue with a paler blaze; 'Victoria Falls' (1977), another mid-blue

with ruffles and a white beard; and 'Wharfedale' (1989), a tall ruffled blue with a white beard.

There are many dark blues and purples available, which include those 'black' iris which are popular simply because they offer such an unusual colour in the garden. The black is not, of course, totally without colour, but, when held to the light, the petals are suffused with deep blackcurrant. Nor is the colour unique to iris: it is present in cornflowers (*Centaurea cyanus* 'Black Ball'), tulips (*Tulipa* 'Queen of Night') and violas (*Viola* 'Bowles' Black' and the deeper, larger 'Molly Sanderson'). 'Black Swan' (1960) is the most commonly available but 'Dusky Dancer' (1967) is a good flaring deep purple and 'Superstition' (1977) and 'Black Flag' (1983) are superior blacks with beautiful ruffling. In these and other blacks the intensity of colouring is enhanced by the velvety matt texture of the petals.

Deep blues really came of age with the introduction of 'Arabi Pashi' (1951) in Britain and 'Allegiance' (1957) in America. Both were deep, purplish blues and this has remained a popular colour with gardeners and breeders. Among the newest are 'Deep Pacific' (1975), 'Festival Crown' (1992), named for the British garden festival in Wales in 1992, and 'Titan's Glory' (1981), which is a large, ruffled purple.

PINK AND RED

Pinks have been rather slower to develop, and though early hybrids were described as pink, they all had mauve or orange tints combined. Most of these had yellow pigments in the petals, but by crossing pinks with blues, cleaner mauve pinks rather than salmon pinks have been produced. Good clean oranges have now been developed and red pigments have been isolated and enhanced in the beards, even on whites and blues, but at present there are no clear, true reds. Those iris that are described as red are actually bright browns, maroon or orange – there is nothing to match the bright red of poppies. Although it appears that the pigments in iris would not allow this colour to be developed, so much has happened in the twentieth century that it would be foolhardy to suggest that reds are not attainable.

'Beverly Sills' is a landmark pink with great ruffling, though not common in Britain; 'Fantasy Fair' (1977) is laced and ruffled; 'Vanity' (1974) is a pale pink; 'Dovedale' (1980) is a lilac pink; 'Paradise' (1979) is a rich pink with contrasting orange beard and plenty of ruffles and lace; and 'Good Fairy' (1989) is a mid-pink with long horns or spoons and extraordinary vigour. Reds merge imperceptibly with brown or orange in iris, and there are a few superb selfs, though for me this colour is at its best when combined with other colour in some of the patterns. 'Ninevah' (1965) is a particularly fine reddish iris that owes its special satin sheen and distinct hues to its aril genes. 'Muriel Neville' (1963) is a good burgundy red and 'Red Kite' (1989) and 'Red Rufus' (1979) are both good modern reds; 'Fort Regent' (1987) has two shades of red, as does my favourite red, 'Purgatory' (1987), which is flaring, ruffled and really a deep rusty orange with a hint of chestnut. It is easy to become seduced by iris catalogues; their adjectival skills put wine tasters to shame.

In the true browns, 'Café Society' (1983) is a favourite of mine, with heavily ruffled flowers in the colour of coffee ice-cream, but 'Blue-Eyed Brunette' (1964) is probably a better garden plant offering mid-tan flowers with a pale blue patch below the orange beards on the falls. This one is not a showy plant but one with real presence.

'Jungle Shadows' always surprises me, the first surprise being that it ever got named at all. The flowers are brown, not a rich orange brown but a rather dirty khaki brown, with standards that huddle together in a cone and strappy falls that seem to show the distortion of virus. Then mine changed one year, with brighter colours and no distortion. I would say that it is interesting rather than beautiful, but it might well be an iris for flower arrangers.

'Good Fairy' is a pink space-age iris with thin horns that remonts in some circumstances.

YELLOW AND WHITE

Yellow has always been a strong colour, ever since 'W. R. Dykes', Sydney Mitchell's 'Happy Days' and William Mohr's 'Alta California' in the USA in the 1930s. However, 'Golden Hind' (1934) was the first real strong yellow. Now there are so many to choose from, but particularly to be recommended are 'Ultrapoise' (1961), a very pretty rich yellow of perfect proportion, not too big, on lovely stalks, 'Ola Kala' (1942), a little old-fashioned but bright and cheerful, and 'Spirit of Memphis' (1976), with ruffles and lace.

Whites too have seen purity of colour, petal thickness and ruffling and beard colour increased so that the old 'Frost and Flame' (1956) with red beards has been replaced by the sparkling 'Bewick Swan' (1980) and then 'Mute Swan' (1985) which will be superseded itself, while there are pure whites with less showy beards such as 'Snowy Owl' (1977).

COLOUR PATTERNS

All the colours described so far are selfs, but it is among the patterns and blends that many of the most attractive iris are to be found. Some of them are too complicated and fussy to work well in the border and, for example, a good strong yellow self among red lupins makes a more striking contrast than a yellow plicata or bicolor. On the other hand, some of the colour combinations are just what gardeners need for colour schemes, and against a plainer background of foliage a few carefully chosen fancy iris can stop you in your tracks.

Plicatas have a light ground colour and are stippled and lined with a darker colour around the edge of the petals. Sometimes the darker patterning will be well defined and limited to the very edge, while in others it will leave only a small central area of white or cream and there may even be a central stripe from the beard to the base of the fall. The standards usually share a similar or almost identical patterning. The classic plicata is blue on white and 'Stepping Out' (1964) is the most famous and generally admired. 'Dancer's Veil' (1959) is less bright but very beautiful and 'Violet Icing' (1993) is a subtle plicata. 'Foggy Dew' (1968) is unusual because the falls have a pale plicata pattern but the standards are grey and lavender, and 'Kissing Circle' (1980) has the plicata pattern enhanced by a solid band of colour around the petals.

This pattern is now extended to nearly all colours

'Braithwaite' shows the neglecta pattern of pale blue standards above deeper blue falls.

but looks especially good with browns and russets as in 'Colorwatch' (1987), 'Wild Ginger' (1960) and 'Autumn Leaves' (1972). A colour pattern that seems to be related (at least genetically) is the striped pattern, which is usually an irregular streaking of blue or purple and white. The only iris of this kind I have grown is 'Bohnsack' (1981), a Border Bearded with a rather small but pretty flower which is basically white but striped in straight lines and segments with purple. It is rather too unstable in its colour patterns to be a great iris but it is fun. 'Purple Streaker' (1981) is bigger and basically purple, with small white splashes and streaks over the whole flower.

The amoena pattern is more specific and applies to iris with white standards and coloured falls. The old 'Headlines' (1953) and 'Wabash' (1936) are both purple amoenas and 'Margharee' (1986) is a modern ruffled pink. Amoenas are not as popular as they deserve to be and, at their best, modern cultivars have a light and airy character.

Neglectas are a larger, similar group, where the standards are pale blue and the falls a deeper blue. 'Braithwaite' (1952) is a good older kind and 'Magic Man' (1979) and 'Dream Lover' (1970) are brighter, more ruffled modern developments. This pattern has been extended to other colours so that there are now yellow neglectas such as 'Golden Alps' (1952).

The flower pattern of the typical *I. variegata* with yellow standards and falls heavily lined or suffused with maroon or brown has been developed to produce a small but important group of cultivars. The colour pattern may be restrictive, but these are brilliantly effective in the garden and no collection can be without at least one. The standard cultivar that is most readily available is 'Staten Island' (1945), which has rather narrow falls. 'Mary Vernon' (1940) is similar. Deeper standards are the attraction of 'Brown Trout' (1959) but modern developments have more even fall colouring, fewer haft markings and brighter colours. 'Doctor Behenna' (1991) is ruffled in gold and brown, and 'Hail to Rome' (1986) is fabulously dark for this pattern.

Bicolors have standards and falls of different colours, such as the exceptional 'Edith Wolford' with primrose standards and lavender falls, all ruffled to perfection. These are some of the most beautiful iris, with fascinating combinations such as the aptly named grey and lavender 'Wood Pigeon' and the subtle tones of 'Chartreuse Ruffles' (1975).

BORDER BEARDED IRIS

Border Bearded iris (BBs) have flowers of similar size to the Tall Beardeds but their stems are shorter – between 41 and 70cm (16 and 27in) high. They flower at the same time and are useful in an iris bed to plant at the front to cover the bare stems of the taller plants. Although the choice of cultivars is poor (or sensible) compared with the TBs, there are many beautiful plants that are better suited to exposed and windy gardens.

In 1994 the British Dykes Medal was given to 'Orinoco Flow', a ruffled, bright white and purple plicata, and other good cultivars are 'Whoop 'em Up' (1974) and 'Cherry Falls' (1949), both variegatas in red and yellow, 'Marmalade Skies' (1978) in orange and peach and 'Zeeland' (1984), a blue amoena. But for my money the best, and one of the best of all iris, is 'Brown Lasso' (1972) which has the combination of butterscotch standards and violet falls, edged with a ring of caramel brown. It shares some of the colours of the TB 'Blue Eyed Brunette' but has a flaring, ruffled form on a short plant and is highly desirable.

MINIATURE TALL BEARDED IRIS

These iris (MTBs) flower at the same time as the TBs and BBs. They are the same height as the BBs but have smaller flowers that should not measure more than 15cm (6in) in either height or width. In general, the shorter cultivars have smaller flowers and taller ones reach the top of the flower size scale. Proportion is the key word with MTBs and to balance the flower size the stems should be thin and elegant. Because of the small size of the petals, ruffling and other fancies are limited. They are often called Table Iris, particularly in America, because they are so suited to picking and flower arranging. They are certainly easier to mix into general border schemes than some of the modern TBs. My favourite is 'Bumblebee Deelite' (1986), a dainty variegata in deep red and yellow, but others include 'Carolyn Rose' (1970), a pink plicata; 'Chian Wine' (1976), in purple; 'Lodestar' (1925), a dazzling red and yellow variegata; 'Lucky Charm' (1986), a deep red and yellow variegata; 'Slim Jim' (1978), very pale mauve; 'Topsy Turvy' (1963), a reversed yellow amoena; Velvet Bouquet' (1983), purple; and 'Puppy Love' (1980), salmon pink.

INTERMEDIATE IRIS

The Intermediate Bearded iris (IBs), also known as medians, are the same height as Border Bearded iris and have flowers of the same size but flower earlier, some time between the dwarf kinds and the taller sorts, at the very end of spring. They have an interesting history and two names that are linked with them are William John Caparne, who may have been responsible for their initial development, and the nursery firm of Kelways at Langport in Somerset, home of the 'Langport' range of IBs.

William Caparne was initially primarily an artist, working from Oundle in Northamptonshire, but through his contacts with various commissioning nurserymen such as Peter Barr and Cornelius Gerrit van Tubergen, founder of the famous Dutch nursery, he became a grower of daffodils and other bulbs and then irises. By crossing dwarf irises with taller cultivars he produced intermediate irises (intermediate in both size and flowering time) and by 1900 he was exporting these to North America.

By this time he had moved to Guernsey, where he established the Iris Plant & Bulb Company, St Martins. Already he was offering 30 intermediates. His aim was 'to obtain the colours of the late tall Summer-flowering irises in the early Spring varieties of so-called pumila'. It was Sir Michael Foster who encouraged his work, advising him to force the tall cultivars in a glasshouse to synchronize their flowering with the dwarf types.

Although at first these hybrids were short, with only one or two buds per stem, the race soon became recognized as valuable and beautiful garden plants. Many were trialled at the Royal Horticultural Society gardens at Wisley, and earned awards. By 1907 Caparne had sold plants to Goos and Koenmann in Germany, who continued his work there with great success. His iris were so popular in America that in 1927, when it was just seven years old, the American Iris Society reported that three-quarters of the iris grown there were from his list. Since 1940 this class has increased even more in popularity, the colour range has improved enormously, and Caparne's dream has been fulfilled. In the USA Paul Cook and Geddes Douglas performed similar crosses to Caparne, but Cook sent pollen of his dwarf iris to Douglas, who lived 800km (500 miles) further south and could use it to pollinate his TBs. The most important of all their seedlings, because it became a useful parent and because it is still so commonly grown, is 'Greenspot' (actually a Standard Dwarf not strictly an IB by today's classification) with its characteristic 'thumbprint' on the falls below the beard.

The Intermediate iris are often not as flamboyant as the taller, later kinds – their petals may be narrower and the flowers are smaller, some only just bigger than the dwarfs. They are ideal for small borders and to edge paths and they are often more reliable in northern and less sunny areas. All the 'Langport' cultivars are reliable and have stood the test of time, but the colours are a little muddied and devotees of cleaner, brighter colours might look at more recent introductions. These include bright pinks such as 'Raspberry Blush' (1975), the beautiful 'Bluebird in Flight' (1986), with white standards, blue falls and a red beard, and familiar patterns such as plicatas illustrated by 'Rare Edition' (1980) and 'Happy Mood' (1967).

SMALL SPECIES

IRIS APHYLLA

This species from Central and Eastern Europe is unusual in that it is deciduous. It is a good garden species, producing well-branched stems up to 30cm (1ft) high. In shorter forms, these stems, which usually branch from the base, produce a fine, compact display. The flowers, borne in mid-spring, are purple or dark blue with a pale beard and stripy hafts, and are up to 8cm (3¼in) in diameter. This species is thought to have been involved in the breeding of Miniature Tall Bearded iris, and it is certainly a pretty and easy plant, albeit prone to virus.

IRIS ATTICA

Less hardy, and less predictable in temperate zones, the tiny *I. attica* from Turkey and Greece is a gem with short, curved leaves and flowers just 10cm (4in) high. The flower colour is typically purple or maroon, but can be yellow. The falls and standards are narrow, giving a spidery but elegant flower. It needs a protected, sunny spot outside where it will often bloom in mid-spring, among the earliest of all iris.

IRIS LUTESCENS

This is the correct name for the plant that has long been known as *I. chamaeiris*. In flower it can be 8–25cm (4–10in) high, and the flower colour also varies from yellow to purple and violet. The flowers have falls that often curl under towards the stem and are sometimes rather small for the size of the standards, but it is a robust plant, forming good clumps in the garden. It blooms later than *I. pumila*, in late spring, and is different in possessing a relatively tall flower stem (as opposed to the long perianth tube of *I. pumila*). It is a native of Spain, France and Italy.

IRIS PUMILA

I. pumila has a very wide natural range from southern and eastern Europe into Russia. It is thought that it may have evolved by ancient hybridization between *I. attica* and *I. pseudopumila*, and it occurs in a confusing array of forms in colours from yellow to purple. However, this natural variation has helped to produce the dwarf bearded iris of gardens. Each short stem usually produces a solitary flower in late spring with a long perianth tube and the leaves die away in winter. It has

given its genes and its name to the dwarf cultivars, which are often called 'pumilas' though they are of more complex hybrid origin.

IRIS PSEUDOPUMILA

This species from Italy, Malta and Sicily has taller true flower stems and is evergreen, but otherwise it is rather similar to *I. pumila* and similarly variable in flower colour.

IRIS REICHENBACHII

This is a rather leafy species from northern Greece and the Balkans with foliage reaching 30cm (1ft) tall, a little higher than the flowers, which may be yellow or purple. They are borne in late spring.

IRIS SUAVEOLENS

I. suaveolens (syn. *I. mellita*) is one of the shortest species, just 15cm (6in) tall when in flower. A plant from Turkey, Bulgaria and Romania, it has curved foliage and attractive flowers, two to a stem, of purple, yellow, or a combination of both to produce brownish shades. It flowers in late spring, a week or so later than *I. pumila*.

IRIS SUBBIFLORA

This species has a more westerly distribution than most of the others, coming from south-west Europe. The evergreen clumps of leaves give rise to stems of two deep purplish-blue flowers in mid- to late spring. It is 30cm (1ft) or more tall when in flower. This is a plant for sunny, limy soils.

DWARF BEARDED IRIS

The Standard Dwarf Bearded iris (SDBs) are among the first to flower, often in mid-spring and certainly by late spring. (The word standard means normal, not that they are grown on a single stem.) They grow between 20 and 41cm (8 and 16in) tall and are sometimes called Lilliput iris, though with such varied pedigrees some do not always fit happily into this size band, and the delineation between these and the IBs is often a foggy area. However, these iris usually have one small branch on the flower stems and produce two to four flowers per stem. Early cultivars did not produce as many flowers and modern breeders have helped gardeners by giving us better flowers on better plants. In general, SDBs are

PLATE III

I. 'Festival Crown'
Tall Bearded

I. 'Fairy Light'
Early Tall Bearded

I. 'Burford'
Intermediate Bearded

I. 'Magic Man'
Tall Bearded

All plants shown at approximately 1/3 *size*

I.'Titan's Glory'
Tall Bearded

I.'Lodestar'
Miniature Tall Bearded

I.'Elizabeth Poldark'
Tall Bearded

I.'Bryn Gwyn'
Tall Bearded

I.'Pascoe'
Tall Bearded

I.'Kent Pride'
Tall Bearded

vigorous and easy to grow. They do not require the sun-ripening that some of the taller iris prefer and, of course, they are weather- and wind-resistant with their compact habit and small flowers.

The species that has given rise to this group is undoubtedly *I. pumila*, though the hybrids are considerably taller. The other species involved in creating the hybrids were probably *I. flavissima* and *I. chamaeiris*. In the UK Amos Perry exhibited 'Canary Bird' and 'Bridesmaid' in 1902, and Paul Cook continued the work in the USA in the 1930s.

Although the short spikes do not produce as many buds as the other bearded iris, the flowers are all carried at one height and, viewed from above, can give a carpet of colour for two or three weeks.

Once again there is a bewildering range of colours to choose from, many with 'thumbprints' of a contrasting colour on the falls, or colourful beards. They are good plants for the front of the border, for the large rock garden or lower beds of a small rock garden where they can be looked down on and will not dry out excessively in summer. They also fit in well with modern ideas of gravel-covered beds interspersed with bronze *Carex* and grasses, eryngiums and bulbs, but they must not be planted in tiny holes through planting membranes because the creeping rhizomes will soon outgrow the allotted soil. Among my personal favourites are 'Double Lament' (1969), a sad name for a very pretty purple flower, although I find its stems sometimes topple over, 'Sarah Taylor' (1979), a pale yellow with blue beards, and 'Sun Doll' (1986), which has sweetly scented bright yellow flowers from buds that open like small roses. 'Bibury' (1975) is an excellent cream; 'Clap Hands' (1976) is an interesting brown plicata; 'Jeremy Brian' (1975) is a pale blue; and 'Triplicate' (1983) is a strange brown with blue beards.

For the very tiniest gardens, where space is at a premium, and for the rock garden, the Miniature Dwarf Bearded iris (MDBs) are perfect. They are similar to SDBs and can have flowers of the same size but are never taller than 20cm (8in) and are usually much smaller. The tiniest have small flowers with narrow and sometimes pendant falls and conical standards. Their small size and graceful flower shape would not offend any but the most fussy of alpine enthusiasts and they suit rock gardens very well, especially if planted in an elevated pocket where the flowers can be raised nearer

'Rare Edition' combines the traditional plicata patterning and blue edging with a crisp white ground colour and flaring falls, a pattern mimicked on small iris such as 'Knick Knack'.

to eye level so that they can be better appreciated. 'Grapelet' (1989) and 'Libation' (1974) are two tiny purples, 'Zipper' (1979) and 'Bee Wings' (1959) are small yellows, and 'Knick Knack' (1959) is a popular white veined with blue.

PLANTING COMPANIONS

The dwarf bulbous iris flower earlier and have more delicate flowers than most bearded iris, but their leaves are taller and very unsightly in early summer. This is not a problem with the dwarf bearded iris. Though their foliage may not be the greatest asset on the rock garden it is rarely a liability and once the flowers have faded and been removed, low-growing annuals may be sown to bring colour to patches of iris. I would never suggest that leafy annuals be sown among delicate or valuable plants as their growth would shade the rhizomes and possibly encourage rot through poor air movement and excessive moisture at the base of the fans. In addition, the annuals may compete for soil nutrients and reduce growth. However, a few small annuals may be sown around the clumps without causing harm and I would recommend the many small and bright *Lobularia* (alyssum) strains, the pretty *Leptosiphon*, *Ionopsidium* and *Eschscholzia caespitosa*. Purists may be horrified at the thought of these annuals on a rock garden but they are easily controlled, bring interesting colour to extend the display and will self-seed.

One of my favourite companions is *Myosotis*, the humble forget-me-not. The plain pale blue combines with white, blue, and especially yellow iris, and the pink and white *Myosotis* extend the number of combinations even more. The flaring falls of the hybrid iris mean that the surrounding mist of flowers does not detract from their beauty. As soon as the *Myosotis* has finished flowering it should be removed before it sets seed or becomes mildewed.

For many gardeners there are no prettier plants than the dwarf species and a surprisingly wide range of colours can be grown, even among a single species. Most are of easy culture if given a gritty, preferably alkaline soil in full sun. They will grow and flower best if they are in fertile soil and are divided as the rhizomes become crowded. The smallest can be grown in pots or a frame. Unfortunately a few are very prone to virus diseases, for which there is no cure, but many set seed readily and this provides a good method of producing clean plants if they are kept away from their infected parents which can reinfect them if aphids (or the gardener's knife) transmit the virus. Seedlings will usually flower within three years of sowing, but because this group of iris are notoriously promiscuous, it is wise to isolate flowers that are to produce seed to keep stock breeding true.

REMONTANT IRIS

Although it occurs in some other groups, especially Siberians (where it is most common for extra flower spikes to be produced immediately after the normal flowering season) remontancy is possibly most important among bearded iris. These have two main periods of growth as described earlier in this chapter, but remontants, which are identical in appearance to other cultivars, are usually very vigorous and continue to grow during the summer after the initial burst of root activity immediately following flowering.

There are two basic types of remontants, each of which is suited to its own climate. The cold-climate remontants have been bred to flower again as soon as possible after their first flowering and these often enter dormancy too early for growers who enjoy warm climates with long growing periods. The opposite problem, the commonest for British growers, is that iris bred for warm climates do not flower quickly, and their flower spikes are beginning to be produced in mid- to late autumn or even early winter. These seem to be frost-resistant while contained within the sheaf of leaves but once above that they are killed by winter cold. The following spring the sideshoots that should be flowering are so small that they do not flower either.

To remont successfully it is important that the plants are grown well, and that means that unlike other iris they should be watered and fed in early summer, along with other border plants. The best reblooming is found in young established clumps.

Remontants have received a mixed reception, mostly because the first were rather old-fashioned flowers with other faults like narrow falls or strong haft marks. In the UK some nurserymen considered them inconvenient because they do not stop growing in late summer, a busy packing time, but their main disadvantage is that they are unpredictable, and it is hard to see that they will be popular until the breakthrough cultivar is produced that will remont every summer in every part of the country. It is said that at present they will only remont in the southern third of the country, but having flowered them at the northern limit of that zone I am sure progress will be made.

Remontant iris are no longer ugly ducklings and the proof is the beautiful 'Victoria Falls', a Dykes Medal winner in 1984. It even performs in Britain. 'Vanity' (1975) is a ruffled pink that is a star even among summer flowers and 'Triplicate' (1983), that odd brown SDB, will throw up spikes throughout the summer. Among important TBs is 'Grand Baroque', a pale green-yellow, raised in the 1970s by Lloyd Zurbrigg in Virginia, America, the breeder of many remontants. 'Corn Harvest' in yellow, 'Lovely Again' in mauve and 'Sign of Leo' (1977) in purple will remont in Britain, but in my experience the best of all (though the flowers have falls that grow too large) is 'English Cottage', a pale plicata that is often almost white in autumn. A clump of this always remonts wherever I grow it, with most spikes flowering in mid-autumn, but sometimes also in late summer and late autumn.

3

THE SIBERIAN IRIS
Section Limniris, Series Sibiricae

The Siberian iris is one of the best-known and best-loved of garden plants. In its natural form it is delicate yet colourful, and a survivor even where it it is left to grow without constant attention. Yet there are many modern hybrids that most gardeners are not aware of, with larger flowers and brighter colours, and there are many more species for the gardener to discover in the Series Sibiricae.

The Siberian iris is a term used by botanists to describe 11 species (one of them not in cultivation) which are divided into two groups according to their number of chromosomes. This may seem to be an unnecessary complication as chromosome numbers are not a convenient aid to identification in the garden, but those with 28 chromosomes are generally considered to be rather easier to grow than those with 40 chromosomes. They also require less moisture and are more tolerant of soils with a pH of more than 7 (neutral). This variance in chromosomes must not be confused with tetraploids, which occur when a plant has twice the usual complement of chromosomes for its type and is often more vigorous than the norm: there are tetraploid Siberians, but these have 56 chromosomes, with all the benefits (or otherwise, depending on your opinion) of tetraploidy, such as larger flowers, thicker petals and brighter colour.

The 28 chromosome species are *I. sanguinea*, *I. sibirica* and *I. typhifolia*, those with 40 chromosomes being *I. bulleyana*, *I. chrysographes*, *I. clarkei*, *I delavayi*, *I. dykesii*, *I. forrestii* and *I. wilsonii*. Though the flowers are smaller, the last seven are useful in the garden because they generally flower a few weeks later than the first four listed, and they are very elegant in habit. They are sometimes split into the subseries Chrysographes.

As Siberians are finding increasing favour with gardeners, breeders are beginning to put more effort into their development and the range of cultivars is expanding rapidly. But the species remain relatively stable, in number and kind, save for the further work of botanists who may decide that a new or more accurate taxonomy is necessary.

I. sibirica is the first iris I really remember as a child, and it grew in heavy wet clay where the few bedding plants I had could barely survive. The clumps grew for many years, without division or feeding, and every year could be counted on to flower well. They were disease-resistant and never received watering or feeding. This is one of the great attributes of the Siberian iris; they tolerate neglect and are good, long-lived garden plants that go quietly about their business. They are not the biggest or rarest or most spectacular iris, but, adopting the pragmatic view, the Siberians are better garden plants than the Tall Bearded iris with their infinite variety of colours and shapes, especially for the gardener who needs foolproof plants to enhance the garden. More than any other group, this is a class of all-round garden plants – even in autumn, when the leaves assume deep brown tones, they still have an appeal. Their appearance suits them to waterside locations and they are perfect planting companions for *Tricyrtis*, *Astilbe*, *Primula* and *Lobelia* at the edge of a pool or stream.

28 CHROMOSOME SPECIES
IRIS SANGUINEA

I. sanguinea is often confused with *I. sibirica* but can be most readily distinguished by its unbranched stems bearing only two flower buds. The stems may reach 70cm (28in) and the flowers may be 8cm (3¼in) across,

'Berlin Little Blue' shows the chubby, rounded flower shape that has been produced in Dwarf Siberians.

larger than those of *I. sibirica*. The leaves may be as long as the flower spikes, which detracts a little from its garden value. It is found from eastern Russia east to Japan and Korea and readily hybridizes with *I. sibirica*, by accident and also by the gardener's design as the purple flowers have extended the blue colour range. Both species and the hybrids flower in early to midsummer.

IRIS SIBIRICA

An elegant, attractive plant, *I. sibirica* is native to Europe and northern Asia, and has the widest and most westerly distribution of the species of the Sibiricae series. It has the useful attribute of flower stems that are taller than the leaves, reaching a height of 80cm (28in) or more. The flower stems carry one or more branches and the terminal spathe produces between two and five (usually three) buds which open to flowers about 7.5cm (3in) across. The falls are arching and elegantly pendulous and the standards are upright. The typical flower colour is blue-violet, and there is a white mark at the base of the falls veined with the ground colour. The seed pods are rounded and no more than twice as long as wide. There is some variation in flower colour and a white variety occurs in the wild. This species also differs from *I. sanguinea* in that its buds emerge from dried, brown spathes, rather than from green ones as in *I. sanguinea*.

IRIS TYPHIFOLIA

This species was described in 1928 but was not introduced into cultivation in the West until 1988. It has very slender leaves, as narrow as 3mm (¹/₈in), and deep purple flowers with little other marking. It resembles a very thin, narrow *I. sibirica*. It is probably a 28 chromosome species, comes from north-east China and may be useful in breeding work because it flowers earlier than other Siberians.

40 CHROMOSOME SPECIES

IRIS BULLEYANA

Much conjecture has surrounded *I. bulleyana*, which was originally described in 1910 by the irisian W. R. Dykes from material obtained from A. K. Bulley. It was supposed to have been grown from seed collected by George Forrest, though he apparently never saw it in the wild. To add to the confusion, Dykes stated 11 years later that *I. bulleyana* did not breed true from seed, a sure sign of hybrid origin, and it was suggested that this plant arose as a hybrid in Bulley's Cheshire garden. It was thought to be possibly a hybrid of *I. chrysographes* and *I. forrestii* or *I. wilsonii*, though this cross could not have occurred in Bulley's garden because the last two species were not introduced to Britain until 1907 and 1908 respectively, and this would not have allowed for a flowering plant by 1910 for Dykes to describe. However the mystery was a step nearer to being solved when *I. bulleyana* was found on the 1994 Alpine Garden Society/Royal Botanic Garden Edinburgh expedition to China. It is a compact species reaching 45cm (18in), with flaring blue/violet flowers up to 8cm (3¹/₄in) in diameter appearing from early to midsummer, usually before full leaf development.

IRIS CHRYSOGRAPHES

The darkest flowers of this group are produced by the lovely *I. chrysographes*, named after the golden markings that look like writing on the falls of the deep purple flowers, which in some forms are almost black. They are carried on unbranched stems about 50cm (20in) tall in midsummer. It is reported to hybridize with *I. forrestii* and *I. sibirica* (even though the latter is a different chromosome group). This species from China

The more typical drooping falls of the Siberian species such as *Iris forrestii* are echoed in 'Cleeton Double Chance'.

and north-east Burma is said to be fragrant and though I have not noticed this it would be a desirable characteristic to introduce to hybrids as this group of plants is generally without much scent.

IRIS CLARKEI

I. clarkei is unusual in that it has solid flower stalks, hardly of importance as a garden plant but useful for identification. It is a pretty species, reaching 60cm (24in) when in flower in early summer, with stems carrying up to three branches and purple flowers with pendent falls and almost horizontal standards. There is a clear white signal patch on the falls, often rimmed with a deeper band, and yellow markings on the hafts. It is not as widely grown as its beauty merits, but then few species are.

IRIS DELAVAYI

The giant of the group is *I. delavayi*, which has flower stems up to 1.5m (60in), dwarfing the leaves. The stem branches carry one or two buds that open to large purple flowers up to 10cm (4in) across of elegant pendent form with splayed but not horizontal standards. They appear in midsummer.

IRIS DYKESII

This species is like a vigorous form of *I. chrysographes* and has deep purple flowers with yellow and white fall markings in early summer. It was sent to W. R. Dykes from St Petersburg, Russia, but did not flower until 1926, after Dykes's death. It is not known in the wild and is rare in cultivation. It may be a hybrid.

IRIS FORRESTII

There are two yellow-flowered species in the group and this one is slender and elegant, with pale yellow flowers with drooping falls and upright standards. The unbranched flower stems reach 40cm (16in), significantly taller than the leaves, and carry two flowers in midsummer. This is a pretty, easy-to-grow plant from Tibet, Yunnan, Sichuan and Burma.

IRIS WILSONII

This yellow-flowered species from China is superficially similar to *I. forrestii* but makes a more robust plant, with leaves as tall as the flower stems. Each stem carries two yellow flowers up to 8cm (3^1/$_4$in) across with flaring standards that stand out from the vertical. *I. wilsonii* flowers later in midsummer than *I. forrestii*, but when grown side-by-side the two plants will hybridize.

DEVELOPMENT OF HYBRIDS

I. sibirica has been cultivated for longer than the other species in this group, probably since the time of Carolus Clusius (1526–1609), and it has been developed through selection and hybridization by gardeners. Clusius named the plant we now know as *I. sibirica* as *I. angustifolia media* and it was the father of modern plant naming, Linnaeus, who in 1753 coined the name we use today. *I. sanguinea* was the next species known in the West, though it was not given that name until the 1950s, having been first described as *I. orientalis*.

The other species were introduced in the late nineteenth and early twentieth centuries and in the 1920s

hybridizing began in Britain, performed largely by Amos Perry. Not only were the Siberian iris used, but also the Pacific Coast Iris, in the latter case producing hybrids known as Calsibes. The first winner of the prestigious Dykes Medal, given to exceptional cultivars by the British and American Iris Societies, was a Calsibe called 'Margot Holmes' (1927). The number of cultivars available now runs into many hundreds, and 30 new Siberians are registered every year. Fortunately not all enter commerce, as very few can really represent something novel or better than those already available. Much of the breeding has taken place in the USA, though British breeders such as Marjorie Brummit – 'Anniversary' (1965), 'Cambridge' (1964) and 'Limeheart' (1968) – and Philip Hutchinson – 'Nottingham Lace' (1959) – are responsible for important cultivars.

The big breakthrough in Siberian breeding came in 1957 when 'White Swirl' was introduced by Fred Cassebeer. Until then all falls were pendent, just like the species, but he had collected a basket of bee-set pods, sown them, and quite by chance, out of the thousands of seedlings, one had the form and class to make it the single most important Siberian in the history of the group. 'White Swirl' had horizontal, flaring, rounded falls, quite unlike anything seen before, and it was also a good grower and performed well in the garden. Though quite old, and undoubtedly fairly small-flowered compared with what followed, it is still a first-class plant, deserving a place in every garden. In fact, it is said that its characteristics can be traced in the ancestry of any iris that is worth growing, so its genes might be in your garden even if the plant itself isn't.

As in the other highly developed types, it is contentious to say what is a good iris flower and what another lacks, though when it comes to showing and judging some traits are less desirable than others. Hybridizers generally set themselves goals, and these usually accord with what are considered improvements by the public, but the development of novelties in the flower should not proceed without thought to the plant as a whole and its value in the garden. To date, the development of Siberians has produced plants that most gardeners would find acceptable, but the turning point has been reached as the flower form has been altered to the point that the grace of the original bloom is about to be changed. There is now a range of heights of flower stalk from 60cm to 120cm (2ft to 4ft) and

Modern Siberians, especially tetraploid cultivars, exhibit deep colours and strong petals to make large flowers like 'Ruffled Velvet'.

flowers can be up to 15cm (6in) across in the newest tetraploids, though diploids are a little smaller. This increase in size is partly due to the flaring flower shape, but the falls are also much fuller, more rounded and are now found with strong ruffling in the latest hybrids. Personally I do not really want to see this, and it would be a shame to see lace and other novelties of the Tall Bearded iris appear, though I find them acceptable in that group. Perhaps inevitably, there are now cultivars with six falls, or what approaches the shape of the double *I. ensata* cultivars (*see page 52*) and these may be popular, but I would rather see flower size restrained. However, the development of more colours, breeding for scent ('Mabel Coday' is said by some to have a fragrance), better petal substance to make flowers last longer in bad weather and better branching to prolong the bloom season are all to be encouraged. Reblooming, or remontancy, in which some cultivars produce more flower spikes intermittently after the main bloom season, could also be progressed. In my opinion this would do more to encourage the cultivation of these plants than grotesquely enlarged flowers.

Good cultivation is necessary to encourage Siberians to flower a second time, though the season is only extended by a month or so, the next set of flower spikes

often being produced just as the first set are fading. The following can be expected to remont quite frequently: 'Welcome Return' (a ruffled violet), 'Ruffled Velvet' (purple), and 'Dreaming Yellow' (flaring cream with a yellow heart).

SERIES TRIPETALAE

Although this series has just two species, one is such a useful and easy garden plant that it cannot be ignored. *I. setosa* is not in fact a Siberian iris but looks like a dwarf one, though it differs from the Siberians in being short-lived – not a major disadvantage as it is easy to grow from seed. It has a remarkable distribution in the wild, from eastern Asia through Japan to Alaska and then reappearing on the east of Canada. Such a wide range of habitats has produced a very variable species, but *I. setosa* (and the rarer *I. tridentata*) are recognized by their reduced standards, giving the flowers the appearance of having just three petals. Though *I. tridentata* is uncommon and tricky in cultivation, *I. setosa* is an easy-going plant that will grow easily from seed in any acid, moist soil in sun or semi-shade. The branched stems, up to 1m (39in) in height but more often less than half that, bear six or more flowers of a bluish shade above mid-green leaves in early summer. There are many variants but one of the smallest is ssp. *canadensis*, which bears fewer flowers on unbranched stems. *I. tridentata* has violet and white flowers, but is very rarely grown in the UK at present.

4

THE PACIFIC COAST IRIS
Section Limniris, Series Californicae

It can be said that with the exception of Bearded iris every group of the genus is undervalued, underused and underplanted, and this is particularly true of the Pacific Coast Iris. Under this general heading are about a dozen species that grow wild on the west coast of North America, largely in California, but also north into Washington and Oregon. They all possess thin, wiry rhizomes and roots and narrow, long, evergreen leaves. The flower stems are usually unbranched and bear two or three flowers, but because a clump produces a number of stems, a remarkably colourful display is provided by many of the species and their hybrids. Most are rather small plants and can be planted in the front of borders in any but alkaline soils. The flowers of most are quite spreading in form, with flaring falls and oblique standards. They often have beautiful contrasting veins on the petals, which is why they are sometimes referred to as orchid iris – not something to be perpetuated. Most flower in mid- to late spring, or occasionally early summer.

In the wild, all these species are found on soils with impeccable drainage, and usually on slopes. However, there is always water deep down in the lower layers of the soil and, because these are plants that grow at the edges of woods, there is often a mulch of leaves or pine needles around the plants, preventing the roots from drying out. As a general rule, the best species for British gardens are those from the more northern regions of the group's distribution, and the biggest threat to their success in cultivation is root disturbance.

Because the different species in this series hybridize readily many beautiful cultivars have been bred, and, having 40 chromosomes, they can even be crossed with the 40 chromosome Siberian iris to produce Calsibes such as 'Golden Waves' which brings extra height to the group.

SPECIES
Not all the species are hardy, or readily available, but all are interesting and have some merit.

IRIS BRACTEATA
I. bracteata is a rather coarse plant that grows in semi-shade in the wild. Its leaves are up to 1cm ($^{1}/_{2}$ in) wide and 30cm (1ft) long, and the pale yellow flowers, veined with brown, are 8cm ($3^{1}/_{4}$in) across. Two flowers are produced in late spring on each stem. The stems are about as long as the leaves and are clothed with overlapping bracts which give the plant its name.

IRIS CHRYSOPHYLLA
This plant from Oregon has pale yellow flowers 6cm ($2^{1}/_{2}$in) across with narrow petals. It is 20cm (8in) tall and blooms in late spring.

IRIS DOUGLASIANA
This is the leafiest and also the most robust species of the group, and as the flower stems are branched and can carry as many as eight flowers when it blooms in late spring it is a good plant for garden display. In the wild it grows near the sea, unlike any other species, and has a wide distribution, largely along the Californian coastal strip and into Oregon. The flowers are large, up to 10cm (4in) across, and are carried on tall, branching stems up to 60cm (2ft) tall. They are lavender, lilac or mauve, with deeper veining. It is an adaptable plant and will grow in light shade, but may not flower so profusely as it does in sun. A useful attribute is its ability to tolerate

less than perfect soil conditions, and for gardeners on neutral or alkaline soils this is the species to try first.

IRIS FERNALDII

This species is interesting because it has a very limited distribution around San Francisco. The flowers, which are up to 7.5cm (3in) across, are pale yellow, although it hybridizes readily and plants under this name may be other colours. The leaves are grey-green and may reach as much as 45cm (18in). It blooms in late spring.

IRIS HARTWEGII

This is a small Californian species with narrow leaves. The solitary or paired rather sparse flowers borne in late spring are also small at 6cm (2¹/₂in), with narrow petals in pale yellow or lilac. There are at least three subspecies – ssp. *australis*, ssp. *columbiana* and ssp. *pinetorum* – which are usually bigger plants, the first two also being more showy than the type.

IRIS INNOMINATA

By any standards this is a first-class garden plant and many nurseries and garden centres that would not sell any other species iris stock this because they know that a plant in a pot in flower is a sure-fire seller in late spring. The evergreen clumps of narrow foliage produce 20cm (8in) stems with one or two flowers in a rich variety of colours, from yellow through orange and mauve to lilac and purple, often veined on the falls and sometimes on the standards. The flowers also show gentle ruffling. They measure 7.5cm (3in).

IRIS MACROSIPHON AND IRIS MUNZII

These two species are unfortunately too tender for general outdoor cultivation but *I. munzii* is worth growing indoors for its large flowers 7.5cm (3in) across on tall, branching stems – up to 70cm (27in). They appear in mid-spring. The flower colour may be true pale blue, violet or purple and the petals have ruffled edges. It should also be considered for cool greenhouse display.

IRIS PURDYI

In late spring this uncommon species bears two pale cream flowers up to 8cm (3¹/₄in) across per stem above dark green, purple-tinged foliage. It reaches a height of 30cm (1ft).This plant is not easy to find as the true species, having hybridized extensively.

IRIS TENAX

This dense, tufty plant was the first of this series to be discovered and is native to south-west Washington State and into Oregon, the most northerly range of any of the species. In continental climates this species is reputed to be difficult but it is quite easy in British gardens, producing its one or, less usually, two flowers per stem in late spring in shades of lavender and mauve, white or cream. They are 7.5cm (3in) across and are produced on 25cm (10in) stems. Unlike *I. douglasiana*, which will tolerate a little lime in the soil, this must have acid soil in order to flourish.

IRIS TENUISSIMA

This plant from North California has narrow-petalled pale cream flowers with brown veining. They measure 7.5cm (3in) across and are borne in pairs on stems up to 30cm (1ft) high.

CULTIVARS

The cultivars are generally more popular than the species, though a selection of seedlings from any of the species will show considerable variation and provide an interesting range of plants for the garden. However, the cultivars available certainly make a splendid display, combining colour and charming form most successfully.

The Broadleigh cultivars offered by Lady Skelmersdale, so long a feature of her stand at Chelsea Flower Show each year, give some idea of the beauty of these flowers, but equally pretty are the Banbury hybrids raised by Marjorie Brummit and introduced in the 1960s and 1970s. Some have almost pure colouring such as 'Banbury Velvet', a deep purple, while others such as 'Banbury Beauty' have dark thumbprints on a pale background, and 'Banbury Welcome' and 'Banbury Fair' are interestingly marked and veined. A standard, famous and reliable PCI is 'Arnold Sunrise', which was raised by V. H. Humphrey and introduced in 1975. It has lilac buds but opens to white with a deep yellow zone on the falls, a clear and bright flower. In the USA in the 1980s Joe Ghio introduced cultivars such as 'Big Money' (yellow) and 'Mission Santa Cruz' (almost magenta), while in Britain, Bob and Eileen Wise produced the Pinewood series including 'Pinewood Poppet' (white and yellow with purple), 'Pinewood Charmer' (yellow and pink) and 'Pinewood Sunshine' (yellow).

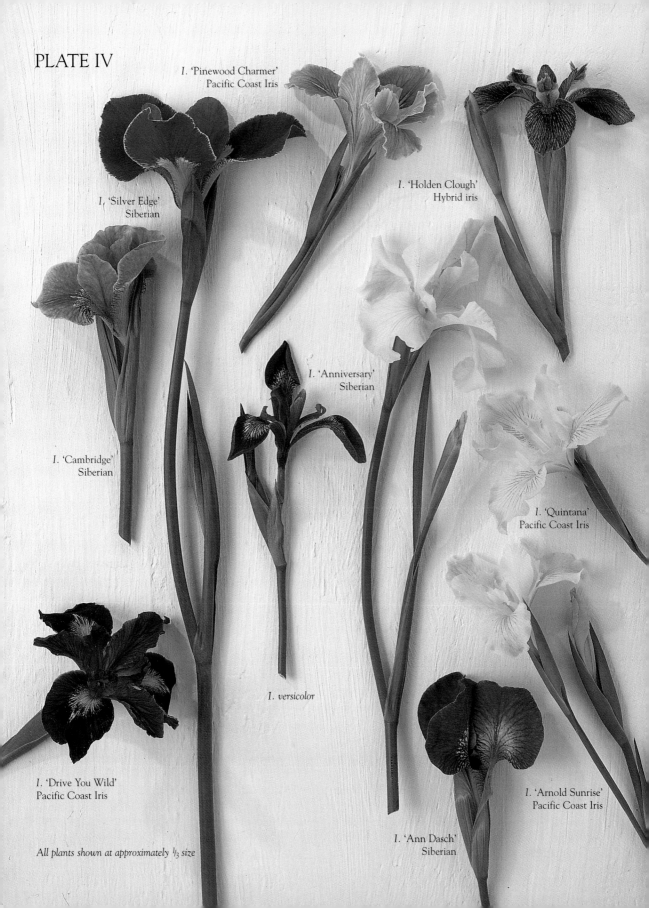

PLATE IV

I. 'Pinewood Charmer'
Pacific Coast Iris

I. 'Holden Clough'
Hybrid iris

I. 'Silver Edge'
Siberian

I. 'Anniversary'
Siberian

I. 'Cambridge'
Siberian

I. 'Quintana'
Pacific Coast Iris

I. versicolor

I. 'Drive You Wild'
Pacific Coast Iris

I. 'Arnold Sunrise'
Pacific Coast Iris

I. 'Ann Dasch'
Siberian

All plants shown at approximately ¹/₃ size

5

THE WATER IRIS
Section Limniris, Series Laevigatae and Hexagonae

SERIES LAEVIGATAE

This series of deciduous iris includes the Japanese water iris, the most revered and beautiful of all water plants when in flower in mid- to late summer. Their image appears in Japanese iconography over centuries and is accepted as a symbol of elegance and restraint in the West. Photographs of the plants in growth with their foliage and flowers emerging from a lake criss-crossed with wooden bridges give a perfect feel of how this iris should be grown – or at least that is the common perception. In fact it will not tolerate such conditions all year, and the grounds are only flooded at flowering time for effect.

The British native *I. pseudacorus* is renowned for its unfortunate tendency to treat water in the same way as duckweed – which is to say to cover it up. It is an irony that many pond plants are expensive to buy, yet become pestilential weeds in a season or two. In large ponds this plant is a positive asset, but for smaller ponds there are two less vigorous species in the series that will grow in wet soil or shallow water.

IRIS ENSATA (SYN I. KAEMPFERI)

This plant achieved a cult status in Japan, where individual plants were revered and cared for like pets, and there is even a ceremony that has evolved to accompany the opening of the flowers. In 1694, a Japanese gardening manual described eight varieties but by 1799 there were hundreds, many of which were raised by Matsudaira Shoo and his father Sadahiro who, it is said, raised double-flowered cultivars in only four generations from wild-collected seeds. They have now been so highly developed that some of today's cultivars bear little or no resemblance to the

wild plant, and have blooms at least 15cm (6in) across.

With so many cultivars available, a number of classification systems have been proposed. The traditional Japanese system is loosely based on the geographical origin of the plants. The Ise types are derived from plants at Ise, 80km (50 miles) south-east of Kyoto, and were developed after 1800. From genetic study it is clear that they were bred from a different wild source to that of the other two groups. Ise cultivars have flower stems the same height as the leaves, were originally single-flowered and have pendent falls. They were bred for pot culture, to be brought into the home and watched as they opened, and the perfection of one flower was the most important goal in breeding.

Edo types can be double- or single-flowered. This doubling of the flowers is something that occurs occasionally in other iris and is then regarded as a fault by all but the most avant garde, but in Japanese iris it is encouraged. The doubling usually takes the form of an extra set of falls, to give an even flower shape, but in multi-petalled types this can be augmented by a tuft or crown of smaller petals made up of the standards or even style arms too. In Edo iris the falls should not overlap at the haft and the flower stalks are taller than the leaves. The stems are often branched because they were bred for garden display rather than solitary perfection of flower.

The Higo types were bred from the Edos from the 1860s for pot cultivation and branching was discouraged (though modern cultivars do show branching as garden use has become more important). Higos can be single or double and have huge flowers, sometimes over 30cm (12in) in diameter. The falls overlap, are held horizontally and are often ruffled.

There is another way to classify these iris, based upon how the flowers open. Most cultivars remain essentially the same shape over the three days that they remain open. However, some, called 'acting' flowers, change shape – in particular, the falls lengthen – and it is these that are particularly desirable for the 'Act'. In this traditional ceremony, which is often accompanied by meditation, a well-grown potted iris with a single bloom stalk is brought into the home as it is about to open and placed before a gold-coloured background. Over three days the flower changes shape discreetly, and to watch a flower over three days is said to leave impressions that last a lifetime. Unfortunately, even in Japan such niceties are becoming rare, and the culture of these iris in pots is not as popular as it was.

The basic flower colour of these iris is blue and purple though white and, less usually, pink flowers occur. However, there is a great variation in patterning, and the falls and flowers may be veined, sanded (stippled), brushed, splashed and rimmed with contrasting colours. The yellow signals can be large or almost absent and often are 'haloed' with a contrasting colour. Yellow is not a colour naturally found in any of these iris, but *I. ensata* has been crossed with *I. pseudacorus*, the yellow flag, which has given rise to hybrids with yellow colouring, for example 'Kimboshi'. As these two species are in the same series they might be expected to hybridize, but many closely related interspecific crosses result in poor seedlings with weak growth and yellowish leaves.

Tetraploidy, the condition where a plant has cells that contain four sets of chromosomes instead of the usual two, is rare in nature but desirable in garden cultivars because such a change is usually associated with visible changes in the plant. These normally include larger leaves, stems and flowers, thicker substance to the petals, which may make the flowers last longer or be more resistant to weather, and brighter colours. Tetraploid cultivars did not appear in *I. ensata* until 1960, when Currier McEwen bred 'Raspberry Rimmed'. This was not introduced until 1979, but breeding along these lines has now escalated and will lead to new, large-flowered cultivars.

IRIS LAEVIGATA

In many respects *I. laevigata* is the best species to begin with because it will tolerate less than ideal conditions, though it must have wet soil or water at its roots. It is more robust in habit (cynics read leafier) than *I. ensata* and the flowers have generally not been so highly bred (cynics read smaller) as that species. As part of a garden scene *I. laevigata* plays a less dominating role, being a better balanced and more rounded personality, a fact recognized by the Royal Horticultural Society, which bestowed an Award of Garden Merit upon the unimproved species.

I. laevigata is widespread throughout eastern Asia, where it grows in swamps and at the edges of water. It is often confused with *I. ensata*, and both are called Japanese water iris, but if the leaves are felt *I. ensata* will be found to have a distinct midrib which *I. laevigata* lacks. The typical species is a plant with class, bearing blue-violet flowers of clean colour and reasonable size – up to 10cm (4in) across – in mid- to late summer. The

'Reign of Glory' develops huge, rounded flowers delicately marked with blue on a white ground, from delicately pointed buds typical of the transformation which inspired the 'Act'.

standards are large and rather floppy and are held at the horizontal to give a flat flower rather like a snowflake, with six points. At present there are also about a dozen cultivars offered for sale, though fewer than half of these are common. The finest of these is I. laevigata 'Variegata' which has leaves striped with pure white, mingling with the deep bright green where they meet. The blue flowers are enhanced by the striped leaves and this is a plant to convert the most hardened 'variegata hater'. Furthermore it looks good throughout the summer and that cannot be said about many pond plants. 'Snowdrift' has pure white flowers, while in 'Colchesterensis' they are a curious (and messy) blend of deep blue and white.

IRIS PSEUDACORUS

The easiest of all water iris to grow in Britain, because it is a native plant, is I. pseudacorus. Its specific name is derived from the resemblance of the leaves to the sweet flag (Acorus calamus), with which it sometimes grows. Although very vigorous, it is a useful plant because it will tolerate a wide range of water levels, from being submerged to barely moist soil, and it will grow in grass at the edge of a pond, making it ideal for natural planting. It is also the only yellow-flowered water iris, the flowers being bright yellow with a deeper yellow mark in the centre of the falls. The blooms are produced for a long season in mid- and late summer, and though not large are showy on account of their colour. In the variety bastardii the flowers are a paler yellow and there is a curious hybrid, perhaps with I. chrysographes (an unusual cross because it is between iris of different series), called 'Holden Clough' which has yellow flowers netted with purple to give a strange brown appearance. Neither will set the world on fire, but are interesting and worth growing if you like something different.

I. pseudacorus 'Variegata' will make an impact, though, and must be one of the best of all variegated plants – reason enough to make a pond. The leaves emerge in spring in the most vivid combination of lemon and lime imaginable, and as they grow retain their colour until the flowers appear to add a touch of gold. Unfortunately the leaves fade to plain green for the second half of the summer, a trait that is often held against the plant. It may be a disadvantage to garden designers who want static effects in their plans, but gardeners should appreciate the changing face of their gardens and compare the months of bright foliage favourably with the leaves of most flowering plants.

IRIS VERSICOLOR AND IRIS VIRGINICA

In addition to the iris that will happily grow right at the water's edge there are many more that prefer moist soil, growing in nature in wet meadowland and associating well with ponds, yet should not be grown with their roots in water. There are two in the Laevigatae series, I. versicolor and I. virginica, both from North America and rather similar. The latter is the more southerly in distribution but quite hardy in temperate zones and is distinguished by a yellow hairy patch on the falls. Both like moist soil; although I have grown I. virginica from seed in ordinary garden soil in the east of England, it has not made the massive clumps it might have in wetter conditions. My plant has produced flower stems about 60cm (2ft) tall, which is about average, each with one branch and four flower buds in total. The flowers are quite large and showy, yet would appeal to the gardener who prefers subtle plants; they are of a fairly pure mid-blue with a large, netted yellow patch on the falls. Although variable, I. versicolor is usually rather more purple than blue.

SERIES HEXAGONA

This group of iris for the water garden, or at least damp soil, are named after the six prominent ribs on the seed pods. Often called Louisiana iris, they are all deciduous, leafy, strong-growing plants with branched flower stems. Most have broad, flat flowers with floppy standards. They are marsh plants from the southern states of the USA and have never been popular in the UK, largely because the plants are rather shy in producing their large and indisputably beautiful flowers and the hybrids have a reputation for being frost tender. Two species, I. giganticaerulea and I. hexagona, are generally considered too tender for cultivation at all in the UK, preferring moist, acid soils and warmer summers and milder winters than the UK enjoys. However, I. brevicaulis (purple), I. fulva (brick red), and I. nelsonii (purple) are quite easy to grow in the southern half of the country, in damp or wet soils above the water line.

'Wine Ruffles' shows the combination of elegant form and colour typical of the ensatas, which is true despite the large size of the flowers.

It is easy to see why the large, colourful, flat flowers of the *Iris ensata* cultivars have been nicknamed the clematis iris.

I. fulva is best suited to general cultivation, as is its hybrid of *I. brevicaulis*, *I. × fulvala*. Both make thick clumps of green leaves and have flowers about 10cm (4in) across in early summer on stems 60cm (2ft) high.

Few named cultivars are available in Britain but remarkable breeding work has created exceptionally beautiful flowers in the USA in a wide colour range. More work, aimed at producing good cut flowers that last for three or more days, has been carried out in South Africa by Eugene Scheepers. With 350 cultivars to work with and 40,000 seedlings a year, it is not surprising that his dedicated work has created flowers that are 20cm (8in) across, last for four days in water and encompass fabulous colour combinations. His work has shown the importance of breeding cultivars for the home climate as he has created plants that tolerate ordinary garden soil, freezing in winter, high temperatures in summer and some alkalinity in the soil.

It is surprising to think that there were virtually no Louisiana hybrids before the Second World War, but their development now parallels that of the TBs. Greatly enlarged floral parts with overlapping petals, bright colours, bicolors, even with striped and splashed petals, ruffling and even tetraploids are now becoming common. They also vary in height, but the shortest and hardiest cultivars – 'Little Miss Sims', 'This I Love', 'Gold Reserve', 'Acadian White' and 'Charjoy's Jan' – seem to be produced when *I. brevicaulis* is not too far back in the family tree. In some, the standards are similar in shape and size to the falls and the style arms provide a striking contrast in the centre of the flowers. However, the modern Louisianas encompass a wider range of colours, including brick reds, maroon, blues and purples, pinks, yellows and pure whites. These may be the next important group in iris cultivation.

6

THE SPURIA IRIS
Section Limniris, Series Spuriae

The spuria iris include the hybrids that provide the last major iris display of summer, and a number of interesting and pretty species for sunny and semi-shaded parts of the garden. Like the Siberian irises, they have been rather neglected by British gardeners. This may be because after the Tall Bearded iris have flowered most gardeners are ready to move on to other flowers for the rest of summer, or because spurias are relatively large plants with small flowers. It is true that they do not relish being moved, which makes them less suitable for instant gardening than some other iris, but they do have staying power and where conditions suit them they are reliable and colourful garden plants that more than repay the effort involved in finding and then growing them.

All have woody rhizomes and wiry roots, and narrow, upright, deciduous leaves that form tough, hardy plants. The flowers are produced in clusters on unbranched stems, or if they are branched the branches are held so close to the main stems that they appear as a single spike. The flowers have rather narrow petals and the shape, of the hybrids at least, is similar to the Dutch iris, but they are readily distinguished, even when cut, by the presence of three nectar drops at the base of the falls and standards. The other obvious feature is the seed pods, which have three pairs of prominent ribs running along their length, terminating in a short, curved beak.

SPECIES

The smaller species are very suitable for the larger rock garden, or a woodland garden where they will enjoy the rich moist soil, but they should be planted on the edge of shade and not in deep woodland. The species are often found growing in very moist conditions in the wild, some in salt marshes, but these conditions do not need to be copied in cultivation for successful results. Heavy soils enriched and improved with copious organic matter will give the most impressive results, and most are quite easy to grow, particularly the hybrids.

IRIS CROCEA

I. crocea (syn. *I. aurea*) is a tall plant from Kashmir, reaching 1.5m (5ft). The bright yellow flowers, borne in early summer, may be up to 18cm (7in) in diameter and the falls and standards have wavy or crinkly edges. Apparently this species is commonly grown in cemeteries, and its origin is rather obscure. In any event, this is a good garden iris, tough and dependable.

IRIS GRAMINEA

This species is totally different in appearance to the average impression of a spuria, though the small, purplish flowers have the characteristic flower shape. The centre of the flower is brownish due to the colour of the base of the falls (haft) and style arms. The flowers are not large, only 8cm ($3^1/_4$in) across, and they are overtopped by some of the leaves, the stems being just 20cm (8in) high when in flower in early summer. However, this is a plant that is grown for its scent – the flowers smell of stewed plums, earning it the name of plum tart iris. This native of central Europe is a tough little plant that thrives in light shade or full sun in rich moist soil, though I have even grown it with reasonable success in dry shade under yews.

IRIS KERNERIANA

I. kerneriana is a delicate and rather elegant species from Turkey. The flower stems are just taller than the very

PLATE V

I. 'Golden Lady'
Spuria

I. foetidissima

I. 'Adobe Sunset'
Spuria

I. 'Clarke Cosgrove'
Spuria

All plants shown at approximately ¹/₃ size

I. xanthospuria

I. 'Essay'
Spuria

I. 'Blue Embers'
Japanese iris

I. 'Sierra Nevada'
Spuria

I. 'Lydia Jane'
Spuria

narrow leaves, at about 30cm (1ft), and the flowers have gracefully arching falls that bend over so that the tips of the falls almost touch the stem. The style arms follow suit, but the standards are stiffly erect. The falls are yellow, fading to cream at the edge, and the standards are cream. This is a charming little plant that flowers in late spring.

IRIS MONNIERI

This plant is found in areas around the eastern Aegean and is certainly an ancient hybrid because in 1808 it is recorded as growing at Versailles as the 'Iris de Rhodes'. It was thought to be a cross between *I. orientalis* and *I. crocea*, but it is now believed to be a hybrid of the former and *I. spuria* 'Turkey Yellow' (which itself should be called *I. xanthospuria*), a tall, vigorous yellow. The pale lemon-yellow coloured flowers of this iris are held on a stem about 90cm (3ft) in height. They have a darker yellow patch on the falls, often covering the greater part of them, though the edge of the petals, style arms and standards are pale.

IRIS ORIENTALIS

I. orientalis (formerly known as *I. ochroleuca*) is an easy species, which is surprising considering that within its range in the Middle East it often grows in areas of salty marsh. It usually reaches 90cm (3ft) with white flowers and a bright egg-yolk-yellow blotch on the falls, but 'Shelford Giant', a wild-collected clone, is twice that height with creamier flowers.

IRIS PONTICA

This is a very dwarf purple-flowered species from Romania, the Caucasus and Central Asia for the alpine house and rock garden, where it will reach just 10cm (4in) when in flower in early summer. The leaves are three times as long. It is rarely seen in the UK.

IRIS SINTENISII

This is another short, slender species of similar stature to *I. kerneriana*. A native of the Balkans and Turkey, it bears purple flowers with purple lines on a white patch on the falls in early summer. They are carried on stems up to 30cm (1ft) high.

Though not particularly large, the flowers of the spuria iris 'Sunny Day' are guaranteed to light up any garden.

IRIS SPURIA

I. spuria is a catch-all name that includes a huge range of variations within this species, all flowering in early and midsummer. Although they are of great interest to collectors most gardeners will not concern themselves with these plants, which are not easily obtained in any case. It is almost impossible to describe a 'normal' *I. spuria* as the colour and habit varies so greatly. Among the most distinct are: *I. spuria* ssp. *carthaliniae*, tall blue or white; ssp. *halophila*, tall yellow with darker veins; ssp. *musulmanica*, violet blue or white with darker veins and a yellow blaze on the falls; ssp. *notha*, a late-flowering violet blue; and ssp. *spuria*, lilac, from central Europe and even found growing in coastal parts of Dorset and Lincolnshire in Britain (where it is presumably an escape from cultivation).

DEVELOPMENT OF HYBRIDS

As has been the case in so many other groups of iris, Sir Michael Foster was largely responsible for the early development of spuria iris. He crossed *I. monnieri* and a form of *I. spuria* to create 'Monspur', a mid-blue. Barr and Sons Ltd introduced 'Cambridge Blue' and 'Premier' which were his next generation, and cultivars from France, but the real breeding work began in California in the 1940s. It was here that Eric Nies used 'Monspur' to create a series of iris that were so important that his name now appears on the top American award for spuria iris. When he died Marion Walker took over his stock and introduced many of his later seedlings, which are still among the best available today and include the popular violet blue 'Ruth Nies Cabeen' (1940) and 'Sunlit Sea' (1956), a mid-blue with a contrasting deep yellow signal on the falls.

What breeders have managed to change in the modern spurias is the flower shape. The old hybrids had long hafts and short falls which gave an elegant but spidery flower, and since the falls face outwards the larger these can be the bigger the impact of the flower. Falls are now much wider, as are the standards, and ruffling has increased. The range of colours has also increased, encompassing mauve-pinks such as 'Clarke Cosgrove' (1974) and 'Essay' (1963); pure white, 'White Heron' (1948); deep blue, 'Port of Call' (1965); and interesting blends and browns such as 'Redwood Supreme' (1976) and 'Janice Chesnik' (1983).

This colourful and elegant spuria is a hybrid between
I. monnieri (itself of hybrid origin) and the long-established
hybrid 'Cambridge Blue'.

At the same time as Eric Nies was working, Carl
Milliken introduced two famous spurias. The first,
'White Heron' (1948) is still available, while the second, 'Wadi Zem Zem' became the first winner of the
Eric Nies Award, and a valuable parent of many later
spurias. Ben Hager, another American who has
achieved great success with his spurias and Tall
Beardeds, introduced his first spuria in 1963. This was
'Elixir', a deep yellow bred by crossing 'Wadi Zem Zem'
with *I. xanthospuria*. Two others in that year were 'Essay'
and 'Neophyte', a deep blue and cream, both derived
from crossing *I. spuria* ssp. *carthaliniae* and 'Morning-
tide'. From then on he produced a steady stream of
top cultivars such as 'Archie Owen' (1970) which is a
deep yellow self of thickset, ruffled form, and 'Ila
Crawford' (1976), a white with a large golden orange
signal on the falls.

Eleanor McCown kept the momentum going in
California with a string of superb introductions based
originally on hybrids derived from *I. ochroleuca* such as
'White Heron' and 'Cherokee Chief'. Further examples
include 'Highline Lavender' (1968) with violet standards and yellow falls edged with lavender, and her
'Imperial' series which includes 'Imperial Bronze'
(1970), a yellow heavily tinted with brown, 'Imperial
Ruby' (1977), a maroon self, and 'Imperial Sun' (1984),
a sulphur-yellow with golden blaze.

The spurias have never received the adulation that
they deserve and perhaps their naming got them off to a
bad start. Linnaeus gave them the name *I. spuria*, from
the Latin word *spurius*, meaning false (he thought it was
a hybrid), perhaps also because they were such a complicated bunch of plants and so difficult to sort out. But
breeders have now created a magnificent race of plants
that are truly wonderful additions to the garden and are
better subjects for the gardener who does not wish to
fuss over his or her plants too much than the Tall
Beardeds.

7

THE STINKING IRIS
Section Limniris, Series Foetidissimae

This series contains just one species, *I. foetidis-sima*. It is not a beautiful plant and its common name of stinking iris is hardly appealing, but a plant as tough as this deserves respect. It is hardy, and the sheaves of mid- to dark green evergreen leaves that may reach 45cm (18in) make solid clumps in the shade throughout summer and look bright enough in winter to make a contribution to the garden. A problem with this plant is leaf spot disease, which often disfigures leaves quite badly. This is especially prevalent in very dry, hot years, in my experience, but that could just be a side effect of the natural loss of vigour in such circumstances – you can only push a plant so far. If you have a collection of iris it is worth noting that masses of sickly *I. foetidissima* can store up problems with leaf spot that can spread among your other plants, disfiguring the bearded species and hybrids.

Fortunately, the name *I. foetidissima* is no real cause for alarm – the plant only stinks if the leaves are crushed and in any case the smell is often likened to roast beef, a harmless enough odour.

The flowers are not large, and barely emerge from the fans of leaves when they bloom in early summer. They are typically a mixture of lilac/mauve and brown on the falls with lilac standards. In the variety *citrina* the flowers are pale yellow and brown and possibly more attractive; certainly they are more showy. There are also paler and even white-flowered plants reported.

COLOUR FROM SEED AND FOLIAGE
Once the flowers have faded, fat green seed pods develop, ripening in late autumn to split open into three segments, each covered with bright orange rounded seeds. Although usually nodding under the weight of the seeds, these pods look attractive in the garden, and can be picked to brighten up winter flower arrangements. The yellow variety *citrina* produces better crops of seeds. In mild winters, *Jasminum nudiflorum* and mahonias with their acid yellow flowers make good companions to *I. foetidissima* in shady places. This plant

The flowers of *Iris foetidissima citrina* are a showy blend of pale yellow and brown.

In autumn the pods of *Iris foetidissima* split into three segments to reveal the startling orange seeds. These last for many months and can be picked and dried for the house.

spreads by seedlings which will appear naturally if the pods are not all picked, and there are now at least two colour variants ('Fructo-Albo' which is white and an unnamed yellow-seeded plant) that will add interest to the winter garden, though none is as common as the orange-fruited sort.

In addition to the variations in seed colour, there is a variegated form, *I. f.* 'Variegata', which could be a really fine garden plant but for two drawbacks: the plant rarely flowers (presumably because the variegation is caused by a chimera) and never (in my experience) sets seed. It is grown solely as a foliage plant, a rather strange reason to grow an iris, but its foliage is pleasant and fills

a difficult space under trees. In parts of New Zealand this plant has been introduced as a garden plant but has escaped into the wild and is now regarded as an aggressive weed and a threat to native plants.

Apart from *I. foetidissima* there is no other iris that can be recommended for deep shade and dry soil beneath deciduous and even evergreen trees. However, a point worth emphasizing is that although this plant can tolerate deplorable conditions it will benefit from better ones, and if conditions are too dreadful it will die. So when you plant it, pretend it is the rarest, most lovely American hybrid iris you have, and improve the soil with garden compost or leafmould, add a little fertilizer and water it well for the first season until it is well established. Only then will it do everything it is supposed to where hardly any other plant will do anything at all.

8

THE DWARF BULBOUS IRIS
Subgenus Hermodactyloides

All bulbous plants have their charm for gardeners as well as great commercial importance to plant producers. They are almost as convenient as seeds in their long storage capacity and perfect for garden-centre sales. The botanical adaptations that led to their development, with dry summers when the bulbs become completely dormant, suit them admirably for the months of sorting, distribution and waiting before they are finally planted in the ground. Such convenience breeds a kind of contempt, which is accentuated by the familiarity of the cut Dutch iris. The dwarf reticulata types are treated with greater respect because they flower so early in spring and seem so brave in the cold and wet, often flowering with snowdrops as soon as the first rays of the weak spring sunshine appear. All have flowers up to 7.5cm (3in) across, held close to the ground, with just a few emerging leaves.

I will never forget my first bulb of 'Katharine Hodgkin', a bizarre cross of the beautiful blue *I. histrioides* with primrose-yellow *I. winogradowii* raised by E. B. Anderson in 1960. It is now quite readily available, but I paid £5 for my bulb (then about a morning's wages) and it was with excitement that I watched the bud push through the layer of gravel in the sink garden. Then, just as I was expecting to see that curious flower, a blend of sky blue, grey and primrose, my morning vigil was rewarded with the sight of a fat green caterpillar and scattered frass where my flower should have been. 'Frank Elder' and 'Sheila Ann Germany' are similar hybrids of the same parentage.

The reticulata iris, as the group of dwarf bulbous iris are called, consist of about 10 species that are uniform and distinct enough to be given a genus (*Iridodictyum*) of their own by some botanists. They can be recognized by the netted (reticulate) skin around their bulb, and by the leaves (usually one or two), which are square in cross section (except for *I. bakeriana*, which has cylindrical leaves). All flower in early spring, before their leaves are fully developed, and bring a welcome splash of colour to the rock garden long before most plants have started into growth; the blue species make a charming contrast with snowdrops. The disadvantage is that their long leaves can present a problem until early summer when they eventually die down and can be cleared away.

The reticulata iris like very well-drained soil and *I. bakeriana* and *I. histrio* succeed best when planted into a bulb frame to give better control of their watering. They are popular subjects for troughs or pots, and are often exhibited in this way, but they do not always flourish for more than one year in these conditions, preferring a less restricted root-run and perhaps deeper planting (to 20cm/8in) as is advised to keep bulbs of *I. danfordiae* at flowering size.

IRIS BAKERIANA

This species is interesting because although it looks very much like a typical *I. reticulata* but two-toned with pale blue standards and deep blue falls, the leaves have eight ridges rather than the usual four. The leaves are usually longer than the flowers. *I. bakeriana* is best grown in a frame, though the plants in commerce, which have come from Turkey, can be grown outside in suitable conditions.

IRIS DANFORDIAE

In garden centres and shops throughout the country this is sold by the million to hapless gardeners who

It is a shame that the bright flowers of *Iris histrioides* 'Major' are so close to the ground because they deserve at least as much attention as the taller iris of late summer receive.

think that it will fill their gardens with golden flowers each spring. Unfortunately, this species from Turkey has the annoying habit of producing dozens of tiny bulblets (rice grains) after flowering, which, though wonderful for nurserymen, are a dead loss for gardeners because they take several years to reach flowering size – longer if allowed to remain *in situ* where they have to struggle for room and nutrients. Deep planting (to 20cm/8in) helps to prevent or at least minimize this problem. The flowers are bright yellow with green speckling on the falls but the standards are tiny bristles, barely visible, and certainly make no contribution to the flower's beauty. As with most of the reticulatas, the foliage, though not obtrusive at flowering time, is very long at up to 45cm (18in) and untidy after flowering,

which makes effective positioning of the plant in the rock garden difficult.

IRIS HISTRIO

This is a large-flowered species from Turkey, Syria and the Lebanon, with blooms up to 8cm (3¹/₄in) across in mid-winter, but it is not easy to grow outside. The flowers are pale blue, the falls are splashed and spotted with deep blue with a yellow ridge, and the leaves usually exceed the height of the flowers. The variety *aintabensis* from southern Turkey has smaller flowers but is easier to grow outside. It also has shorter leaves at flowering time. Both tend to produce rice-grain bulblets.

IRIS HISTRIOIDES

Compared to *I. histrio*, which it resembles in colour, this has even bigger flowers. It is hardier, though still very early flowering, and its bulbs tend to stay at a flowering size, making it a far better plant for general cultivation.

'Natasha' is a recently introduced white cultivar of
Iris reticulata that is best grown in pots to fully appreciate its
delicate beauty.

It is native to northern Turkey. Several clones are
offered by nurseries, the commonest being 'Major', but
'Lady Beatrix Stanley', 'G. P. Baker' and 'Angel's Tears',
all varying slightly in colour, are sometimes sold.

IRIS RETICULATA

This is the best known but also the most variable
species, with many flower colours. The bulbs sometimes
produce rice-grain bulblets but they may divide into
comparatively large offsets that soon flower. Fortunately this is quite an easy species to grow outside,
flourishing in limy soils. It will even grow on quite
heavy clay soils if they are dry in summer and not too
wet in winter, but the flowers are susceptible to slug and
snail damage because they appear at a time when little
else is available for them to eat. They are also suitable
for pot culture, to bring indoors when in flower, where
their fragrance can be best appreciated.

Recently, a large number of cultivars have become
available in every shade from deep red, purple and blue
through pale blues to white. Among these, 'Cantab' in
Cambridge blue is hard to beat, 'Clairette' has the
colouring of *I. bakeriana* with deep blue falls, 'Harmony'
is a large dark blue with short foliage at flowering, 'J. S.
Dijt' is a vinous purple with good scent, 'Natasha' is
almost white and 'Pauline' is a deep wine red.

IRIS WINOGRADOWII

This is a yellow-flowered species from the Caucasus of a
paler, more delicate shade than *I. danfordiae*. Unlike
that species it has large standards and the falls are
longer, the flowers being generally of a more typical iris
shape. It is suited to outdoor growing if it can be given a
light but not poor soil that is free of chalk.

9

IRIS FOR THE SPECIALIST

The majority of iris mentioned in this book are both easy to grow outside in most temperate zones and relatively easy to obtain from commercial sources, albeit often specialist iris nurseries. The iris in this chapter differ because they offer a challenge to gardeners who want to test their cultivation skills and will require a fair degree of detective work to find a source of supply. Without doubt joining a specialist iris society is the best course of action, but even then it may be necessary to grow some of these plants from seed as plants will not be available.

These are not just iris exclusively for experienced growers; beginners can grow them just as successfully, and may indeed be more inclined to make a special effort if they do not already have a collection of several hundred other iris to care for. In many ways these could be the best iris for beginners, because the sense of satisfaction that will accompany success will inspire further exploration of the genus.

Apart from the challenge that these iris present, the flowers of some are the most interesting and beautiful of the genus, their fleeting appearance and capricious temperament only adding to their mystique.

ONCOCYCLUS IRIS:
SECTION ONCOCYCLUS

This group, consisting of about 50 species and many more varieties, subspecies and probably hybrids, are similar to the regelia iris that follow (and the hybrids between these two sections are often referred to as regeliocyclus) in that the seeds possess a large fleshy appendage (often as big as the seeds) called an aril, which is sweet in taste and is provided to attract ants which carry the seeds away. Therefore this group is also called the aril or arillate iris. To the gardener they are distinct and sought-after for their striking flowers.

These are structurally similar to the bearded species but the oncocyclus iris are generally of small stature, with flowers that are grossly out of proportion with the size of the plants – a trait that would be considered a failing in a man-made hybrid. One constant factor is that each stem bears just one, marvellous flower. The size of the falls and standards varies widely, but a large dark blotch on the falls and dark veins on a paler ground are characteristic of most species. The falls have the familiar beards of the quite closely related bearded iris, but these iris are adapted to even hotter and drier climates and their adaptations are the principal reason why they are so tricky to please in northern temperate zones. These are iris from central Turkey, the Caucasus and Syria, Lebanon, Israel, Iraq and Iran. The taller species tend to come from southern lowland areas and dwarf species from northern, more mountainous habitats. In general they grow in areas with very little or no summer rainfall. They do receive rain in spring and autumn, and the winters are generally dry and mild in the southern habitats or dry and with a protective blanket of snow in the mountainous areas. These are conditions that are rarely found but must be recreated by gardeners if success is to be achieved.

SPECIES

This is a large group but few are in cultivation. The following list includes some of the most distinct.

I. acutiloba is a sombre species about 20cm (8in) high with pointed flower segments, lined and streaked with brown or dark grey. The flowers reach 7.5cm (3in) in diameter. Both it and its subspecies *lineolata* are dwarf and are among the best suited to growing in pots.

I. antilibanotica has very short, sickle-shaped leaves but flower stems reaching 40cm (16in). The 15cm (6in) flowers have purple falls with a black blotch and yellow beard and paler standards.

I. assadiana is a short species, only 15cm (6in) tall, with deep purple flowers 7.5cm (3in) across.

I. atrofusca has flowers of purple-brown with lighter standards. They measure 20cm (8in) across and are borne on stems 60cm (24in) tall.

I. atropurpurea has almost black flowers, but as with most of these species, the form and reflective texture of the petals is as important as the flower colour. They measure 8cm (3¼in) across, on stems 20cm (8in) high.

I. barnumae and its subspecies are small spreading plants up to 30cm (12in) high. Their flowers are purplish with large arched falls, more colourful than some others in the group, and measure 7.5cm (3in) across. It is one of the least demanding species.

I. bismarckiana has huge flowers, up to 12.5cm (5in) across, pale with reddish-brown dots and veins and a large black patch on the falls. They are carried on stems as much as 80cm (30in) tall.

I. camillae is very variable and the 7.5cm (3in) flowers may be blue, yellow, purple or bicolored. This plant reaches a height of between 20 and 40cm (8 and 16in).

I. damascena has narrow, curved leaves but quite large flowers up to 9cm (3½in) across on 30cm (24in) stems.

I. gatesii is one of the must-have species, with stems up to 60cm (24in) high topped with huge grey flowers that may reach 20cm (8in) across. The falls are broad and curve down gracefully, the standards arch to meet at their apex and the style crests are rounded to bring the perfect finishing touch to this magnificent plant.

I. haynei has flowers 12.5cm (5in) across, attractively veined brown on purple, held on 60cm (24in) stems.

I. iberica is a short species, only 20cm (8in) high, with densely veined dark falls with a darker blotch and very pale standards to create a stunning flower 10cm (4in) across. The subspecies *elegantissima* has larger standards and the subspecies *lycotis*, with rather open standards, is just as attractive.

I. kirkwoodii is one of the tallest species, reaching 75cm (30in) with 10cm (4in) veined flowers with purple patches on the falls.

I. lortetii is a tall species, 50cm (20in) high, with pinkish flowers that are 8cm (3¼in) across. The white standards are veined in purple and the falls are spotted and veined and have a deep maroon spot. This is a very beautiful plant, the falls and standards making great sweeping curves.

I. meda usually has yellowish flowers with thin but undulating falls and standards, veined in brown to produce an elegant effect. They are 7.5cm (3in) across on stems 20cm (8in) high.

I. nigricans has 10cm (4in) black flowers on 30cm (1ft) stems but is universally considered to be a difficult species to grow.

I. paradoxa is one of the most distinct and easy to grow of all. The 8cm (3¼in) flowers have tiny falls, reduced to a large furry beard, but huge billowing standards on stems 20cm (8in) high. The falls are usually dark purple and the standards paler, but many variations exist.

I. samariae is similar to *I. lortetii*, with large, dark-veined cream flowers 10cm (4in) across, held on 30cm (1ft) stems.

I. sari is a compact species, less than 30cm (1ft) high with large but rather untidy flowers, up to 10cm (4in) across, that are pale yellow veined with brown or red. The signal patch is red or brown. A vigorous form is known as *I. lupina*.

I. sofarana is rare in its native home on the mountains between Beirut and Damascus. It has 10cm (4in) cream flowers, heavily spotted and veined with purple, on 30cm (1ft) stems.

I. susiana is not just one of the easiest of this group, often surviving in general garden conditions, but is also one of the oldest iris in cultivation, having been brought to Vienna in 1573. The cultivated plant differs from the wild plants and the clone grown today could be the very one introduced 400 years ago. The 10cm (4in) grey flowers are veined purple, with a black signal patch and a purple beard, and are borne on stems 30cm (1ft) high. Its sombre colouring has earned it the name of the mourning iris, but it is a beautiful flower.

CULTIVATION

Root growth begins in autumn, when the rains start, but stops for the winter and leaves are rarely produced before the warmth and life-giving rains of spring. In the garden it is important that after the autumn watering, which will stimulate root growth, water must be withheld or leaves will be produced which are unlikely to survive a cold-mild-cold erratic winter. Winter leaves are also likely to be attacked by aphids, which spread virus diseases that can ruin these plants.

Despite their adaption to drought, these iris enjoy rich soil and in the wild their deep roots have little competition for nutrients. This makes them less suitable for pot cultivation than their strict water requirements might suggest and the best way to grow them is either in raised beds 30–45cm (12–18in) high, constructed of brick, wood, stone or even turf, or in frames. Because the plants are basically hardy but must be protected from winter wet, a raised bed with overhead transparent protection is the best combination; as most of the species are rather low-growing a structure 60cm (2ft) high above soil level is usually quite sufficient. The structure does not need to have sides, and indeed good air circulation is essential to prevent rots, but removable sides are a good idea to keep windblown rain off the soil unless the top cover has a significant overhang. The growing position must be in full sun – no spot is too hot. Put a layer of broken pots, bricks or other drainage material on the base of the raised bed, then fill it with soil that has been improved with organic compost (some growers specify that this should not include animal manure, but others find this acceptable) and very coarse grit in the proportions of one part soil to one part compost and two parts grit. If your soil is very heavy clay it would be advisable to buy some good loam. Lime is necessary and should ideally be added in the form of coarse dolomite or magnesium limestone. Some growers add well-rotted manure to the top of the compost, while others prefer to control feeding more carefully with liquid feeds throughout the growing season.

In mid-autumn, plant the rhizomes about 5cm (2in) deep. Water the beds immediately and then cover them to prevent any more moisture reaching the plants until spring. The idea is to encourage root growth but prevent leaves being produced. However, if leaves do appear they can be protected from frost by covering them with dry grit or gravel in small mounds. It makes the beds look more attractive and helps to show off the flowers if the soil is covered with gravel or stone chippings (which could be limestone to good effect) and these can be simply pulled up over the leaves should the need arise.

Throughout the growing season the plants need watering and feeding. Some growers prefer to give high-nitrogen feeds, but a general liquid fertilizer at weekly intervals may be easier to begin with for plants growing under permanent shelter and relying on artificial irrigation. Flowering is usually in late spring and at all times the plants should be watered well and kept free of aphids. In mid- to late summer the foliage will begin to die down, when watering must cease. The plants can be lifted and stored dry in sand, perhaps in a greenhouse, to 'bake' them for the summer; or if grown in a frame they can be left in the soil.

Some growers prefer to use very deep clay pots and peat and grit-based composts. These plants are regularly and heavily fed with soluble fertilizer throughout the growing season, and this method does have the advantage that complete control over the growing conditions can be achieved – ideal if you wish to exhibit plants.

REGELIA IRIS: SECTION REGELIA

The regelia iris require similar conditions to the oncocyclus, but in the wild they come from areas further east. One in particular, *I. hoogiana*, is sometimes grown outside in temperate zones and is one of the classic iris, of superb form and colour. They are distinguished from the previous group by having two flowers per stem and beards on the falls and the standards. The flowers are usually elegant with elongated segments and are a little less unusual than the oncocyclus, though they are still noteworthy. Those described here are the most commonly grown.

I. afghanica is a lovely plant 30cm (1ft) high, bearing flowers with pale yellow standards and falls that are veined with rosy purple. A purple blotch completes the blooms, which may reach 10cm (4in) across.

I. hoogiana is a tall species reaching 60cm (2ft) and producing bluish flowers 8cm (3¼in) across with a yellow beard and pleasant scent. It is a comparatively easy species to grow.

I. korolkowii has purplish, elegant, narrow flowers 7.5cm (3in) across. It is sometimes grown in borders because it is vigorous, but it does best in a frame. It reaches 60cm (2ft) high.

I. stolonifera has 8cm (3¼in) flowers of a pretty blend of pale lilac edged with rusty brown on the standards and falls. They are carried on 60cm (2ft) stems.

ARIL HYBRIDS

The aril iris have attracted the attention of many breeders and, as well as combining the species to create new (but not necessarily better) flowers to tempt growers, it has been possible to combine the exquisite appearance of these exotic beauties with the comparative ease of growth of the pogon or bearded iris.

The taller of these exciting hybrids are called arilbreds, while the smaller ones, developed from crossing aril iris with short bearded species and hybrids, are known as arilmeds. The species that have been used most in these developments are *I. gatesii*, *I. iberica*, *I. barnumae* and *I. korolkowii*.

The first hybrid was probably 'Alkmene', a hybrid of *I. paradoxa* and *I. sweertii*, raised by Dammann in 1896. The idea was to produce an exotic flower that would be more likely to survive western European conditions. One of the greatest problems in this work is that the hybrids have low fertility but occasional 'mistakes' in the production of pollen and egg cells have periodically led to tetraploids, which have enabled fertile crosses with large tetraploid iris and great leaps forward in breeding. The first fertile arilbred was 'Ib-Mac' (*I. iberica* × *I.* 'Macrantha'), introduced by Van Tubergen in 1910, and in 1923, 'William Mohr' (*I.* 'Parisiana' × *I. gatesii*) was introduced, bred by William Mohr. These were combined by Frank Reinelt, a Czech who was inspired by the plant-breeding work of Luther Burbank to move

Iris stolonifera is bizarre and beautiful, but difficult to grow in most gardens in northern temperate zones.

to California, where he produced 'Capitola', a fully fertile plant that was crossed extensively to introduce aril 'blood' into bearded iris.

The American Iris Society has two awards for these beautiful hybrids, the C.G. White Award for 'half bloods' and the William Mohr Award for 'quarter bloods'. The more aril blood there is in the genetic make-up of the cultivar the more exotic the appearance of the flower. Often those that have just a small number of aril genes look very similar to ordinary bearded iris in flower shape, but their falls may be curiously shaped, the petals may have a strange metallic lustre or the combination of colours may be unusual. Their culture depends upon their breeding, but in general they are likely to survive if planted in the sunniest spot in well-drained soil and never allowed to have other plants flop around them, which would encourage rot.

Some of the older and proven cultivars which would make a good introduction to the growing of all aril iris in general (but are unfortunately not commonly available) include:

'Big Black Bumblebee', with large pink flowers with a black blotch on the falls.

'Bionic Burst', reddish-brown.

'Esther the Queen', an amazing blend of lilac, green and red.

'Genetic Artist', lavender, gold and brown.

'Genetic Burst', grey standards and blue falls with blue beards.

'Genetic Dancer', a brown bicolor.

'Loudmouth', lilac and violet with a black blotch.

'Ninevah', brown and reddish-purple, the only arilbred that is offered by nurseries in the UK. It flowers with the Tall Beardeds and is of the same height.

Newer developments are producing flowers that show almost pure red and also whites. Aril iris offer hybridizers great challenges, and great opportunities. The challenges are to overcome breeding systems that lead to sterile offspring, and the battle to create plants that will survive in cool temperate conditions, but the opportunities are the beautiful and bizarre flower shapes and colours that the aril iris possess.

JUNO IRIS:
SUBGENUS SCORPIRIS

This major group of iris, encompassing about 50 species, are so distinct that they have even been given their own genus – *Juno* – by some botanists. They are bulbous iris, but the bulbs are usually small and accompanied by thick, fleshy roots which help the bulbs to survive during the dormant season; care is needed not to damage them during transplanting. The plants have two ranks of long leaves, though these may not be fully developed when the flowers appear. Others have their blooms held on tall leafy stems that look a bit like leek plants. The leaves have a thin white margin which in some cases is quite prominent and ornamental, especially when the leaves are young. The flowers are very distinctive because the standards are much smaller

than the falls and are usually horizontal or even pendulous and the falls have a ridged crest.

The habitat in which these iris grow, in central Turkey east to Pakistan and south to Jordan, is similar to the habitats of the groups above, with hot dry summers and cold but dry winters. These conditions make the culture of Junos very similar to the oncocyclus and regelia iris, and they also like lime.

Unless specialist growers are located, these are not easy plants to buy, and few would be brave (or foolhardy) enough to risk such valuable plants outside. Occasionally, however, *I. bucharica* is offered for sale in garden centres and department stores as dried bulbs at reasonable prices. This is a pretty and easy species with which to become acquainted with the Junos and if you do see them, the bulbs should be snapped up immediately because the fleshy roots do not enjoy being out of the ground for long periods of time.

CULTIVATION

Some Juno species can be grown successfully outside, but their large leaves tend to collect water at the base against the stem, which can exaggerate the problems associated with rotting. Although when in growth they require moist soil, great care should be taken when watering that the leaves do not get wet.

In a frame it is convenient to install 'leaky pipe' (perforated hose) or other subterranean irrigation. Plants grown outside can be protected from wet by sheets of glass. Provide supplementary feeding by means of a slow-release fertilizer in spring or regular liquid feeding. Deep planting is not essential, just 8cm (3¼in) for most, but if grown in pots, 'long toms' (tall, narrow pots) are needed to accommodate the deep, fleshy roots that search down for water in native soils.

Those that are quite successful grown outside in well-drained soil in sunny places include I. bucharica,

Iris bucharica is the best known and most commonly available Juno and grows well in many gardens.

I. cycloglossa, I magnifica and I. orchioides. Of these I. cycloglossa, which grows in a rather damp soil in its native habitat, is reputed to be of easy culture, though it is not commonly grown. It has flowers that are scented of cloves.

Few of the many beautiful Juno species are sold by nurseries but the following are sometimes cultivated, a number of them just by botanic gardens. All of them require cultivation in a bulb frame or pots in a greenhouse (except in exceptionally mild areas) apart from the species recommended above for general cultivation.

I. aitchisonii, from Pakistan and Afghanistan, is a tall species (often more than 30cm/1ft) with lilac, purple or yellow flowers.

I. albo-marginata is a species with pale blue and yellow flowers which reaches 30cm (1ft) in height. It is a native of Central Asia.

I. aucheri (syn I. sindjarensis) is a beautiful small species from Iraq, Iran, Turkey and Syria with pale to deep blue flowers, that is transformed from being just pretty to beautiful by its amenable disposition. It may be grown in the open garden in warm areas.

I. bucharica, with many yellow and white flowers, is the easiest of all the Junos and a pretty garden plant that reaches about 30cm (1ft) when in flower. A native of Bokhara, Uzbekistan, it prefers a soil containing lime and often thrives at the base of old walls, where the extra heat stored by the wall returns to the soil and helps summer ripening of the bulbs. A pure yellow form is sometimes offered as I. orchioides.

I. caucasica is short-growing, with up to four pale yellow or green flowers.

I. cycloglossa differs from all other Junos in its large erect standards and is tall and slender. The clove-scented flowers are bright blue and large, up to 10cm (4in) across. This species comes from moist soil in north-west Afghanistan.

Iris cycoglossa was introduced into cultivation as recently as 1969 and is an unusual Juno iris with large standards and a tall, slender profile.

I. galatica (syn. *I. purpurea*) is a tiny species with a few small flowers that may be purple or lime green.

I. graeberiana is a small blue-flowered species from Central Asia that some gardeners report to be as easy to grow as *I. bucharica*.

I. magnifica is a robust and easy species. The large pale lilac and yellow flowers are produced in heads of up to seven. It is twice the size of *I. bucharica* when in flower and a fairly safe bet in the sunny rock garden.

I. nicolai is a stunning dwarf species that needs to be grown in a frame and is very early to come into flower. The blooms are pale purple, striped with deeper colour, and are fully exposed, appearing when the leaves have barely emerged from the soil.

I. palaestina, from the eastern Mediterranean, has pale green flowers and is less cold-tolerant than other Juno species.

I. persica is variable in colour, and very dwarf. Although it has been cultivated for hundreds of years it is not easy to grow and requires a frame.

I. planifolia is the only Juno native to Europe. The blue flowers are carried on short stems. Unfortunately it is very prone to virus diseases and should always be grown from seed, which is the best method of propagation for all Junos.

I. vicaria is like a more colourful I. *magnifica*, with pale violet flowers.

I. warleyensis is a colourful tall species with violet or purple flowers that can succeed outside.

HYBRIDS

Junos have not as yet caught the attention of hybridizers, although many species do form natural hybrids. There is a case for creating hardy hybrids that are adapted to temperate climates, using I. *bucharica* and I. *magnifica* as a starting point. However, two established hybrids that are moderately easy and vigorous are 'Sindpur' (I. *aucheri* × I. *galatica*) and 'Warlsind' (I. *warleyensis* × I. *aucheri*).

HIMALAYAN IRIS: SERIES NEPALENSIS

I. *colletti* and I. *decora* are two interesting species with fleshy roots that come from the Himalayas, where they receive moisture when growing in summer and then dryness for the winter. I. *collettii* is rare in cultivation, but I. *decora* is quite easy to grow in a pot from seed and has purple or lavender, scented flowers. It would be more popular if its flowers were longer-lived, but unfortunately each lasts less than a day.

CRESTED IRIS: SECTION LOPHIRIS

This group of beautiful evergreen iris contains the Evansia or crested iris. Most are rather tender, which is why they have been placed in this chapter, but I. *tectorum* and I. *milesii* are both good garden flowers. The Evansias are natives of Asia and North America and tend to prefer semi-shaded, rather moist conditions. Most of the Asian species, apart from the two mentioned above, are not reliably hardy although in sheltered borders I. *japonica* will survive at least, if not give its best performance. All have rather flat flowers with spreading falls and, instead of a beard, the falls have a crest – a ridge of tissue like a cockscomb. Many make delightful pot plants with exquisite flowers.

Unlike most other iris, some have tall, leafy stems that after a year's growth produce branched flower stems carrying dozens of attractive small flowers. These are often white or pale blue, with intricate blue and gold markings. They require nothing more than protection from frost, and are interesting and attractive evergreen flowering plants for an unheated conservatory that is well ventilated in summer. They are not fussy about soil, though they prefer it acid and with a fairly high humus content. They do not have dormant periods and consequently should never be allowed to dry out completely.

TENDER SPECIES

I. confusa is a lovely foliage plant, reaching 1m (33in), with bamboo-like leaves and stems. The white flowers are small, no more than 5cm (2in) across, and they are short-lived, but produced in large numbers over many weeks. It flowers in early spring if protected from frost. Flowered stems should be removed completely after blooming to keep the plant tidy.

I. formosana is a short plant with stems up to 10cm (4in) high, bearing pale blue flowers flecked with yellow. It is larger-flowered and more attractive than I. *japonica*, but will not tolerate any frost.

Iris nicolai is a striking Juno that will grow best in the protective environment of a bulb frame.

Iris wattii is not hardy in cooler areas, but makes a fine evergreen plant for a conservatory or cool greenhouse and a good outdoor plant for warmer zones.

I. japonica is the best-known of the species, with 5cm (2in) flowers that are typically white with a yellow crest and deep blue markings on the falls. It has the potential to form great mats of leaves 30cm (12in) high and flowers for a month or more. It will grow outside in warmer areas, but then often has tatty foliage at flowering time in late spring. Pot or greenhouse cultivation suits it well. There is a form with variegated leaves, I. j. 'Variegata', worth growing just for the foliage, and 'Ledgers Variety', though visually identical, is reputedly hardier. It is the most common plant sold, though the name may not always be accurately applied. In Japan this iris was traditionally encouraged around castles on the tops of hills, the slippery fans of leaves slowing marauding invaders sufficiently to allow defending armies to muster their troops and weapons.

I. wattii is twice the size of I. confusa and the flowers are also much bigger, and typically pale lavender. The falls are rather drooping, but this is a superb greenhouse plant. There are a number of interesting and very beautiful hybrids, including 'Bourne Graceful' with deep green, purple-flushed leaves and large lilac flowers, which are worth every effort to obtain.

HARDY SPECIES
I. cristata and **I. lacustris** from North America and **I. gracilipes** from Japan are dwarf woodlanders which are quite hardy. They have lavender-blue flowers.

I. milesii This tall plant has rather small, flat, mauve flowers, just 7.5cm (3in) across, on thin, branched stems rising to 45cm (18in) above leafy clumps. These grow from thick green rhizomes which are unusual for this section of the genus. It is an easy and interesting plant for sun or semi-shade and sets plenty of seed.

I. tectorum This is a compact plant with large blue flowers (white in 'Alba') which are very decorative. Also known as the Japanese roof iris, it requires good soil in full sun and regular division to thrive. It can be easily raised from seed.

10

IRIS AS CUT FLOWERS

The current fashion is to regard the garden as an outdoor room, an extension of the domestic living space, but in reality few gardeners actually treat their garden as such unless it is a small patio or courtyard. Even the ubiquitous French windows do not really bring the garden into the home, so it is inevitable that gardeners will either want to pick some of their iris to enjoy them in the home, or even grow them specifically for cutting and flower arranging.

Iris are rewarding as cut flowers on account of their intricate shape and coloration, and for their perfume, which may be undetectable in the open garden. All iris take up water when cut, and the flowers will last almost as long as they would on the plant (and in some cases longer, if they bloom at times of adverse weather or if wind or drought are causing damage). Because the flowers are either borne without a real stem (for example *I. reticulata*), or on a flower stem that is not an important photosynthetic (food producing) part of the plant, almost all iris flowers can be cut without damaging the plant (notable exceptions are the bulbous Dutch iris and Juno iris, which should be cut carefully with as few leaves as possible to avoid weakening the bulb).

If flowers do not have to be transported far they can be cut in full bloom, though obviously fresh blooms that have just opened are the best to pick, if only because they will have the longest vase life. Most iris flowers last for a maximum of three days in full bloom. It is best to cut them in the morning or evening rather than in the hot sun, when they would be most prone to wilting.

BEARDED IRIS

The Tall Bearded iris share a number of the common problems of all iris, and have a few of their own. The first is the elegant placement of blooms. If they are being used just as an informal display of flowers this is not a hindrance, but for flower arrangers it can be a significant restraint to their artistic endeavours. These iris are best used in vertical arrangements, or as the vertical component of arrangements, as otherwise the angle of the flowers will appear very odd. For special arrangements, however, there is no reason why the stems cannot be staked at an angle while they are young so that the buds will adjust their angle to face upwards, but this does require careful planning, and may not be successful if the timing is wrong.

While the individual flowers of most iris do not last more than three days, there is usually more than one bud per stem. Unfortunately, on a branched Tall Bearded iris stem, the flowers are widely spaced and in a carefully designed arrangement this coming and going of flowers can be a problem. Also, the individual flowers of many modern cultivars are too big for some arrangements. A further disadvantage of bearded iris is that as the blooms of the dark cultivars fade they may drip inky liquid that will stain fabrics and furnishings.

Then there is the problem of perfume. In bearded iris this is on the cusp of scent and stink, and once the flowers are picked and brought into the home it becomes rank and overpowering. There are exceptions, even among the Tall Beardeds, and species such as *I. pallida* can never be offensive (to my nose!). I have found that the perfume is most noticeable when the flowers are first brought into the house and seems to be less strong on the second day, though this may be due to familiarity rather than a loss of fragrance once in water.

Among the bearded iris, the best for cutting are undoubtedly the Miniature Tall Bearded cultivars, which have slender, branched, tall stems and extremely elegant, well-proportioned flowers that look well either on their own or with mixed flowers. The Tall Bearded iris are displayed best either in a huge vase cut with full-length stems, or as solitary stems with carefully chosen foliage in the simple Japanese style.

BULBOUS IRIS: SUBGENUS XIPHIUM

Of all the other iris that can be cut it is the tall bulbous species that are the most important, and their horticultural use is almost completely confined to commercial cut flower crops. The group consists of about eight species, all from western Europe and North Africa, but it is the hybrids of a few that are most grown in gardens. There are three groups of hybrids, confusingly known by regional names: English iris, derived from *I. latifolia* (syn. *I. xiphioides*) from the Pyrenees; Spanish iris, bred from *I. xiphium* from the countries bordering the Mediterranean (including Spain); and the Dutch iris, bred from *I. xiphium* and *I. tingitana* from Morocco.

English iris have the largest flowers of the three groups, in blue, purple and white shades with a yellow patch on the falls. There are usually two flowers per stem on a strong bulb and they make excellent cut flowers, though they are not seen for sale as often as the smaller Dutch iris. Unfortunately, only mixtures are usually offered, but in well-drained soil in a sunny position these make a colourful display for several weeks and will fill many vases.

I. xiphium, from which the Spanish and Dutch iris are descended, grows in marshy soils that dry out in summer. Like all these cultivated iris, they prefer soil that has been improved, such as in the vegetable plot, and do not relish barren borders. The leaves appear in autumn, unlike those of the English iris, which do not show until the spring, and they flower earlier, in many shades of blue, white and yellow. Again only mixtures are usually offered but their crisply shaped, bright flowers are perfect for cutting.

The Dutch iris, particularly its pale blue 'Wedgwood', its selection 'Ideal' and the darker blue 'Professor Blaaw' cultivars, are standard florist flowers sold by the million each year. This is not solely due to the admiration of the public but also to the fact that its cultivation has been controlled to such an extent that it can be brought into flower all year round, and thus has become as dependable as the chrysanthemum. 'White Elegance' (white) and 'Lemon Beauty' (yellow) and a whole host of shades in between are also available. Named cultivars are often offered for sale, as well as mixtures. The largest bulbs that may produce more than one flower per stem are best for garden use, while smaller bulbs are quite sufficient for cutting.

SIBERIAN, SPURIA AND PACIFIC COAST IRIS

Siberian iris also offer a great deal of potential as cut flowers and their thin stems are easy to arrange, especially in floral foam. The wide range of flower shapes allows their use in all sorts of arrangements and even on short stems the flowers do not look out of proportion. It is surprising that they are not grown more frequently as a cut flower crop. Modern, flaring cultivars such as 'White Swirl' can be used in arrangements so that the top of the flower faces the viewer, while the 'wild' flower type still looks best in an upright position.

The spuria iris, with their strong upright stems and flowers rather like large Dutch iris, make admirable cut flowers and with modern hybrids available in a wealth of interesting colours they are very popular.

Pacific Coast Iris make dainty, short-stemmed flowers for small vases and the water iris *I. ensata* and *I. laevigata* are ideal for modern arrangements and ikebana. The Louisiana iris too make good cut flowers and offer a wide range of colours and elegant flower shape but are not as popular as garden plants in Britain, though modern developments in breeding tough, hardy cultivars could change that.

A feature that almost certainly has not been deliberately bred for but which is an asset in many groups, particularly the Siberians, is the shape of the seed pods. Siberian iris have shapely pods on long, thin stems that dry well without dispersing their seeds if picked before they are fully ripe. Other species that can also be used in this way include Pacific Coast Iris and spurias; bearded iris with their stout stems and fat pods are less elegant. Either air drying or standing the pods and leaves in a solution of glycerine to enhance the brown colour and gloss should produce satisfactory results.

WINTER IRIS

There are two iris in the Series Unguiculares of very different habits but similar appearance that must also be considered as iris for cutting. The first and, from the point of garden display the most important, is *I. unguicularis*, the Algerian iris, sometimes still known by its previous name of *I. stylosa*. This species comes not only from Algeria but other countries around the Mediterranean and varies considerably; some variants, such as those from Greece and Crete, are sometimes referred to a separate species (*I. cretensis* or *I. unguicularis* ssp. *cretensis*). In the wild it grows in rocky places among low shrubs, and in cultivation it requires the hottest, sunniest position in the garden, even at the base of a south-facing house wall where little else will survive. However, even if planted in the proper place, it may grow but resolutely refuse to flower. The narrow leaves arise from closely set, wiry rhizomes and make untidy clumps about 30cm (1ft) high. It is evergreen and in winter, often as early as Christmas, begins to send up buds. Although it is strictly almost stalkless the peri-anth tube is several centimetres long and the flowers are typically lavender blue, with a superb crystalline tex-ture on close examination, and have a sweet perfume. Cut the stems and bring them into the house just as the buds are about to unfurl; they will open the following day and last for another day or two. *I. unguicularis* combines prettily with other winter flowers such as *Mahonia*, *Viburnum × bodnantense*, *Helleborus argutifolius* and *Jasminum nudiflorum*. The main flowering period is from late winter to early spring in most seasons, but it is quite possible for the same clump to be in bloom for both Christmas and Easter. However, the flowers are often damaged by winter weather because although the buds are frost-hardy the open blooms are not. Snails and slugs decimate the flowers and find the dense masses of foliage a perfect hiding place.

Although the usual colour of the flowers is lavender, as characterized by the wonderfully scented, large 'Walter Butt', there are white-flowered varieties (which tend to have less than satisfactory, thin-textured flowers) and deeper shades, such as the violet 'Mary Barnard', deep violet 'Speciosa' with a deep yellow signal on the falls and 'Marginata' with a thin white edge to the petals. There are also pink-flowered forms. All need baking hot soil and lime. No soil is too dry and when I first grew this iris on heavy limy clay I dug out a large hole, filled it with brick rubble and stones and planted the young potful in less than 15cm (6in) of soil. It grew and flowered well, though snails were always a problem.

I. unguicularis is not a tidy plant, and it is often said that the leaves should be trimmed back after flowering to allow sun to reach the roots. This is not necessary and may weaken the plant, but some tidying of the old, dead leaves is to be recommended, simply by running your fingers through the clumps in late summer and in spring. The autumn groom in particular is useful to remove snails that have set up home, and leaving a few slug pellets containing methiocarb among the clumps in mild spells through winter will reduce damage.

This plant does not like to be disturbed, but if it has to be moved or divided the job is best attempted in late summer. It is vital that divisions are watered in their first season to help them establish, even if the increased leafy growth means missing flowers for a season.

Despite the rather exacting cultural requirements, this is a very fine garden plant and everyone who has a suitable border should plant it. For those lucky garden-ers with moist soil and dappled shade, the closely related but smaller *I. lazica* is a good substitute. Its leaves are greener and arranged in looser clumps, in fans at an oblique angle to the soil, but the flowers are super-ficially similar, if shorter-stemmed.

SNAKESHEAD IRIS

When I first grew *Hermodactylus tuberosus* (syn *Iris tuberosa*), I planted the long, finger-like tubers in a sunny dry place, in the sort of conditions that *I. unguicularis* demands. This iris is grown for its unusual, sweetly scented flowers which are a mixture of green and deep purple, almost brown-black. Although known as a commercial cut flower, it is rarely seen out-side expensive city florists. It is rarely grown in gardens, probably because of its colouring which, although very pretty, is sombre and no use for garden effect. But the biggest problem with this plant is its leaves, which are very long at 30cm (1ft) and scruffy. They start to droop as the flowers open on stems that are slightly shorter, pulling the stems down and hiding the flowers. The best thing to do is cut the flowers for the house. The blooms appear in mid-spring and the leaves die down soon after.

This is another plant from the Mediterranean. It needs well-drained soil and prefers some lime, and given these conditions it will increase happily for years without attention. The tuberous roots should be divided after flowering and before new root growth begins, in mid- to late summer.

11

THE VALUE OF IRIS
IN THE GARDEN

It is a common misconception that iris prefer wet soils, or even need a pond to thrive, while other gardeners believe that they will only flower in full sun. In fact iris will bring colour and beauty to every part of the garden, though the right iris has to be chosen for each particular place. Above all, iris provide both grace and colour, an unusual combination for any plant. Their stiffly upright stems and grassy leaves suit both formal and informal schemes. They look right in cottage gardens, yet may be the only flowering plant in a minimalist garden composed of hard surfaces and man-made materials.

To gain an unbiased view of the value of iris in the garden it is best to look at them through the eyes of a garden designer, someone who is not interested in unusual cultivars or particular patterns on the flowers but wants plants for form, texture, structure and colour. For a designer, the flowers may be the least important thing of all – possibly a healthy counterbalance to the breeders of the Tall Bearded cultivars who have so often bred almost solely for flowers and ignored the qualities of the rest of the plant.

The modern Tall Bearded iris is very much a florist flower, improved (if that can be generally accepted as fact) beyond recognition in many cases, and the colour range enhanced so that the group has been split into sections to classify it for exhibition and practical purposes. As in the case of the show auricula and striped ranunculus of our ancestors, the more effort that has been put into the development of the flower, the less use to average gardeners, who wish to decorate their

gardens, the plant has become. This is, of course, a controversial generalization, and I believe that breeding will continue, particularly in the UK, to improve branching, bud count, vigour and bloom season – all necessary attributes of a good garden plant.

CLASSIC PLANTS

Many gardeners will be more than satisfied with older hybrids and species, a predilection based on more than pure nostalgia. In a horticultural world that is full of change – when no sooner is a plant introduced than it is superseded by something bigger, brighter, bolder or more expensive – there is a reassuring security in growing a plant that is a classic. Plant species are the classic plants in our gardens, fashioned by evolution over centuries; they are tough, designed to succeed and, as in the best contemporary design, there is nothing that is without function as nature does not squander materials. Some have an illustrious pedigree – you can grow the same plant that Gertrude Jekyll, or E. A. Bowles, or even Gerard or Parkinson grew in their gardens, and who can argue with their choices. The species can also be grown from seed, and be relied upon to look almost exactly the same as the parent plant. And there is the guarantee that if you did not garden for a thousand years that same plant would still be there in the wild, getting on with life happily without you.

This is fine if humankind does not inadvertently destroy the plant's habitat, and that is another attractive reason for growing plant species – to preserve for future generations the gene pool of wild plants that can otherwise never be replaced once lost in the wild.

It is also true that many of the beautiful colour combinations and variations of the modern cultivars are

'Waterboy' shows the flaring form of modern dwarf iris that makes the flowers look more colourful from above.

Variegated *Iris pallida* leaves catch the sun in the garden of the late Frances Perry.

lost in the larger scale of the designed border and garden, and although many of the cultivars with pure colours are quite suitable for mixing with other plants, the (generally) smaller flower size of the species is more convenient for mixing with other garden flowers. Choice depends upon whether the grower wants a flower that steals the show or one that is an team player.

FLOWERS

There is no doubt that the most striking feature of the majority of iris is their flowers. Although they vary enormously in shape, from the point of view of garden value it is their size and colour that is most important, though when selecting cultivars it must be remembered that if the stems are upright, flaring (horizontal) falls are less colourful from a distance than drooping falls. Low-growing Pacific Coast Iris are always viewed from above, and their flowers are not seen from a distance

unless they are planted as an edging or among dwarf plants. Spurias produce their flowers in a sheaf at the top of their stems, giving a line of colour in the border, and Tall Bearded and Border Bearded iris, if well branched, give a broad and deep mass of colour that may be more useful for mixing with other flowers.

Many thousands of words have been written about how to use iris and how to blend and combine the colours and patterns in the garden. Most of these suggestions are made in books in the first half of the twentieth century and they often include suggestions such as 'plan for a small formal iris garden in a rural home'. These must have reinforced the idea that iris cannot be mixed with other flowers, and though a bed of iris in full bloom is a marvellous sight, most gardeners will want to mix them with other plants. But if a bed is to be dedicated to iris how should they be arranged? There is no set answer to that. The gardener who needs to create beautiful garden effects will choose a limited range of iris, carefully selected, to create the exact effect that has developed in his or her inner eye. The collector who loves his or her iris may arrange them according to size, colour, pattern, raiser, awards or country of origin. Exceptional skill is needed to achieve a gradation of colour, and it is probably best to group colours, so that all blues, pale, frosty, deep and purple, are placed together, supporting each other yet accentuating their differences, with plicatas and other patterns arranged with them. Like variegated plants in the garden, bold patterns like plicatas should be used sparingly or they lose their effectiveness.

Even within a small group, particularly the bearded iris, but also within the Siberians and the Dutch and Spanish bulbous iris, there is a large range of colours to use. Perhaps it is because the bearded iris show such variety that many gardeners do not look elsewhere in the genus for garden plants. This is a mistake, however, because although the deep, blackcurrant purple of 'Superstition' may have a velvety sheen, a ruffling and size that are hard to match, the deep purple of forms of *I. chrysographes* are augmented by bright golden markings on a flower of refinement and poise that makes the other look clumsy and almost grotesque.

Many of the bulbous iris, and all those hybridized for the cut flower markets such as the Dutch iris, are so cheap to buy that they can be treated as bedding plants. While it might be expensive to plant dwarf reticulata iris thickly enough to make a showy display, the Dutch, English and Spanish iris are suitable alternatives for spring bedding. They flower a little later, but if combined with *Hesperis matronalis* (sweet rocket), *Lunaria* (honesty) and tall species of *Allium* they can be very effective.

No individual iris has a particularly long flowering season and, while it is true that it is possible to have iris in flower for six months of the year, a great many would need to be grown. It is unfortunate that the best known, the Tall Bearded iris, do not have a particularly long flowering season, especially in the old forms that are passed to new gardeners as rejects from knowledgeable gardeners. They are almost bound to kill, rather than kindle, any love for these flowers.

The iris with the longest season of flower of all is the Algerian iris, *I. unguicularis*, which in mild winters will be in flower at Christmas and will continue until early spring or beyond, depending on the season. It provides colour and scent in the darkest months of the year and thrives in the driest, poorest soil imaginable. In fact knowledgeable gardeners dig out the soil at the base of sunny walls and fill the hole with rubble and mortar to make a dry, alkaline patch which the plant prefers and which the snails which devour its flower buds dislike.

FOLIAGE

Foliage is important to iris because, with a few unusual exceptions, iris have creeping stems or bulbs and leaves that originate at ground level. To get to the light they have to be long, and they do not like close competition from other plants. Iris leaves can be big, and often beautiful, and they make interesting shapes in the border.

In particular, spuria iris have what must be some of the longest leaves in the garden, beaten only by lanky phormiums or the massive spread of *Gunnera*. These

'Saxon Surprise' makes a traditional, soft and fragrant scene with *Rosa* 'Mme Grégoire Staechelin'.

leaves are tall and thin but superbly strong, held in narrow sheaves that form upright clumps like narrow shuttlecocks. They disappear in winter like those of most iris, but those that do not become dormant immediately after flowering are exceptionally fine accent plants in summer, or as a background to lower plants such as *Tricyrtis* or *Helenium* that flower later in the season.

The spuria iris can be used in most soils, and even in positions of light shade. They can be planted at the edge of a shrub border, for instance, or even used to divide a piece of wild grassland from the more formal border, for spurias are generally tough and quite suitable for naturalizing where they are given protection from invasive weeds and can be left to grow unhindered by the gardener.

The group of Siberian iris are just as versatile, but they do not have such a striking silhouette. Instead, they form rounded humps of narrow foliage that is often as fluid in the wind as some grasses. Unlike the spurias, the habit of the clumps changes through the season, starting upright and often tinged with purple at the base, then later becoming less stiff, and finally collapsing as it turns a deep brown in winter, leaving the flower stems and tulip-shaped seed pods standing stiffly erect. These are iris to soften edges and give informality.

The flowers of Siberian iris are delicate and, depending upon the cultivar and species, look good in well-manicured borders or schemes that are on the edge of chaos. Because they thrive so well without attention once planted, they are suited to naturalizing and to naturalistic herbaceous planting where informal drifts of perennials are planted as though by nature.

Stiff, sword-like foliage is the merit and downfall of bearded iris. The leaves of a few can be said to provide accents in the border, but many are ugly. In addition, if the bases of the fans are crowded by other plants rot may occur. In gravel and drought-resistant gardens the foliage of Tall Bearded iris may be tolerated but the large flowers of the hybrids may not be what you need.

Annuals associate well with these plants, provided delicately foliaged plants such as *Eschscholzia*, *Cladanthus*, *Delphinium* (larkspur), *Leptosiphon*, *Gilia* and *Papaver* (poppies) are chosen rather than fat leafy *Calendula*, though *Tropaeolum* (nasturtiums) with glaucous leaves may complement the iris, especially if the dark-leaved 'Empress of India' is chosen.

Siberian iris such as 'Splashdown' are permanent garden plants that can be left to establish and grow with minimal attention for many years.

The greyish iris leaves suit other grey-leaved plants and, since these may come from similarly sunny climates, they make good companions. If summers continue to be dry, with restrictions on watering becoming the norm, iris could be used as the colour in a planting of drought-tolerant plants such as *Salvia* (sages), *Convolvulus cneorum*, *Phlomis*, *Rosmarinus* (rosemary), *Lavandula* (lavender), *Romneya*, *Artemisia*, *Corokia*, *Caryopteris*, *Eryngium*, *Dianthus*, *Festuca* and *Erysimum*. However, none of these plants look their best in winter and should be pruned in spring.

In the very mildest gardens, or alternatively in pots in cool greenhouses in cold ones, the tall stems of *I. confusa*, which are reminiscent of bamboos, add a tropical flavour to a collection of ferns, *Bletilla* orchids and *Eucomis*, even without the airy sprays of delicate white flowers in spring.

VARIEGATION

If used with discretion, variegated foliage is a valuable tool in making a good garden and fortunately the few iris that do possess variegated leaves show restraint and order in their colouring; they exhibit stripes of contrasting shades and avoid the splashes, blotches and distortion that affect other variegated plants. Indeed, even the most pragmatic of gardeners would agree that *I. pallida* 'Variegata' is among the best of variegated plants. It inherits the healthy foliage of its parent and is blessed with a primrose-coloured stripe that often takes up half the leaf blade. It is vigorous and flowers well too. The white-striped *I. pallida* 'Argentea Variegata' is less strong and flowers less freely, but is still good. The latter is a happy part of any white garden, and its blue flowers are pale enough to break the monotony rather than dominate the scene. There are variegated hybrids, but they are rare. The only one I have grown is 'Striped Breeches', the white flowers of which should make it a useful plant for sophisticated and tasteful planting schemes, but the variegation is very unpredictable and it is not as good a garden plant as the two forms of *I. pallida*.

Where conditions are less than favourable for most plants, the variegated form of the evergreen *I. foetidissima*, 'Variegata', will thrive but, unlike the typical species, it will not flower or produce its bright orange seeds to brighten the dry shade under trees.

In water, or in the dampest soils, there is *I. laevigata* 'Variegata' and, for the early summer at least, *I. pseudacorus* 'Variegata', which adds a ray of sunshine before becoming green after the effort of flowering. In mild gardens, *I. japonica* 'Variegata' makes a good low-growing foil for autumn bulbs. The bright stripy leaves are the perfect partner for candy-pink nerines and mauve colchicums and, although the foliage of the latter is a little coarse, if it is removed as soon as it yellows it should not cause too much damage to the iris. A light mulch of good garden compost at the same time will not only encourage new growth and flowering, but also maintain the iris at its peak through the summer.

CONTAINER GARDENING

Many iris are very happy to grow in pots and containers. The best are the bulbous or clump-forming species rather than those that move rapidly in a horizontal direction such as the bearded iris. This method of cultivation also means that plants with very different cultural requirements can be grouped together in a series of containers.

In sinks and troughs, the smallest bearded iris can be grown for many years, along with bulbous reticulata and Juno types. If well watered, the tiny *I. cristata* will grow with other peat-lovers such as *Cassiope* and autumn-flowering *Gentiana*. In larger half-pots and pans the Japanese roof iris, *I. tectorum*, is an elegant addition to any patio, and larger pots could be home to any Pacific Coast or Siberian iris. With some winter protection, *I. confusa*, *I. wattii*, *I. japonica* or beautiful Evansia hybrids such as 'Bourne Graceful' make striking garden features.

IRIS FOR SCENT

Not all iris are fragrant, but in some it is an extra asset. The tiny bulbous *I. reticulata* and its cultivars and related species are sweetly scented, but this is a little academic unless they are grown in pots and can be lifted to the nose on warm days.

However, the taller bearded iris have flowers at a more convenient height, and many have fragrances that are wafted on the wind. Many are fruity, described as grapy or plummy, but when the flowers are cut and taken into the house these perfumes can become rank

Iris graminea has small flowers and large leaves, but a wonderful scent. It is not a typical spuria iris.

The purity of the white form of *Iris tectorum* makes this flower one of the prettiest of all iris. The usual colour is lavender blue.

and overpowering – they are often better left in the garden. Dwarf bearded iris too show an amazing range of scents, and some are as sweet as roses. Few, however, can compete with the perfume of *I. pallida*, a plant that is almost faultless.

Some iris are named for the scent – the plum tart iris (*I. graminea*) really smells like stewed plums, but it is another scent only appreciated by those who are prepared to bend over to smell it. The stinking iris (*I. foetidissima*) does not in fact smell at all unless the leaves are crushed, and then the scent is by no means as unpleasant as the name suggests.

IRIS FOR SHADE

The very word 'shade' suggests a problem area to the gardener, a place where few plants will grow. Yet even the iris genus has a few species that will tolerate shade – depending on the type of shade.

Basically, a shady area is one that does not receive full sun. There are many different degrees of shade and semi-shade, the most commonly occurring phrase, means that an area is shaded for part of the day. Dappled shade means that sunlight reaches the soil in small patches, constantly changing as the sun moves across the sky. Neither of these are great enemies of plants, though the intensity of the sun in northern latitudes as compared with southerly gardens must be considered in the case of certain iris that need high light levels in order to flourish.

What causes the shade is often more important than how much there is, and the difference is all about water availability. In the wild, in areas not shaded for part of the day by mountain ranges (or, in micro-climates, by rocks) most shade is provided by trees. When in leaf, trees suck up vast quantities of water. They produce 'dry shade' and it is this condition that is so very difficult to cope with in gardens. In nature, plants have come to adapt to this; they are either evergreen, with very deep green leaves (which maximize the little light there is), or they grow and flower in the winter, while the trees are relatively dormant. That is why woodland gardens are filled with flowers in spring – anemones, bluebells, celandines and primroses. The shade cast by buildings is not such a problem unless the wall prevents rainwater reaching the ground, which is why it is sometimes difficult to establish plants under the eaves of a house.

The worst type of shade is the dry shade cast by an evergreen, because here even spring-flowering plants cannot thrive. It is surprising that anyone encourages this situation, but thousands of gardeners do it every year when they plant × Cupressocyparis leylandii as a hedge. The problem is compounded if they clip it regularly, because the necessary trampling compacts the soil and squashes any vegetation that may be attempting to colonize the dusty soil.

But there are plants that will grow in this situation, and one of the best just happens to be an iris. In addition it is an iris that is evergreen, and has showy seed pods that split open to bring colour to the garden or home in winter – the stinking iris, I. foetidissima, a valuable landscape plant. I have grown a number of other species and hybrids including Pacific Coast Iris, I. fulvala, I. milesii, I. tectorum, I. graminea, many

Siberian iris and others in semi-shaded or lightly shaded positions, but they would almost certainly have flowered more freely and attained more compact habits if grown in full sun.

The shade of a north-facing wall is very useful in the garden. Although this is often dismissed as being dark and cool, it does ensure that the micro-climate is fairly constant, and because plants of all types are less likely to burst into growth prematurely at the first hint of spring weather, they are also less likely to be caught out by late spring frosts. This is a perfect place to build a peat garden in warmer areas because these are very prone to drying out in sunny places and prove difficult to keep moist without the profligate use of water.

An acid soil rich in humus, be it leafmould or peat, a cool root run and a steady supply of moisture are good for a number of the smaller species in the genus that are difficult to establish in ordinary beds. Among the prettiest of these are the Evansia or crested iris, including I. cristata and I. gracilipes (and the hybrid between the two). I. cristata is the smallest of the three, with leaves less than 15cm (6in) high and thin, creeping rhizomes. It is a native of the eastern states of the USA, where it grows in moist deciduous woodland. It does not mind neutral or slightly alkaline soils, and will grow in sun or semi-shade, but it must not dry out or be forced to compete with taller plants. It eventually spreads to leave a tired, dead area in the centre that can be top-dressed with some rich compost which may induce fresh rooting and the growth of new shoots. Alternatively, divide and replant it. This is best done after flowering if transplanted pieces can be watered as they establish, otherwise it should be done in spring as growth starts. Although autumn division has the advantage that the soil is moist and warm, important factors for most plants, iris generally make new roots in spring and immediately after flowering. Also, autumn division of small iris (and indeed other plants) allows too much chance for blackbirds and other animals to rummage among them and disturb them before they have a chance to root.

The flowers of I. cristata are less than 5cm (2in) across but are beautifully formed with erect, narrow standards, each stem producing one or two blooms. They are held on short stalks and are in varying shades of lavender-blue, all having a white patch in the centre of the falls

'Sun Doll' combines well with forget-me-nots at the edge of
a path or in a rock garden.

with three ridged crests running along its length,
touched with yellow or gold. There is also a white form,
'Alba'. *I. cristata* is a gem of a plant, perfectly in proportion and a lovely companion for small erythroniums
and anemones, flowering from mid- to late spring.

The flowers of *I. gracilipes* are rather similar, but are
carried on more slender plants and the crest has less yellow in its colouring. This is a native of Japan and China,
again found in moist deciduous woodland.

IRIS IN THE ROCK GARDEN

There is a certain amount of snobbery when it comes to
rock gardens and alpines, and the alpine gardener may
shudder with horror at the thought of a rockery plas-
tered with aubrieta and arabis. However, in this chapter
I simply refer to areas of the garden that will probably be
augmented with rocks, may be raised above ground
level to assist drainage, and are planted with small
plants. These may be home to choice alpines but they
may also contain a less sophisticated selection.

Strictly speaking, an alpine plant comes from an
upland, even mountain region, the term encompassing

bulbs, herbaceous plants, small shrubs and annuals. A
rockery often means an area of soil implanted with
rocks, and all too often the surface of the soil is the
infertile subsoil excavated from making a pond or other
construction – only the hardiest of plants can survive.
However, provided the rock garden has been constructed. with moderately good soil many iris will
succeed, and if it is very dry in summer the dwarf bulbous iris in particular will be very happy. Bear in mind
that the dwarf bearded iris, like all pogon species, need
a period of growth after flowering to make increases for
the next season, and tolerance of drought can be taken
too far. Water in well-drained alpine soils is often abun-
dant in spring as the winter snow melts.

The great advantage of a rock garden is the control
over cultivation it gives, especially if the soil mixture in
different pockets is varied. Small cloches and other protection can be provided in winter for delicate plants.
Very delicate species are for enthusiasts only, but there
are many little gems that even the casual irisian will
want to grow. Many of these small iris are very early
flowering, pushing up their blooms when there is little
else in flower in the garden, and the anticipation of
waiting for that first bud of a new iris to open is one of
the greatest pleasures in gardening.

12

CULTIVATION

Most of the commonly available iris are quite easy to grow in gardens where the conditions roughly approximate those of their natural habitats, but any account of the cultivation of iris is necessarily complicated by the diverse nature of the genus – the very reason that iris are so valuable·to gardeners. While conditions can be adapted if need be, certain parts of any country are more suited to particular groups and it is wise to begin with the plants that are most likely to thrive with the least effort on your part.

Apart from the ease of culture, the other good reason for growing plants that suit your own climate is that if a plant is not suffering from stress caused by severe drought, waterlogging, cold, heat, shade or scorching sun, it will be better able to resist pests and diseases – the basics of organic gardening, which is relevant to all gardeners whatever their chosen approach. However, most gardeners do like a challenge, and if all our garden plants grew like weeds there would be less satisfaction to be gained.

The other principle of gardening is that there are too many variables to give an explicit and accurate set of instructions about how to·grow any plant; if the same treatment were applied three years in a row to the same plants, the results would all be slightly different. However, this chapter does describe the basic cultivation requirements of all the groups of iris except the specialist iris, for which cultivation details are given in Chapter 9.

BEARDED IRIS: SECTION IRIS

The whole group of tall, short, species and hybrid bearded iris require similar conditions, which is to say sunlight and good drainage. Without sun the fussiest

will die and the toughest will not flower as they should, while without good drainage all might rot.

A position in full sun for the whole day will suit all, but if the border is shaded by a building or by a plant (though not an overhanging one) for a part of the day some should perform quite well; the Dwarf Bearded and Intermediates in particular will flower successfully if the sun shines on them for at least half the day. Obviously it is better if that half is in the middle of the day, when the sun is strongest – a little sun early in the morning and in the evening at midsummer is not really enough.

SOIL

A good soil with a balance of clay, silt and sand is best for most types of plant and iris are no exception, with the addition of organic matter improving growth. Heavy soils are not necessarily badly drained, but in winter a soil that contains a large proportion of clay particles will retain more moisture between rainfall than sandy or silty soils. In this case digging in coarse sand, grit and gravel is important more for drainage than fertility because clay soil is naturally quite rich in nutrients and does not leach them as sandy soils do. If this is not practical the rhizomes may be planted either in raised beds or on ridges of raised soil, about 20cm (8in) or less above the natural soil level. This obviously limits their aesthetic use in the border, but it is useful for growing collections or for specific iris beds. In the border they can be planted on mounds but this is not easy to accomplish without damaging surrounding plants if replanting in late summer. Deep double digging, incorporating well-rotted organic manure into the bottom spit, is of benefit, as it is with most garden plants, especially in ground that has not been cultivated for some

PLATE VI

I. 'Stepping Out'
Tall Bearded

I. 'Sable'
Tall Bearded

I. 'Curlew'
Intermediate Bearded

I. 'Braithwaite'
Tall Bearded

All plants shown at approximately ¹/₃ size

I. 'Wood Pigeon'
Border Bearded

I. 'Sugar Biscuit'
Tall Bearded

I. flavescens

I. 'Ola Kala'
Tall Bearded

I. 'Wabash'
Tall Bearded

I. 'Gudrun'
Tall Bearded

time or in soil that has already grown iris and needs to be revitalized.

Organic matter is the essential ingredient in any soil, and will be present in soil in all its stages of decomposition, from coarse partially decomposed material to the sticky brown substance that is called humus – although that term is loosely applied to anything that will eventually become humus. Humus is like an organic glue, sticking soil particles together and also grabbing hold of plant nutrients in solution. It creates the crumbly texture sought after by gardeners and the nutrients that it retains indirectly increase soil fertility.

It does not really matter what the raw material of this humus is, but some forms of organic matter contain more plant nutrients than others. Conversely, some contain less desirable additions such as weeds. Sandy and alkaline soils in particular benefit from added organic material because they provide the perfect conditions for the bacteria that decompose it. However, in order to be effective the organic matter must be added regularly or the improvements to the soil will not be maintained.

SOIL IMPROVERS

Leafmould is a universally admired organic soil improver and is simply decomposed leaves. The leaves that produce the best leafmould are those that contain the largest amounts of lignin – the woody substance in plants like oak and beech. Unfortunately these leaves take a long time to break down so an activator should be added to help. For example, grass cuttings, if mixed thoroughly with the leaves, can speed up the process and produce a reasonable leafmould in a year.

Garden compost can be a useful addition to soil and it is free, but unless materials are added as small pieces and well mixed the results can be disappointingly variable. It is inadvisable to add perennial weeds and diseased material to the heap.

Spent mushroom compost is one of the most valuable soil conditioners there is. It is based on composted horse manure but, because the crop mushrooms have taken a large proportion of the nutrients, it is unlikely to overfeed any garden plants. It contains traces of lime which may be useful to some iris and it is clean to work with and pleasant-smelling. Bought in bags it can be expensive, but if bought by the trailer-load it is very economical.

Many bearded species occur naturally on alkaline soil, and it is often recommended that soil is heavily limed before planting. This is not strictly necessary and there is little evidence that the addition of lime produces better plants or flowers. However, calcium (in lime and chalk) is an essential plant nutrient, and some believe that limy soils produce healthier foliage through disease resistance. A neutral (pH7 or more) alkaline soil is ideal, and you may wish to add lime if the soil is acid (pH less than 7). This may cause chlorosis (yellowing of leaves) in surrounding plants, so it is best to give their requirements preference if they are more sensitive. If an iris bed is edged with *Matthiola* (stocks) or *Cheiranthus* (wallflowers) liming in spring may help to reduce the incidence of clubroot, a fungal disease of the roots of brassicas such as *Matthiola* that thrives in acid soil, but if the surrounding plants are phlox or even azaleas and rhododendrons, leave well alone.

FERTILIZER

Before planting, the soil can be augmented with a fertilizer to encourage growth. Many gardeners prefer organic fertilizers, but for the plants themselves there is probably little difference between these and inorganic sources of nutrient because plants can only absorb chemicals as very simple compounds. Inorganic sources supply food in a readily available form, while organic ones usually require weathering or the action of bacteria and fungi in the soil to release them. Organic fertilizers do encourage the soil flora and fauna, thus contributing to the general health of the soil and, because they generally release their nutrients slowly, they are useful if you are not quite sure when to apply the feed. The exception to this is dried blood, but as this is a source of nitrogen it is not something that will usually be given to garden iris except to stimulate leafy growth.

Of the three major nutrients – nitrogen (N), phosphorus (P) and potassium (K) – the most important are phosphorus and potassium, the former encouraging root growth and the latter flowering and disease-resistance. Excess nitrogen leads to sappy leaf growth which is prone to aphid attack and in winter may be less able to withstand cold. Before planting, a balanced fertilizer such as Growmore or fish, blood and bone can be raked or forked into the soil at the recommended rate. Any garden fertilizer designed for roses, flowering shrubs, flowers or tomatoes is recommended because it will be balanced to contain a smaller proportion of nitrogen.

It is always best to replant into fresh soil that has not grown iris for several years, but if this is not possible dig the soil well and incorporate some well-rotted garden compost, or spent mushroom compost. Animal manure is not always recommended for iris but I have used it without harm, though it should not be fresh, nor applied in autumn when it may encourage a surge of leafy growth or cover the rhizomes. If you are spreading it as a thin mulch take care to keep it away from the necks of the fans, as if it accumulates around the base of the leaves it is very likely to cause rot. However, one reason why mulches are not often recommended for bearded iris is that blackbirds love to throw the material around as they look for insects and they can easily bury small iris under any kind of mulch.

Dried calf's milk is used as a fertilizer in the USA and this may provide the plants with traces of vitamins that give stronger growth. However, although vitamins may be a useful foliar feed I doubt their efficiency when applied to the soil. The dried milk may even encourage bacteria that lead to rhizome rots, and American growers have used antibiotics to control bacterial infections. This practice is not to be condoned because the excessive use of antibiotics in all parts of our environment is leading to the development of resistant strains of bacteria.

Calcified seaweed is a splendid fertilizer, and contains calcium and other plant nutrient. Fertilizers based on crushed crab shell (which may be locally available) should also be ideal and are reputed to inhibit bacteria with a natural antibiotic.

PREPARING FOR PLANTING

The optimum time to plant is six weeks after flowering. This is usually in midsummer, allowing time for the new rhizome to become established and make sufficient growth to produce fans to flower the following year. New roots that began growing immediately after flowering will then be strong enough to help anchor the new plants. Early spring is another suitable time, just as the other main period of root growth is about to start, but flowering may be forfeited, and if flowers are produced the stems will almost certainly need staking. Planting later than early autumn will nearly always

result in flowers missed for a year, though it might encourage late summer flowering of remontant cultivars. Bearded iris cultivars are tough, and if the rhizome is large they can survive out of soil for many weeks. This is not an ideal situation, but it makes transport of the plants easy.

If you have bought new rhizomes they may be ready to plant, but if you are dividing an established clump (most need replanting after three to five years) or you have received rhizomes as a gift they will need to be trimmed before planting. Each fan of leaves is cut away from the old rhizome with the part of the rhizome that has been formed in the previous 6–12 months. This may be 15cm (6in) long in Tall Beardeds but just 1cm ($^{1}/_{2}$in) long in Miniature Tall Beardeds. Any rhizome older than that is worthless unless you wish to bulk up large numbers of plants, when you may wish to wait for old, dormant buds to break. The retained rhizome will probably have 5–10 leaf scars or ridges. Choose the largest fans, only planting small fans if they are required to make up numbers; they will grow, but there is usually a surplus when dividing and replanting and it is best to chose the healthiest and plumpest. As a precaution, dip the rhizome and roots into a fungicide solution to discourage rot. The rhizomes can then be planted immediately or allowed to dry out for just a few hours first. Although severe drying out is tolerated it will lead to root death, and this puts an unnecessary strain on the food reserves in the rhizome.

Extraordinary individual beauty combines with great garden impact in Japanese water iris like 'The Great Mogul'.

It is usual practice to trim the leaves. This can be done with a knife or secateurs, but if there is a chance of virus being present I recommend sterilizing tools between the preparation of each cultivar to prevent cross-infection. Dipping the blade into methylated spirit and touching this with a lighter to ignite it is an easy way to do this. The leaves are usually cut across horizontally at about 15cm (6in) high. This not only looks neat and avoids the inevitable die back of the leaves after transplanting, but it also prevents the wind from rocking the young plants before they become established. It also allows the first signs of growth to be seen, always reassuring after replanting.

HOW TO PLANT

The traditional advice is to dig a shallow hole and form a mound in this so that the top of the mound is just lower than the surrounding soil level. The piece of rhizome is then placed on this, with the roots radiating out quite shallowly, and the soil is then replaced and firmed so that the top of the rhizome is above the soil surface. However, anyone who has dug up plants will be aware that the roots do not just grow outwards but downwards as well. A far easier, and just as effective, method is to remove a fairly deep hole with a trowel and tuck the roots into this. Replace the soil, working it between the roots to avoid burying them in a bunch, and firm once or twice as the soil is replaced. It is not difficult to hold the trimmed fan of leaves with one hand, shaking the plant to distribute the soil around the roots, and fill the soil with the other. Because the roots are firmly held in place using this method there is less movement after planting. Where the roots are present along the length of the rhizome, fill in the soil from the side rather than from the back.

On heavy soils it is important that the top of the rhizome is on the soil surface, but in light sandy soils covering the rhizome a little will aid stability – the plants will soon pop up to the surface as growth continues. It is not necessary to water immediately, but if there has not been any rain within a week it is best to apply water to spur the plants into growth or at least help settle the soil around the roots.

The planting distance between the rhizomes will depend upon the particular iris, but 15cm (6in) is required for dwarf kinds and a minimum of 30cm (1ft) for taller types. Clumps are more effective than single

fans, although the latter will increase in future years. If possible, in the northern hemisphere, plant the rhizomes so that the cut end of the rhizome points to the south and the fan to the north, so that they will initially grow to the north; reverse the procedure in the southern hemisphere. The fan of leaves would shade the rhizome from the sun if planted the other way round, and it is important that sun 'ripens' the rhizome in summer. This principle also gives a neat effect after planting. However large or small the group, this pattern will give an even clump and is better than planting with the growths radiating out from a central point, which can produce a clump with a hollow centre.

CARING FOR THE PLANTS

Once the iris start to grow the weeds will too. Hand-weeding is the best solution, though the soil between the clumps can be hoed or sprayed with weedkiller

'Silberkante' demonstrates just how special a good clump of some Siberian iris can look.

down to 20cm (8in) or so to prevent winter damage and wind rock. This trimming should not be too extreme – the result may look tidy, but the leaves are there to nourish the plant, and overtrimming can reduce plant vigour and thus flowering.

Take off old flower stems at ground level by snapping the stem forward – a gentle push forward will cleanly sever the stem from the rhizome and leave no remnant for rot. It is quicker, neater, and better for the plant than cutting off the stems, and because there is no contact with the cut surface there is no chance of cross-infection with virus.

SIBERIAN IRIS: SERIES SIBIRICAE

Many of the Siberian species grow in damp soil in the wild, but this is damp in spring not waterlogged in winter; their roots should never be waterlogged. However, they respond well to rich moist soil, and should not be planted in poor, dry, stony soil in full sun.

Siberian iris should be transplanted in spring as growth is about to start, or after flowering if watering in dry weather can be assured. When transplanted in spring plants may bloom the same year, while summer planting should result in flowers the following year, if the plants survive. Autumn planting is possible, but it is not followed by a period of root growth and plants may succumb to cold before they become established. The soil should be improved with well-rotted organic matter and plants set so that the base of the leaves and the wiry rhizome is just 2.5–5cm (1–2in) below the soil surface. Shallow planting, with the plants set in a dish-like depression, is a useful habit as it allows easier watering and, over the season, the soil will wash in, finally leaving the plant at the correct depth.

PACIFIC COAST IRIS: SERIES CALIFORNICAE

These species and hybrids require sun or semi-shade and prefer an acid soil. This should preferably be enriched with organic matter, but they are not such gross feeders as the spurias and do not need the moisture required by the Siberian iris. They dislike disturbance and should be left alone as much as possible, but may be replanted in autumn; do not cut them into tiny pieces

provided this is not allowed to come into contact with the foliage of the iris. It is important to clear the ground of perennial weeds before planting as they are extremely difficult to remove once the bed is planted. After a few weeks the plants should be checked to see that they are stable, and gently firmed if necessary.

In the first season it may not be necessary to apply another fertilizer after planting but after that it is beneficial to feed in spring as the buds start to show in the fans of leaves, and again after flowering when the fans for the following season are growing.

Watering in summer is not essential, but it will help the plants to make more and better increases for the following year's display. Summer watering and feeding is essential if you are expecting summer and autumn flowers from remontant cultivars.

Remove dead and dying leaves by pulling them down and backwards at soil level; in autumn trim the leaves

'Sultan's Sash' is one of the deeper coloured spurias of a shade that almost smoulders in the garden.

but keep them as clusters of three or five strong shoots for easiest establishment. As with all the beardless herbaceous iris, if small offsets are made it is best to place these into small pots and keep them in a cold frame until they are established and growing well for up to a year before planting into the open garden.

They need light shade or full sun, and a light, gritty, acid or neutral soil, though they will grow in a humus-rich soil provided it is not waterlogged. They can be combined with heaths and dwarf conifers or dwarf rhododendrons to add a little extra interest. In the wild, most grow at the edges of conifer woods where their wiry roots and rhizomes hold them fast in the loose leaf litter. Moisture is required in spring and at flowering time, though they will tolerate dryness in summer, which makes them ideal in many parts of Britain.

They have a reputation for being difficult to move, but they may be divided in early autumn or in spring, and if kept as chunks of a reasonable size they do not sulk for long. It is most important that their roots do not dry out when they are out of the ground, however, which is one reason why they are so difficult to move, compared to bearded iris.

Alternatively they may be grown from seed, which, even if the species are grown, will result in a range of colours, as the species are very variable. Pot-grown seedlings certainly establish easily and there is always the surprise of seeing the first flowers.

WATER IRIS

It is not necessary to have a pond to grow the water-loving iris. In the garden, *I. ensata* like moist soil and can be grown with their crowns covered with water, but they must not be left waterlogged in winter. It is reported that if planted in very deep water so that the crowns are protected from frost the plants will survive, though they are not as vigorous as normally grown plants. They are gross feeders and liquid fertilizer is of benefit in early summer. In dry areas it is possible to dig out borders, line them with polythene and replace the soil, enriched with rotted manure and peat, to create a damp bed. A soil pH of 6.5 or less is required in all situations. Plants are divided in spring and single crowns are usually potted into 10–18cm (4–7in) pots of good, rich, acid compost, containing moss peat, rotted manure, moss and sandy loam. The crowns are planted no more than 2.5cm (1in) deep, rather more shallow than usual, and placed in shallow containers of water. This water level should remain constant, as although gardens in Japan are flooded when plants are in flower for aesthetic purposes this is not necessary for their cultivation and a fluctuating water level can weaken plants. Once plants are in full growth, liquid fertilizer can be given – that sold for ericaceous plants is ideal. Stop feeding as soon as the flower buds show colour. Pot cultivation is not only ideal for growing perfect blooms, it is also a useful method of cultivation in gardens where the natural soil is unsuitable because it is dry or alkaline.

In general cultivation, *I. laevigata* and *I. pseudacorus* can be treated in the same way as *I. ensata* but they are not fussy about water around their roots and can be grown in both damp soil or where the roots are constantly in water. The Louisiana iris prefer damp or wet acid soils above the waterline and are divided in spring or grown from seed.

SPURIA IRIS: SERIES SPURIAE

Spurias are not fussy about soil but prefer more humus and more water during the growing season than bearded iris. Most are tolerant of lime, and all like soil enriched with garden compost or well-rotted manure worked into the whole soil profile. Because they dislike disturbance, soil preparation is even more important than for bearded iris – spurias will remain in the same spot for a decade or more. If they are divided this is best done in early or mid-autumn, or even early spring, but at no time should the roots or rhizomes be allowed to dry out. Unlike the bearded iris, they will not flower the year after division and may even sulk for a few years before settling down to regular flowering. The rhizome should be planted about 5cm (2in) deep on heavy soils and slightly deeper on sandy soils. Feeding as flowering starts is useful, and those species and cultivars that die down after flowering and become dormant for the

summer (*I. monnieri*, *I. crocea* and *I. orientalis* for example) should have their old foliage cut away. *I. spuria* itself retains its leaves through to late autumn, when they can be removed.

BULBOUS IRIS: SUBGENERA HERMODACTYLOIDES AND XIPHIUM

Although the general rule when planting all bulbs is to plant them so that the top of the bulb is covered with soil twice the height of the bulb, the dwarf reticulata iris usually perform better and are less likely break into tiny bulblets if they are covered with at least four times their height of soil. A general fertilizer can be applied as soon as their growth is seen in spring. The bulbous iris are generally planted in early to mid-autumn as they become available from nurseries. All require a well-drained but not impoverished soil. *I. reticulata* flourishes in limy soils and will even grow on quite heavy clay soils if they are dry in summer and not too wet in winter, but the flowers are susceptible to slug and snail damage on heavy soils because they appear at a time when little else is available for them to eat.

I. reticulata grown in pots for indoor flowering should be potted with the bulb tips covered with 1cm ($\frac{1}{2}$in) of

The blue and white flowers of the spuria 'Protégé' bring a cool shade to the midsummer border.

compost and then plunged into a bed of peat outside in mid-autumn, preferably in a cold frame where watering can be controlled, until mid-winter, when they may be brought into very gentle heat and light in late winter. If the bulbs are covered with a 5cm (2in) layer of peat or grit, they can be brought into warmth as soon as the tips of the shoots show. High temperatures before the flowers show colour will cause flower buds to abort, so do not be tempted to force early flowering and do not attempt to grow them in the home for any length of time. After one year of pot growth, plant them out into the garden.

PESTS AND DISEASES

Most problems associated with iris are related to growing conditions, especially in those species with very specific requirements, as iris are remarkably free of pests and diseases.

The most common pest is aphids, that scourge of almost all garden plants. They spread viruses and can cause distortion of flowers if the buds are heavily infested. As a general precaution it is wise to control any aphids as soon as you see them. Systemic controls are difficult to use effectively because the leaves of bearded iris are waxy and do not absorb spray. If the infestation is minor, just crush the aphids between finger and thumb or by drawing a leaf between your fingers. If not caught quickly, aphids on the leaves will move to flower buds and these cannot be sprayed without damaging the blooms or threatening pollinating insects. Aphids are drawn to plants that are under stress, perhaps suffering from inadequate soil or drought, and heavy infestations can be a sign that something else is wrong.

Caterpillars and earwigs sometimes attack flower buds of remontants that flower in autumn but fortunately this is not a common occurrence. They can be sprayed or dusted with derris, or hand picked. Voles or mice sometimes attack rhizomes; poison them if necessary, taking great care not to endanger other wildlife.

The two biggest problems of bearded iris are rhizome rot and leaf spot. Rhizome rot (or wet rot) can show at any time but is most common in spring, when it is spotted as developing flower stems fail to develop and collapse. If you suspect the presence of rot, inspect the rhizome and cut away any areas that are soft. This can mean severe cutting, but as long as there is an area with root initials on the lower surface and potential

This space-age iris 'Thornbird' is suffering from accidental weedkiller damage caused by glyphosate drifting onto iris foliage and developing flower stems.

sideshoots at the side of the rhizome there is a good chance of success. In such circumstances it may be easier to dig up the plant to clean it thoroughly. Rot is most common in wet, sunless seasons, on heavy soils or on plants that are smothered by other vegetation.

Before replanting soak the rhizomes in a fungicide solution or dust with sulphur. Good hygiene, which means regularly clearing away dead iris leaves and other vegetation, is the best way to control this problem. Avoid high-nitrogen fertilizers and use those high in potash or superphosphate to 'harden' growth in preparation for the winter.

Hard rot or scorch causes severe browning of the leaves and fan death, and is differentiated by the rhizome dying but remaining hard. It is controlled in the same way.

Leafspot does not do much harm to iris (though in severe cases it can cause temporary defoliation), but it does look unsightly. At first small brown spots appear on the leaves, then these grow larger and can join together to cause large dead areas of leaf tissue. Cut away and burn affected leaves, spray with a fungicide and use high-potash fertilizers. Large native stands of *I. foetidissima* can be a pool of infection so should also be sprayed regularly to prevent disease.

Reticulata iris suffer from ink spot disease which causes black lesions on the surface of the bulbs and kills them. Soaking the bulbs in a fungicide before planting can eliminate the problem. Affected bulbs should be destroyed and never planted with existing stocks.

Virus diseases are serious and show themselves as leaf and flower mottling, stunted growth and distorted petals. Once infected a plant cannot be cleared of the problem and must be dug up and destroyed. Aphids and other sap sucking insects (and the gardener's knife) all spread viruses, and plants that are resistant and show no symptoms act as undiscovered reservoirs of infection in the garden. Fortunately most viruses are not seed-borne, which means that if seed can be produced and germinated to produce new plants these can be grown to replace the ailing parents. Cultivars will not breed true and cannot be freed of virus in this way, which is one of the reasons why cultivars do not last in cultivation as long as the toughest species. However, this is not to say that modern cultivars are not tough plants. In Utah, the US Forest Service has been planting unwanted bearded iris on bare soil to stabilize banks at altitudes of 1500–3000m (5000–10,000ft). They have to survive soil erosion, foraging deer and feet of snow, but they have performed well – although there is a conservation question about the ecological ethics of introducing such plants to the wild.

PROPAGATION

Apart from division, which is described on page 93, the other main way to propagate iris is by seed. Almost all species can be treated in the same way, though those iris that require careful watering will need a gritty compost and specific growing conditions almost as soon as they have germinated. Except for species that are not frost hardy, which can be sown and placed in a heated propagator, seed should be sown in autumn so that it can be stratified (subjected to frost which will break any dormancy that may be built into the seed). Sow the seed in pots or trays of loam-based compost (John Innes No 1 is ideal, with the addition of grit where necessary or moss peat if lime-hating species are being sown). Cover the

seed with 5–15mm ($^1/_8$–$^1/_2$in) of sharp grit, which discourages moss and liverwort growth, water the pot and place it in a cold frame, where the compost can be kept moist and the worst of winter cold can be avoided. In spring the seedlings, often looking like grass, should appear. Bearded iris seedlings can be lined out into the open ground soon after they appear to encourage fast growth, others may be potted singly into the appropriate compost and bulbous species should remain in the pot, unless very crowded, until they die down in the autumn and can be spaced out evenly. Flowering will take from two to five years depending on how well they are grown and the species concerned.

Where bearded iris are required in large numbers, the older parts of the rhizomes, usually discarded once the young vigorous shoots have been removed, can be used to make new plants. Cut the old rhizome into sections, either across the rhizome or along its length, soak it in fungicide because of the extensive cut surface, and plant as usual in the soil. Because the green growing points have been removed, a vigorous cultivar will respond by sending out tiny sideshoots. These should be removed later in the season or the following year and grown on.

LABELLING YOUR COLLECTION

Labelling is important with all garden plants but especially so with a collection of iris where, out of flower, they can look bewilderingly alike. When moving them it is easy to write the names on the leaves of bearded iris with a felt tip pen, but these are cut away when replanting. Some garden markers are permanent on white plastic but I have not found anything easier or cheaper than pencil on white stick labels. Copper and zinc labels are possibly better and do not snap, but are expensive. Other gardeners write on paper and place this in a plastic film container that is buried under the rhizome like a time capsule. However, although it is a chore at the time, there is nothing better than making a plan of the beds and keeping this on record. Labels are pulled out by birds and scrabbled out by cats whereas a plan is an (almost) foolproof way of keeping track of your plants, and can be accompanied by notes of how the plants fare each season. Recording is especially important for bulbous iris, which retire underground for long periods and are easily dug up or speared with a trowel when adding new plants to the garden.

13
HYBRIDIZING

A species is a group of plants that, given the opportunity, will reproduce itself without significant variation – in other words, it breeds true. However, many plant species produce occasional white-flowered forms, due to lack of pigment, and such albinos occur throughout the plant and animal kingdoms. In some species variations in flower shape, colour and even plant habit occur, and it is the job of botanists to decide the parameters of a species. However, it is not in the interest of a species to produce genetically identical offspring, and the wider the genepool the more variation there is within a species' DNA, and the greater the capacity for adaptation in case climate, pollinators or other factors change.

The style arm, with the two upright crests, has a stigmatic flap that receives the pollen and protects the stamen, above the fluffy beard on the fall.

To ensure this genetic diversity, many flowers are adapted to prevent self-pollination. The bearded iris is a good example, with flowers that are structurally adapted so as to encourage cross-pollination. As a bee enters the flower it pushes open the stigmatic lip, which receives pollen from the insect's back. As the bee leaves the flower, with fresh pollen on its back, self-pollination is prevented because the stigmatic flap is pushed shut. The downfall of this system is that the iris flower has three falls and three stigmatic lips and if the bee immediately moves to another fall on the same flower, self-pollination will occur.

There are other systems to prevent hybridizing with different species. The pollen may be unable to fertilize the ovules, even if they land on the stigma, because they just do not match, structurally or genetically, or the plants flower at different times. However, all these systems have evolved to work in the plants' natural habitat. If plants are brought together in an artificial environment, although they may never interbreed with other species in their natural habitat, they may make a multitude of hybrids in their new home because the mechanisms they have evolved to prevent hybridizing have not been developed to take the new plants they are growing with into account.

Hybrids have some advantages, if only in terms of vigour. They may bring together good attributes from different species (although such values are subjective). They may increase flower size, disease resistance, plant health, ease of growth and the range of colours; they may even create new flower forms. The iris flower is so varied in its natural forms that there is tremendous scope for work and 'improvement'. There are therefore good reasons for wanting to create new hybrids, but the natural species must represent the building blocks of the work. They should be regarded as an invaluable raw material that once lost, through habitat destruction, loss of pollinators or just evolutionary pressures, can never be replaced.

Plant breeding also brings immortality, for a few. Just a small number of iris live through the decades and become classics loved by generations – though with the increasing number of cultivars being produced this is becoming less likely. The famous iris of tomorrow are just as likely to be those that are resistant to weedkillers and diseases and are commercially viable as those that are beautiful.

There are too many bearded iris being produced and named, and they cannot possibly all be improvements on the plants that went before them, nor can they be truly novel combinations of characters. But the introductions go on, and while catalogues print tempting descriptions, gardeners will buy the latest iris. Creating your own plants is also fun, and though the chances are that you will not produce an iris that everyone will want, at the least you will make plants that you can call your own to fill your garden.

HOW TO HYBRIDIZE

The basic procedure for pollinating all iris is fairly similar but, because the flowers are large and they are a popular group to work with, I will describe the procedure for Tall Bearded iris. This group also have the advantage of producing flowers at a convenient height to work with.

Before starting it is worth spending a while considering your goals. These need not be set in stone, but results are always more forthcoming if you are working with a clear purpose. The breeding may produce other results along the way, or you may wish to change tack, but apart from anything else you need to have an aim in view to help decide which of the hundreds of seedlings to keep and grow on. Whether it is a specific colour, good branching, or a particular marking that you seek, write it down.

It is also important to start with the best, and that often means the latest, cultivars that exhibit the characters you like. If you are trying to breed a dark blue with red beards it stands to reason that those cultivars that most resemble your goal will give the quickest results. Of course there may be an ancient cultivar with

red beards and good branching that you may wish to add to the mix. However, do not try to achieve all your aims in just one cross or you may never find suitable parents.

Select the female flower, which will receive the pollen and produce the seeds. Early in the morning, just as the flower is opening, snap off the three falls and, if you wish to make sure that self-pollination cannot occur, remove the stamens. Once the falls are removed it is very difficult for a bee to pollinate the flower because there is no landing platform. (In some small iris it may be necessary to bag the flowers with muslin before and after pollination to prevent insects causing pollination but this is rarely the case with bearded iris.)

Then choose your male parent. Remove the anthers from a fully open flower. If they are ripe they will have split down their length to reveal two rows of pollen. This can then be brushed directly over the inner (upper) surface of the stigmatic lip of the female. One anther will pollinate all the stigmas of several flowers. In dull weather and on dewy mornings the pollen can be damaged by water, which ruptures the pollen grains, so do your hybridizing in dry weather.

Then label the crosses. Paper labels on cotton threads are easy and cheap, and if written in pencil are weather-proof. Whatever is used, it must be tied around the base of the seed pod, or around the stem immediately below the flower if there is only one. There is no point in labelling the base of the flower above the seed pod because the withered bloom may drop off, and the label with it. Some gardeners write the parents on the label, but it is even better to code the crosses and make a note of every one in a book. This way you can use smaller labels. It is always useful to have an assistant to keep notes as you are 'pollen daubing'.

Choosing parents is not necessarily easy. Some female parents do not accept the pollen of some males, and some flowers do not produce any pollen at all, the anthers being reduced to thin claw-like stalks. It is always a good idea to repeat every cross the other way round, using each plant as both male and female.

Within a few days the flower will fade and it may drop off with a yellow seed pod, which means failure, or cleanly above the pod, which may mean success. If the weather following pollination is wet, check the state of the dead flowers and ease them off if they are clinging to the pods in case they cause rot.

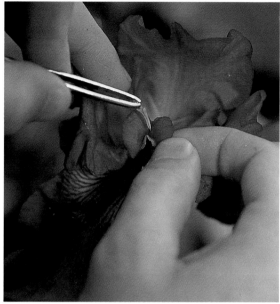

Step 1: Remove the pollen on the anther with tweezers from the male parent (not shown) and take it to the female parent that has been selected to set the pod.

Step 2: Pulling back the style crests to reveal the stigmatic flap, transfer the pollen by stroking the anther over the inner surface of the flap, where some pollen should lodge.

If fertilization is successful the pods will develop into fat green structures. As soon as they begin to split open at the end, pick them and put them somewhere dry to complete the ripening. Although they are even more unpredictable, any pods that are set by bees still offer a chance of something good. If all the plants in your collection are good cultivars, there is the chance that a bee is a better judge than you and some of the great introductions of the past have been from bee pods – for example the Siberian 'White Swirl'.

Seeds can then be kept cool and dry for sowing in autumn or early spring. The seedlings should be transplanted into nursery rows about 20cm (8in) apart and grown on until they flower. In warmer climates the growing season is longer, which means that the flowers are often produced more quickly. Although the colour of the first flowers will be representative, habit and flower form may not be, so it is worth giving 'possible' seedlings another chance to show their best next season, while scrapping those that are downright poor. Selection is difficult because there will probably be good points about most seedlings. The best can be given names and be a useful part of your garden display, but do not distribute any with names because

these will certainly be passed on and cause future confusion. If you believe that an iris of your raising has special qualities and is really worth naming it should be registered with the Iris Society in your country (*see page 134*).

SETTING GOALS

New colour combinations and more ruffling, lace, horns, spoons and flounces are the recent developments by hybridizers. There are many ways to take future breeding and fortunately there are no rules, so your tweezers can follow your own imagination. I would like to see more contrasting beards, especially red on blue, with high bud count, good branching and healthy foliage. True reds are still elusive, and fragrance could be worked on. There is also a need for controllable and reliable remontancy. Height is probably as great as it needs to be, but the space-agers could be improved and a greater selection of iris with variegated foliage would be useful in the garden. For those who like real controversy, how about having a go at doubles or even cultivars for hanging baskets! Arilbreds have great potential, although sterility with some of the wild species presents problems.

Step 3: If desired the falls may be snapped off the female parent to prevent insects contaminating the cross, and the flowers should be carefully labelled.

This pod holds the promise of fertile seed, though the label is in danger of falling off with the withered flower. Ideally, code the new crosses and make a note of each in a book.

Then there are all the other sections. The Evansias in particular hold great potential; *I. tectorum*, such a good plant already, can be crossed with *I. pallida*, in a different section of the genus. Junos could be bred with better weather resistance, greater remontancy could be bred into Siberians, and dwarfer spurias and water iris could be created.

Fashion and the aims of a single hybridizer often have a profound effect on the way a plant develops. One of the most striking cases in recent years is the breeding work on diascias by Hector Harrison. A decade ago the south African plants were considered to be rather tender alpines but now, as a result of some patient work by this hybridizer, they have become a staple of summer hanging baskets and tubs.

The space-age iris may have been far more common today if it had been considered more desirable when the characteristic traits were first discovered in 1884. Described then as 'petaloid over-extension', the flowers were already producing upright spoons and flounces, but they were considered anomalies and ignored. The same 'extras' appeared on flowers raised by Cayeux in France in the 1920s but it was not until 50 years later, in America, when the time was right and enough people

were prepared to accept the changes, that the space-age iris really took off.

Modern hybridizers have the advantages of genetics to help them. By studying the chromosome count of different species and hybrids it is possible to ascertain, even before a cross is made, whether it is likely to be successful. And, even if it is not, in vitro cultivation methods, where an embryo can be cut out of a seed that could not sustain its development and grown in sterile conditions on a nutrient jelly, can allow unforeseen crosses to be accomplished. But knowledge can work against us. If the early hybridizers had known that it was almost impossible to cross their tetraploids and Oncocyclus iris they may never have bothered. As it was they persevered and, by strokes of luck and genius, nature created plants that we know now should never have been possible. That is the power that enthusiastic amateurs hold today.

The sky really is the limit, and there is no way to predict what the next century will produce. W. R. Dykes and Sir Michael Foster could never have guessed at what has happened to their favourite flower, and we all have the chance to take part in the next great period in the iris' celebrated history.

14
PEOPLE & THEIR PLANTS

Like most gardeners, iris growers are friendly, enthusiastic and generous, with their advice as well as with plants. However they began to grow iris, the result is usually the same – a deep loyalty to their favourite flower that often brings criticism from friends who are better disciplined at choosing their garden plants for effect rather than affection. In some cases their iris growing and collecting is purely for satisfaction and the love of beautiful plants; in others the hobby turns to an obsession that results in them rushing to buy the latest releases or hybridizing their own plants, or even devoting their gardens to iris and creating a National Collection.

For the acquisitive there are many different ways to collect plants: by plant groups such as all Pacific Coast hybrids and species or all Miniature Dwarf Bearded iris; by colour, for example all white iris for a white garden; by colour pattern, especially if you prefer bearded iris where there are distinct colour categories such as plicatas and variegatas; or by breeder – many growers are fans of a particular hybridizer, especially in the USA. This may be a breeder producing new cultivars that accord with the taste of the grower, or the collection may be historical, rare, often ignored hybrids, perhaps the work of someone long since dead such as Dykes, Bliss or Caparne.

MARGARET CRIDDLE

Margaret Criddle, who gardens in Lincolnshire, on the east coast of England, still treasures the iris that her mother grew, though others may not share her enthusiasm for such historic plants. Margaret has five plants from her mother's collection, and though they were unnamed, she has traced four of them through the British Iris Society – just a yellow remains to be identified. 'Whitehall' (white with some violet shading) and 'Marshall Ney' (rich brown) are both described as beautiful, and the first, which sets regular seed, has been sent to America where a keen hybridizer friend is using it in his breeding programme because he believes that backcrosses will reveal valuable characteristics in its long-forgotten genes. *I. pallida* is another of her mother's plants and the fourth is 'Dominion', a world-class iris in its time that led to a whole race of hybrids. This may have been partly due to its proclivity for setting seed and Margaret finds that bee pods hold viable seed that germinates around the plant to produce fine seedlings. Unlike the huge flowers of modern cultivars, the older ones can be pollinated by bees and this ability to produce seed that may germinate among the rhizomes of the parent plant only exacerbates the confusion in naming historic or 'heirloom' iris.

While iris gardens in the past were designed with formal beds filled with masses of iris to create a spectacular display, the modern enthusiast's garden is smaller, with more cultivars but in smaller groups. Though the different sections of the genus all prefer different conditions, that does not stop the dedicated grower from packing their plants in. Margaret grows mostly Intermediate and Tall Bearded iris on her heavy clay soil, and struggles to find remontants that will cope with her often too shady garden. Siberian iris and Pacific Coast Iris came later but she now saves seed and grows her own seedlings, which is just as easy as buying plants and gives her the excitement of seeing the first flowers. By growing a wide range of species and hybrids, and a mass of *I. unguicularis* where the sun does reach, she is rewarded with a long season of her favourite flowers.

JACK GRINT

Jack Grint first made contact with Tall Bearded iris in 1963, and has grown them ever since. He does not understand the sneering comments made by some about these flamboyant giants of the iris world and does not condemn them just because they are man-made. Even so, he concedes that in winter they are not the best of garden plants, but the memory of what will come in early and midsummer reassures him that they deserve space in his Buckinghamshire garden. His interest has led him to grow Siberian and Pacific Coast Iris also, but getting the latter sent from America and established is a perennial problem as they will not tolerate any drying of the roots – hard to solve when the soil has to be washed off for shipping. Jack's soil is light, and he is convinced that it is the reason why his Tall Beardeds do not always thrive as he would like, flowering well the first year but then deteriorating in the second. He adds mushroom compost to the soil to retain moisture but would love to swap his soil for clay, which retains moisture and nutrients. His bearded iris are mostly American because that is where most of the latest developments are taking place, but French and Australian cultivars, the latter especially from Barry Blyth, form substantial parts of his collection. In America especially, the hundreds of cultivars raised and brought into commerce every year create a fast-moving and exciting marketplace for iris growers compared to the British nursery scene, which tends to be more conservative. Jack's favourite group are the true blues, which are surprisingly rare, and though he finds that some space-agers are attractive he thinks that their features are largely irrelevant compared to the other factors that go to make up a good iris.

BRYAN DODSWORTH

Novelty is not a priority for Bryan Dodsworth in Nottingham either. He is the British hybridizer of Tall Beardeds who has dominated the British Dykes Medal listings in the last two decades. He grows a wide range of types, partly because his garden is one of the British Iris Society's trial gardens. His love affair with iris began after he saw plants in a neighbour's garden. He began hybridizing in 1963, though his first attempts to produce good new iris were not particularly successful. He imported many cultivars from the USA, but he found that the flower shapes, blends of colours and concentration on the flowers alone did not add up to the irises that he wanted; for him, colour was not the main consideration and he sought flowers that had strong structure and petal texture that would hold their form in the often windy and wet iris flowering season in Britain. His most successful iris have been self colours as these show up best in the garden and 'Annabel Jane' is, in his opinion, probably his finest – it has received acclaim in the USA and Australia, which is no mean feat. Wide crosses (between very different parents) mean that when they are used as parents many American hybrids give an unacceptable range of progeny and it is difficult to isolate or stabilize any particular characteristic. Bryan concentrates instead on line-crossing, using a few known parents repeatedly to get closer to his particular goals. He has now produced good reds, oranges and pinks, though true reds still prove elusive.

NORAH SCOPES

Norah Scopes in Hertfordshire, who has also been successful in hybridizing, wanted to create new plants as soon as she started to grow her first iris. Her interest dates from childhood when, on a trip to France, she saw *I. albicans* and *I. kochii* growing. She then visited an iris show at the Royal Horticultural Society Halls in Westminster. In the 1950s and 1960s the shows were much larger than now, and the massed display prompted her to join the British Iris Society.

A move of house presented her with the chance to acquire a south-facing garden, but it also had compacted heavy soil that required much cultivation to get it into good order. However, it has produced a number of good hybrids including the Dykes Medal-winning creamy yellow 'Early Light', which was the result of crossing the pale 'Cup Race' onto a yellow amoena.

CY BARTLETT

Cy Bartlett is Secretary of the British Iris Society, which he joined in 1961. As is the case with many iris growers, his interest was kindled by the magnificent iris garden at the Royal Botanic Gardens Kew (alas no longer extant). Though it is something that not many gardeners would contemplate now, a dedicated iris garden filled with Tall Beardeds is a magnificent sight. His TBs were followed by others in the pogon section and then Siberians, which he considers to be better garden

'Harpswell Happiness' is one of the many iris that are trialled by the British Iris Society at the Royal Horticultural Society's garden at Wisley.

plants and ideal for those who want trouble-free, colourful iris. The Pacific Coast Iris do not suit his heavy alluvial soil but spurias thrive and are a current interest, and recent shorter imports from Australia have fuelled a breeding programme to produce compact spurias for planting at the front of the border. His efforts with Tall Beardeds have largely been with amoenas and reverse amoenas (where the falls are white and the standards are blue, pink, yellow and many other colours), but he is still searching for a good rich yellow with excellent branching and flower placement. The late Bob Nichols produced what he considers to be one of the best of all and it is under trial at Wisley and British Iris Society gardens under the name 'BNY'.

Apart from Siberians, Cy Bartlett would recommend the Intermediates for beginners because they are not as particular about receiving sunlight on their rhizomes, they flower early and can be trimmed back in time for the bedding season and they are weather resistant, with what they lack in bud count per stem being countered by the number of stems each produces.

EILEEN AND BOB WISE

Eileen and Bob Wise, who have grown iris in their present garden since the 1950s, also began their iris-growing with Tall Beardeds. However, their Berkshire garden is shaded by tall trees and is in typical rhododendron-growing country – the soil is acid and well-drained, and not ideal for this group. After 20 years of breeding and showing TBs Bob bought some Pacific Coast Iris, read that bee-set pods give good seedlings and decided to cultivate these instead.

When he began breeding these iris, which flourish in the Wises' garden conditions, he used the British 'Banbury Welcome' and 'No Name' and the American 'San Lorenzo', with lovely flowers but flopping stems. Fifteen of Bob's seedlings were submitted for trial and many have been given awards and entered cultivation. His favourite is 'Pinewood Dazzler', a yellow with deeper stippling (or sanding).

Bob and Eileen grow an immense variety of other iris, but the Pacific Coast Iris remain favourites. However, they do not recommend them as beginner's plants because they are temperamental about being moved. The iris that they think has given them the most pleasure over the years is *I. unguicularis*, which thrives where few other plants will even grow, and flowers from mid-autumn to early spring.

15
IRIS RELATIVES

The iris family contains about 100 genera and is represented in most countries of the world. Although the genus *Iris* is confined to the northern hemisphere, the majority of genera are found south of the equator. Almost all are either herbaceous or form bulbs or corms, but at least one, *Klattia*, from Cape Province in South Africa, is shrubby and bears little superficial resemblance to the rest of the family, with its narrow, tubular flowers on branching woody stems. Unfortunately many of the most beautiful *Iridaceae* are not frost-hardy, and are unknown outside their native habitats, but many would make interesting plants for a cool greenhouse and would benefit from the hand of the restrained hybridizer. Less rare plants in the family include ixias, gladioli, crocus and freesias. A few of the genera with 'iris-like' flowers are described here in order of familiarity.

TIGRIDIA

Some of the most interesting *Iridaceae* are those that have flowers in which the inner petals and outer petals have dissimilar shapes, like iris. Of these, the best known are the South American *Tigridia*, represented in cultivation mainly by *T. pavonia*, the shell or tiger flower (though the flowers are spotted rather than striped, a distinction that many botanists do not seem to have appreciated) from Mexico and Guatemala, and cultivated forms. The flowers of this popular plant last just a day, but usually a succession are produced on each stem. The flowers are bold and beautiful in the case of *T. pavonia*, showing clear, pure colours, with three large outer petals and three smaller inner ones that are curled and spotted in the base of the bowl-like centre of the flower. Although the bulbs are tender they sometimes survive British winters if planted in well-drained soils. Otherwise they should be lifted and stored, dry, in a frost-free place until they are planted in spring. Seed is set readily and is easy to grow, and seedlings often flower in just their second year. The natural species is pretty enough, with flowers up to 15cm (6in) across, but the selected forms have wider, more rounded outer petals and are available in shades of white, yellow and orange, and red. Other species, such as *T. durangensis*, have flowers in mauve or purple shades, and the curious *T. galanthoides* has small nodding flowers in white veined with brown. These are rarely seen in cultivation.

FERRARIA

Another flower of sombre colouring, though shorter in habit, is *Ferraria crispa*. The *Ferraria* genus is based in South Africa and the flowers have three large outer petals and three smaller inner ones (often marked with a central blotch), though the disparity of size is not so great as in *Tigridia*. *F. crispa* is one of those plants that is often described as more curious than beautiful because the flowers are brown, spotted and flecked with cream, but the patterning is exquisite and the petal edges are intensely curled and ruffled, hence the name. Unfortunately the same cannot be said for the smell, which might be described as unpleasant. This a rewarding bulb for the cool greenhouse, although, as in the case of many of these tender bulbous *Iridaceae* that require good sunlight and a dry atmosphere, the leaves are prone to red spider mite attacks.

CYPELLA

Cypella, from Mexico and Argentina, have a more easily appreciated charm, looking like small *Tigridia*,

Even in its wild form, *Tigridia pavonia* is a showy and exotic flower. The bulbs most often sold are selected forms with more rounded petals in brighter colours and they always attract attention when planted in a block.

except that the outer segments have a slight twist to give a propeller-like appearance – something that would be shunned in an iris hybrid. The petals open flat and the flowers face upwards. The commonest is *C. herbertii*, and each wire-thin stem, 30cm (1ft) high, is branched and bears many small flowers of egg-yolk yellow. It is easy to grow in a pot and flowers in its second year from seed.

Other genera that have similar-shaped flowers include *Cardenanthus* from South America, *Alophia* from Central and South America, *Anomalostylus* from South America, *Ennealophus* from Central America and *Mastigostyla* from the Andes.

NEOMARICA

Neomarica are a fascinating group of largely evergreen herbaceous plants from South America that can be grown in a greenhouse or conservatory that can maintain an absolute minimum winter temperature of 10°C (50°F) but preferably a few degrees higher. The leafy plants produce stems of flowers that sometimes develop plantlets that root in the manner of *Chlorophytum* (spider plants). The flowers are usually short-lived, are often fragrant, and look very like *Tigridia* but in the case of *N. caerulea* are a beautiful purple-blue, a colour not found in that genus. *N. northiana* has white outer petals and blue-and-white striped inner petals attached to a brown-and-white striped bowl. It is a 'leap-frogging' species that spreads by new plants at its stem tips.

MORAEA

Moraea rival iris in the complexity of their flowers, and are truly the African equivalent because the flowers even have upright or very distinct standards and style arms that are a significant feature of the flower. There are two distinct flower shapes. The first has three large outer petals that are often beautifully zoned at the base with contrasting and iridescent colours. The standards are very reduced and the flower has the appearance of being constructed of three petals, with quite small style arms in the centre of the flower. The other flower shape is almost exactly the same as the iris, but the petals are not joined together at the base to form a perianth tube as is found in all true iris. The leaves are pleated, again a character that is not found in iris. All are found naturally in Africa south of the Sahara, but the most beautiful and large-flowered are found in the western Cape.

Although most require cultivation under glass in temperate zones and are rarely available, at least one can be grown outside with some success. *M. huttonii* is a tall species, reaching at least 1m (3ft) in flower with narrow, long, floppy leaves. The flowers, though not large for the size of plant, are bright yellow and look rather like *Iris pseudacorus*. A number of flowers are produced from each branching stem and each has a bright golden blotch on the fall. In eastern South Africa it often grows alongside or even in streams, which might explain its tolerance of cooler conditions.

Other moraeas have even more exciting flowers: those of *M. unguiculata* have pendent falls and upright trident standards; *M. polystachya* is a tough and hardy plant in the wild, producing bright blue flowers with spreading standards and yellow-blotched falls; *M. gawleri* has reddish, yellow-blotched flowers; and *M. tortilis* is a tiny plant with flowers shaped like *Iris tectorum* but thread-like leaves curled into corkscrews.

PARDANTHOPSIS

One of the closest relatives of iris, which in fact was classified as an iris until 1972, is *Pardanthopsis*. The distinguishing characters are the lack of perianth tube, the regular forking of the flowering stem and the fact that like *Belamcanda (see below)* the flowers drop off with the ovary if not fertilized. There is just one species, *P. dichotoma*, from China, Manchuria, south-east Siberia and Japan. The flowers closely resemble iris, with small spreading standards and falls striped on the upper half. The flower colour varies from mauve to purple, and though the flowers are nicely marked, they are just 4cm (1¹/₄in) across on stems that may reach 1m (3¹/₄ft) in height. The flowers are short-lived, lasting less than a day. It will grow outside in temperate zones and can be raised from seed but is not a showy or long-lived plant.

BELAMCANDA

This genus is native to China, Japan and northern India. The plants look like iris, with fans of quite wide leaves. Given a moist, humus-rich soil they will grow outdoors in temperate zones and should survive most winters, but they are not long-lived plants. There is just one species, *B. chinensis*, which usually grows to 60cm (2ft) when in flower. The inner and outer petals are very similar except that the inner ones are slightly smaller, and the flowers open flat, facing upwards. The petals are orange, spotted with red at the base, and are attractive but not showy. This plant is called blackberry lily because the seed pods open to reveal shiny black seeds. It is easily raised from seed and should flower in its second year if not the first. It hybridizes with *Pardanthopsis*, and Samuel Norris of Kentucky in the USA has created hybrids called × *Pardancanda norrisii*. These resemble *Pardanthopsis* but come in a wide range of colour due to the influence of the orange *Belamcanda*.

GYNANDRIRIS

One of the most interesting genera is *Gynandriris*. Like *Pardanthopsis*, the flowers, which are more iris-like, have no perianth tube, but are even shorter-lived, opening in the afternoon and wilting within just a few hours. To botanists the genus is interesting because it seems to be a link between the moraeas of South Africa and the iris of the northern hemisphere. Not only do its physical characters reflect this, but its range also crosses over that of the two genera. *G. sisyrinchium*, which is thought to have the widest distribution of any iridaceous plant, is native to an area stretching from Portugal through Europe and North Africa to Central

Asia and Pakistan. A clump with its short-stemmed bright blue flowers with yellow signal patches is a beautiful sight and, as the stems are branched and can carry many flowers, the flowering display is extended. In very well-drained soil it can be grown outside in temperate zones and flowers in late spring. *G. monophylla* was until recently considered a short, pale blue variant from coastal areas of the Mediterranean, but it has now been given specific status.

The other species are native to South Africa, where they come from winter rainfall areas. They start into growth in autumn and need to be cultivated under glass in cooler climates with the exception of *G. simulans*, which grows in the wild in summer rainfall areas and may be more suitable for outdoor cultivation.

This selection of *Iridaceae* shows just a tiny part of the variation within the family. It would be very rewarding to collect these largely tender plants, though frustrating at times because so few are in cultivation. They are mostly easy to grow from seed, which is often the only way to obtain them, but challenges usually inspire rather than deter gardeners.

Cypella herbertii is not often grown, but is an intriguing bulb for the cool greenhouse.

PLATE VII

I. 'Orville'
Siberian

I. 'Pink Haze'
Siberian

I. 'Brynmawr'
Siberian

I. 'Nottingham Lace'
Siberian

I. 'Ruffled Velvet'
Siberian

I. 'Soft Blue'
Siberian

I. 'Butter and Sugar'
Siberian

I. 'Fourfold Lavender'
Siberian

I. pseudacorus

I. 'Navy Brass'
Siberian

I. 'Reddy Maid'
Siberian

I. 'Forncett Moon'
Siberian

All plants shown at approximately ⅓ size

APPENDIX A
LIST OF CULTIVARS

This is not a definitive list, but it is representative and up-to-date. The name of the individual who raised the plant is followed by the date of registration, where applicable.

E = early in the season

M = mid-season

L = late in the season

* = remontant iris

TALL BEARDED
White and cream

'Allenette' (L) (DeForest 1969) Ruffled cream self

'Arctic Tern' (M) (Dodsworth 1984) Ruffled white with the merest hint of blue, and white beards

'Bewick Swan' (M) (Dodsworth 1980) Superb white with red beards

'Champagne Elegance'* (Niswonger 1987) A blend of white standards and pale pink falls, ruffled and laced. Sometimes the flowers have lilac tinged standards and buff falls, especially in cool weather, and on remontant stems, a good re-bloomer

'Champagne Music' (M) (Fay 1964) Lilac-white

'Christmas Angel' (L) (DeForest 1959) White

'Cliffs of Dover' (M) (Fay 1952) A classic cultivar of ruffled form

'Coral Joy' (M) (Niswonger 1989) White with a hint of pink and orange-tipped beards

'Creme D'Or' (M–L) (Blyth 1987) White marked with yellow with yellow beards

'Denys Humphrey' (M) (Bartlett 1992) Ivory cream with self beards

'Designer's Choice' (E) (Brown 1982) White with yellow centre to flower

'Edale' (M) (Dodsworth 1989) Ruffled cream with pale yellow beards

'Elizabeth Poldark' (L) (Nichol 1987) Ruffled and fluted white with yellow tints

'Frost and Flame' (M) (Hall 1956) Reliable old white with red beards

'Loveday' (M) (Nichol 1992) Ruffled white with gold in the throat

'Madeira Belle' (L) (Quadros 1967) Ruffled palest blue

'Mute Swan' (M) (Dodsworth 1985) Ruffled white with red beards

'New Snow' (E) (Fay 1946) Ruffled white with yellow beards

'Offenham' (M) (Taylor 1986) White with blue hint in the petals and beards

'Rime Frost' (M) (Zurbrigg 1976) Ruffled white with dirty hafts

'Robert J. Graves' (L) (C. & K. Smith 1957) White with pale beards

'Snowshill' (L) (Taylor 1981) White with blue hints and red beards

'Snowy Owl' (M) (Blodgett 1977) Ruffled white

'The Citadel' (M) (Graves 1951) A famous white self

'White City' (M) (Murrell 1939) Blue tinged white

Yellow

'Arctic Star' (M) (Kelway 1959) Lemon yellow with deeper mark on the falls

'Baroque Prelude'* (Zurbrigg 1973) Pale yellow standards and deeper falls, of full, ruffled shape. Quite a reliable remontant iris

'Buttercup Bower' (M) (Tompkins 1960) Lemon-yellow slightly ruffled flower with white flare on falls

'Colonial Gold' (L) (Brown 1973) Ruffled dark yellow with deeper beards

'**Colwall**' (M) (Taylor 1983) Primrose-yellow standards and white falls with yellow beards

'**Dame Judy**' (Kelway 1958) (M) Large clear yellow

'**Demelza**' (E) (Nichol 1984) Ruffled cream with yellow markings and tints

'**Early Light**' (L) (Scopes 1983) Lemon-cream standards and darker falls

'**Eirian**' (M) (M. Foster 1991) Lemon standards and paler falls

'**Fall Primrose**'* (Brown 1953) Not a modern flower, but renowned for its late summer bloom

'**Godfrey Owen**' (E) (Owen 1986) Yellow, fading with age, yellow-edged, white falls

'**Golden Alps**' (M) (Brummit 1952) Pale standards, deeper falls and blue beards

'**Golden Encore**'* (Jones 1972) Bright yellow with pale flare on the falls below the yellow beards, but with an old-fashioned flower shape – the sort of flower that gave remontant iris a bad name because it is about 30 years behind the times in flower shape, but it is a reliable remontant

'**Golden Planet**' (M) (Kelway 1968) Slightly ruffled yellow with orange beards

'**Gold Galore**' (M) (Schreiner 1978) Bright ruffled yellow

'**Green Ice**' (M) (Kelway 1960) Strange greenish yellow

'**Halo in Yellow**' (M) (Niswonger 1989) Yellow standards above white falls edged with yellow

'**Jitterbug**' (E) (Keppel 1987) Bright yellow overlaid with deeper shades

'**Lemon Brocade**' (L) (Rudolph 1973) Bright yellow with lace edging

'**Lemon Drop**' (M) (Kelway) White flares on the lemon-yellow falls

'**Lemon Mist**' (M) (Rudolph 1971) Ruffled pale yellow, white falls edged lemon

'**Lemon Tree**' (E) (Jones 1965) Pale yellow self

'**Nampara**' (M) (Nichol 1984) Interesting flower with pale yellow standards and falls of cream edged lemon, with brown hafts and a purple flash below the beard

'**Ola Kala**' (M) (Sass 1941) Small bright flowers of good form on well-branched stems

'**Pale Primrose**' (M) (Whiting 1946) Primrose self

'**Pinnacle**' (M) (Stevens 1948) A popular old cultivar with white standards with pale yellow falls

'**Soaring Kite**' (L) (Nelson 1957) Pale primrose with deeper beard

'**Temple Gold**' (M) (Luihn 1976) Large ruffled flowers of bright rich yellow

Orange

'**Arab Chief**' (M) (Whiting 1944) Deep orange with ruffled petals

'**Cable Car**' (M) (Luihn 1981) Orange and bronze with paler flare on the falls

'**Feminine Charm**' (E) (Kegerise 1973) Ruffled apricot with pink and yellow toning

'**Gala Gown**' (M) (Corey 1958) Pale ruffled orange

'**Halloween Pumpkin**' (M) (Byers 1986) Light orange with horns

'**Mission Sunset**' (M) (Reckamp 1962) Apricot with red beards

'**Nectar**' (M) (Kelway) Apricot with red beards

'**Olympic Challenge**' (E) (Schreiner 1985) Slightly ruffled flowers of rich orange with white flares on the falls

'**Olympic Torch**' (M) (Schreiner 1956) Ruffled deep orange with deeper beards

'**Orange Dawn**' (L) (Howe by Linnegar 1981) Clouded orange standards and brighter falls

'**Smart Girl**' (M) (Kelway) Apricot with red beards

'**Tangerine Sky**' (M) (Schreiner 1976) Bright modern orange

'**Tangerine Sunrise**' (M) (Dodsworth 1979) Spectacular orange and apricot flower

Pink

'**Albatross**' (M) (Burt 1937) Large, very pale pink flowers

'**Anastasia**' (M) (Whiting 1977) Deep apricot pink with tangerine beards

'**Beverley Sills**' (M) (Hager 1978) An almost perfect iris with pale pink, ruffled and laced flowers, and scent

'**Blue Chip Pink**' (M) (Niswonger 1989) Pink with lilac tint with orange and blue beards

'**Bryngwyn**' (L) (M. Foster 1990) Pink with magenta falls and red beards

'**Cannington Sweet Puff**' (L) (Bartlett 1990) Pale pink with pale magenta falls and red beards

'**Carnaby**' (L) (Schreiner 1973) Ruffled pink shades with orange beards

'Autumn Leaves' is frilled, ruffled and richly coloured like its namesake.

'Charming' (M) (Kelway) Light pink with tangerine beards

'Elizabeth Arden' (M) (Kelway 1957) Apricot-pink standards and paler falls with tangerine beards

'Halo in Pink' (M) (Niswonger 1989) Pink standards over white falls

'Jean Guymer'* (Zurbrigg 1976) A pretty but unexceptional apricot pink made exceptional by its freely remontant habit

'Karen Maddock' (L) (Longley 1964) Pink standards with lighter falls which have a pale flare and orange beards

'Lodore' (M) (Randell 1958) Large ruffled flowers of raspberry pink with tangerine beards

'Margharee' (L) (Blyth 1986) Deep pink falls edged with pale pink to match the standards

'Mulberry Rose' (M) (Schreiner 1942) Bright mulberry pink with orange beards

'Paradise' (L) (Gatty 1979) Peachy pink with paler falls and orange beards

'Party Dress' (L) (Muhlestein 1950) A really good and popular shell pink

'Peach Spot' (M) (Shoop 1973) White flowers veined or marked with peach

'Pink Clover' (L) (Whiting 1953) Violet pink with peach flushes

'Rose Caress' (M) (Brown 1977) Pale bright pink ruffled flowers with red beards

'Satin Gown' (L) (Gatty 1977) Ruffled pale pink

'Saxon Princess'* (Bird 1985) Peachy pink, a British-bred remontant

'Saxon Surprise'* (Bird 1985) Mauve pink, usually remonts well

'Spring Festival' (M) (Hall 1957) Ruffled pale pink with red beards

'Ursula Vahl' (M) (Tamberg 1978) Pale pink with pink beards

'Windsor Rose' (M) (Schreiner 1977) Pale pink standards over deeper falls which have red beards

Blends

'Autumn Leaves' (E) (Keppel 1972) Heavily ruffled flowers of crimson and bronze, aptly named after the leaves of autumn

'Baccarat' (L) (Gaulter 1967) Rose brown with violet mark on the falls

'Brummit's Mauve' (L) (Brummit) Strange blend of mauve, blue and brown

'Cregrina' (M–L) (M. Foster 1990) Cream, yellow and orange standards above ruffled purple and yellow falls

'Deputé Nomblot' (E) (Cayeux 1929) Lilac and copper flowers of no great beauty compared to modern cultivars but nonetheless, historically an important iris

'Jubilee Gem' (M) (Kelway 1960) Pale coffee standards and violet falls

'Oriental Glory' (M) (Salbach 1952) Buff pink with violet central flare on falls

'Pipes of Pan' (L) (Brown 1963) Mid-purple falls and paler, buff standards

'Pretender' (M) (Cook 1951) Pale yellow standards are veined with lavender and the deep purple falls are white-edged

'Sagar Cedric' (L) (Trinder 1991) Pale purple standards with white falls heavily edged in the same colour

'Sand and Sea' (M) (Bennett Jones 1973) Well-named flower of honey brown with blue falls, also rimmed with bronze

'Trevaunance Cove' (M) (Nichol 1992) Ruffled flowers of cream and lemon with lots of tan shading and dark hafts

Lavender and pale purple shades

'Annabel Jane' (L) (Dodsworth 1973) Wonderful ruffled lilac self, a superb garden plant

'Crispette' (M) (Schreiner 1954) Lightly laced flowers of mauve

'Edge of Winter' (M) (Schemer 1983) Shades of lavender that are darkest at the centre of the flowers

'Gay Parasol' (M) (Schreiner 1973) Pale lavender standards and rim to the deep violet falls

'Lamorna' (L) (Scopes 1990) Very pale lavender standards over deeper falls with even deeper edges

'Mary Frances' (M) (Gaulter 1971) Ruffled flowers of lavender blue with white flare on the falls

'Paradise Bird' (M) (Dodsworth 1980) Two shades of magenta

'Rainbow Trout' (M) (Dodsworth 1978) Clean lilac flower

'Ringo' (M) (Shoop 1979) Pleasing flower with purple falls edged with palest lilac, the colour of the standards

'Royal Ascot' (M) (Scopes 1975) Ruffled lavender self

'Susan Bliss' (E) (Bliss 1922) Pale mauve – one of the few Bliss cultivars still sold, and historically interesting

'Wabash' (M) (Williamson 1936) Rather small flowers with deep falls and pale standards but still pretty

'Warleggan' (M) (Nichol 1990) Pale blue standards and violet flared falls

'Wyevale' (M) (M. Foster 1988) Pale blue standards and lavender falls with deeper central mark and pale beards

Plicata

'Beckon' (M) (Daling 1979) Violet on white, with heaviest marking on the standards

'Blue Shimmer' (E) (Sass 1942) Blue on white, large

'Cannington Bluebird' (M) (Bartlett 1987) Blue standards and falls with white centres and violet plicata markings on the falls

'Dancer's Veil' (M) (Hutchinson 1959) One of the classic plicatas with wonderful ruffled flowers of white with violet

'Eagle's Flight' (E) (Schreiner 1985) This is ruffled and has purple standards, white falls edged purple and orange beards

'Earl of Essex' (M) (Zurbrigg 1979) Pale lilac on white, frilly and ruffled

'Firecracker' (E) (Hall 1942) Yellow with brown plicata markings

'Going My Way' (M) (Gibson 1972) Superb garden plant with purple on white plicata marking

'Golden Spice' (L) (Muhlestein 1959) Ginger on yellow plicata

'Jesse's Song' (M) (Williamson 1983) Lacy, frilly, ruffled methyl-violet on white plicata

'Kilt Lilt' (M) (Gibson 1972) Ruffled, laced with gold-brown standards, and russet-edged white falls

'Matchpoint' (L) (Scopes 1980) Copper on white plicata

'Meg's Mantle' (M) (Donnell 1982) Buff standards and falls, the latter edged with magenta

'Minnie Colquit' (M) (Sass 1942) An old but fine plicata of deep mauve on white

'Needlecraft' (M) (Zurbrigg 1976) Violet blue on white with most marking on the falls

'Provencal' (M) (Cayeaux 1978) Unusual combination of wine-red on pale yellow

'Queen in Calico' (M) (Gibson 1980) Modern shape with purple standards above heavily edged purple on white

'Sally Jane' (M) (Trinder 1991) Almost variegata colouring with yellow standards and yellow falls heavily edged with purple

'Violet Icing' (L) (Bartlett 1993) Ruffled white with violet plicata markings, especially on the standards

Pale blue

'Broseley' (M) (Taylor 1986) Pale blue with tangerine beards

'David Chapman' (L) (Bartlett 1990) White standards above pale blue falls

'Derwentwater' (L) (Randall 1953) Pale blue

'Eleanor's Pride' (L) (Watkins 1952) Powder blue self with lemon beard, a fine daughter of 'Jane Phillips'

'Fantasie' (M) (Cayeaux 1968) Pale blue standards above deeper falls of a lilac hue

'Jane Phillips' (M) (Graves 1950) Popular standard pale blue iris, a good all-rounder

'Lady Isle' (M) (Smith 1950) Pale blue with deeper veining

'Mademoiselle Yvonne Pelletier' (L) (Millet 1916) Antique iris with small, pale flowers

'Mary Frances' (M) (Gaulter 1973) Pale lavender blue
with good ruffling and branching

'Morwenna' (M) (Nichol 1984) Ruffled pale blue with
deeper midribs on the standards

'Out Yonder' (M) (Wickersham 1969) Pale blue
standards above deeper falls

'Patterdale' (M) (Randall 1955) Pale blue self

'Quiet Thought' (L) (Scopes 1980) Lavender blue
with paler falls

'Song of Norway' (M) (Luihn 1977) Famously good
ruffled pale blue with deep beards

'Sullom Voe' (M) (Dodsworth 1989) Ruffled turquoise
with white beards

'Sylvia Murray' (M) (Norton 1943) Pale blue

Dark blue

'Allegiance' (L) (Cook 1957) Classic in all senses of
the word, tall, deep colouring and yellow beards

'Amethyst Flame' (M) (Schreiner 1957) A daughter
of 'Crispette', this is well named, and a lovely colour

'Arabi Pasha' (L) (Anley 1951) A deep blue self of
clean, crisp colouring and shape

'Blue Rhythm' (M) (Whiting 1945) A hugely popular
ruffled blue with nice scent and good in every way

'Breakers' (M) (Schreiner 1986) Bubble ruffled flowers of great size in deep blue with a hint of violet and
golden beards

'Dark Bury' (M) (Luihn 1961) Flaring and ruffled dark
blue

'Deep Pacific' (L) (Burger 1975) Another classic deep
blue

'Dusky Challenger' (M) (Schreiner 1986) Flared,
ruffled, huge and satisfyingly dark

'Festival Crown' (L) (M. Foster 1992) Ruffled velvety
deep blue

'Lovely Again'* (Smith 1963) Not the best shape,
rather old fashioned, but lovely violet colour and a
good remontant

'Sapphire Hills' (M) (Schreiner 1971) Mid blue ruffled
blooms

'Titan's Glory' (E) (Schreiner 1981) Broad, ruffled
flowers of immense presence and beauty, a hard
flower to better

'Tom Tit' (M) (Sturtevant) Old with small violet
flowers

'Victoria Falls'* (M) (Schreiner 1977) Frilly blue
flowers with white flares on the falls, a real beauty

'Wharfedale' (M) (Dodsworth 1989) Ruffled deep blue
with contrasting white beards

Dark purple

'Benton Nigel' (M) (Morris 1955) Purple and violet

'Braithwaite' (M) (Randall 1952) Pale blue standards
above deeper falls, a good garden plant

'Cardew' (M) (Nichol 1990) Pale blue standards and
violet falls

'Crushed Velvet' (M) (Ghio 1976) Ruffled deep violet

'Dovedale' (M) (Dodsworth 1980) Heavily ruffled
dark flowers with a bright orange beard on each fall

'Evening Gown' (M) (Ghio by K. Keppel 1986) Two
shades of purple with blue beards

'First Violet' (L) (DeForest 1951) Ruffled violet self

'Magic Man' (L) (Blyth 1979) Light standards but deep
falls with lighter edges and orange beards

'Pasco' (L) (Nichol 1993) Pale lavender standards
above much deeper falls

'Penrhyn' (L) (M. Foster 1987) Ruffled deep violet with blue beards

'Royal Ruffles' (M) (Purviance 1962) Deep violet

Brown shades

'Action Front' (M) (Cook 1942) Copper red standards and maroon falls with orange beards

'Arctic Wine' (M) (Brown 1963) Maroon with bronze beard

'Caliente' (M) (Luihn 1967) Deep red

'Captain Gallant' (M) (Schmelzer 1957) Copper-red self

'Chief Moses' (M) (Plough 1967) Ruffled yellow and brown

'Jungle Fires' (M) (Schreiner 1960) Deep red

'Muriel Neville' (M) (Fothergill 1963) A stunning deep red with ruffled form and good petal texture

'Ninevah' (Keppel 1965) Arilbred with red and brown shades and velvety gloss

'Jane Phillips' is nearly 50 years old but is still one of the most popular blue Tall Bearded. It is valued both for its colour and vigour.

'Purgatory' (M) (Moores 1987) Deep maroon falls and coppery open standards

'Red Kite' (E) (Dodsworth 1989) Ruffled deep red flowers with bronze beards

'Red Revival'* (Preston 1975) Rusty red falls and lighter standards of old flower shape but remonts well

'Red Rufus' (M) (Taylor 1979) Deep red

'Right Royal' (L) (Wills 1950) Pale red

'Ruby Mine' (L) (Schreiner 1961) Dark, purple red with open standards, modern form

'Solid Mahogany' (E) (Sass 1943) Dark red with contrasting yellow beard

'Tall Chief' (M) (DeForest 1955) Deep brown flowers

'Tintinara' (M) (Donnell 1988) Pretty brown with bluish hint at the hafts

'Tuscan' (M) (Kelway) Copper brown with gold beard

Variegata pattern

'Crispen Rouge' (M) (Kelway) Golden yellow standards and falls with a large maroon zone on the falls

'Doctor Behenna (L) (Nichol 1991) Deep gold and brown

'High Command' (M) (Long 1945) Rather dull but pleasant combination of bronze standards and brownish falls

'Rabelais' (M) (Cayeaux 1950) Yellow and plum red with yellow beards

'Rajah' (M) (Smith 1942) Reliable and floriferous old variegata with bright colouring

'Smokey Dream' (M) (Kelway 1965) Cream yellow standards and russet brown falls

'Staten Island' (M) (Smith 1947) Old-fashioned flowers with droopy falls and stripy hafts, but bright colouring and a good grower, hence commonly available

Black

'Black Flag' (E–M) (Stahly 1983) Two tones of deep violet

'Black Swan' (M) (Fay 1960) A popular and memorable name for a popular flower, now superseded by bigger flowers but still worthy of a place in the garden where a black iris is desired

'Dark Rosaleen' (L) (Scopes 1976) Purple black with yellow style arms

'Deep Black' (L) (Cook 1953) Not as dark as 'Black Swan', with lighter standards

'Forest Hills' (M) (Kelway 1956) Very deep blue with long droopy falls to give an old-fashioned flower shape

'Sable' (E) (Cook 1936) Dark purple, older, less full flower shape

'Superstition' (M) (Schreiner 1977) Not the darkest, but beautifully ruffled and elegant, one of the best

'Wild Echo' (M) (Kelway) Dark, blue-black with yellow beards

INTERMEDIATE BEARDED
White

'Avanelle' (Jones 1976) Ruffled white with yellow beards

'Cheers' (Hager 1974) Vigorous white with red beards

'Cutie' (Schreiner 1962) White with pale blue thumb-print on the falls

'Doxa' (Sass 1929) Cream, veined with pale green and brown

'Early Frost' (Gatty 1976) Pretty pure white

'Happy Mood' (Brown 1967) White with blue markings

'Langport Hope' (Kelway) Pale bluish white

'Langport Star' (Kelway) White with yellow beards

'Little Snow Lemon' (Gaddie 1984) White with yellow spot on the falls

'Tidle de Winks' (Stern 1957) Absolutely pure white

'Whiteladies' (Taylor 1975) Pure white

Yellow

'Brighteyes' (Darby 1957) Pale yellow with brown marks on the falls

'Curlew' (Taylor 1967) Pretty bright yellow with white flare on the falls

'Dresden Candleglow' (Reath 1964) Clean lemon yellow flower with white flare on the falls

'Fantasy World' (Brown 1975) Apricot yellow with orange beards

'Golden Muffin' (Niswonger 1986) Yellow with deeper falls with paler edge

'Hagar's Helmet' (Nichols 1976) Yellow with orange beards – a space-ager that can sport horns

'Harlow Gold' (Black 1982) Golden yellow with paler flare

'Honey Glazed'* (Niswonger 1982) Yellow and amber that has the potential to remont

'Indeed' (Hager 1963) Yellow standards and white falls rimmed with yellow

'Innocent Heart' (M Howe 1974) Yellow with red flush on falls

'Lady of Nepal' (Muhlestein 1959) Cream standards and yellow falls

'Langport Song' (Kelway) Ruffled lemon yellow

'Langport Sun' (Kelway) Bright yellow

'Langport Sunbeam' (Kelway) Gold standards and deeper falls with bronze patch

'Lemon Flurry' (Muhlestein 1965) Greenish yellow ruffled flowers

'Listowel' (Zurbrigg 1957) Golden yellow

'Lookin' Good' (Hager 1979) Light yellow with deeper beards

'Maui Moonlight' (Aitken 1987) Bright lemon flowers with self beards

'Midas Kiss' (Roberts 1973) Yellow and white veined with yellow

'Pony' (Hager 1977) Tall golden yellow

'Sherbert Lemon' (Bartlett 1991) Ruffled lemon yellow with good scent

'Sing Again' (Plough 1966) Pale yellow standards and deeper falls

'Sugar' (Warburton 1961) Creamy yellow with yellow flare on falls

'Wenlock' (Taylor 1979) Deep yellow with white flash on the falls

'Why Not' (Hager 1979) Bright apricot with showy orange beards

Pink shades

'Art Gallery' (B. Jones 1984) Cream standards and falls with apricot zone on the falls

'Ask Alma' (Lankow 1986) Coral orange with white and tangerine beards

'Dancin'' (Shoop 1983) Apricot pink with paler falls and a deeper spot

'Fairy Time' (Roberts 1974) White standards and pale pink falls

'Honey Glazed' can be doubly rewarding as it often flowers again in late summer.

'Voila' (1972) is a popular American Intermediate iris coloured a deep, sometimes reddish, violet with blue beards.

'Peachy Face' (Jones 1975) Pale peach-pink with deeper marking on the falls

'Raspberry Blush' (Hamblen 1975) Aptly named raspberry pink shades

Blends and browns

'Alien' (Brown 1958) Brownish standards and lavender falls with rusty spot

'Confederate Soldier' (Nichols 1974) Lavender grey and white with orange beards

'Foxcote' (Taylor 1977) Dark brown self

'Jungle Shadows' (Sass by Graham 1959) Khaki brown with bronze tones

'Langport Curlew' (Kelway) Lavender standards and coffee and red falls

'Langport Haze' (Kelway) Caramel standards and lavender falls

'Langport Tartan' (Kelway) Smoky bronze shades

'Langport Wren' (Kelway) Purple brown with black veins

'Oriental Baby' (Guelthier 1963) Copper standards and reddish falls

'Pogo Doll' (Christlieb 1967) Arilbred with dull lavender standards and gold falls, amber beards and blue signal markings

'Prophetic Message' (Nichols 1978) An arilbred with violet standards and brownish falls

'Shampoo' (Messick 1975) Strange bronze/yellow/green/grey

Pale blue

'Az Ap' (Ensminger 1980) Silvery blue with deeper beards

'Blue Asterisk' (Greenlee 1955) Light blue with deeper blue splash on the falls

'Bluebird in Flight' (Niswonger 1986) A patriotic combination of white standards, blue falls and red beards

'Dew Point' (Plough 1970) Pale blue with deeper markings and blue and yellow beards

'Eardisland' (Taylor 1985) Ruffled blue with white beards

'Miss Carla' (Taylor 1985) The palest blue over white

with blue beards

'Short Distance' (Gatty 1970) Clean blue flower with white beards

'Silent Strings' (Dyer 1978) Modern, open flowers of pure blue

'Wisteria Sachet' (Palmer 1972) Lavender blue

Dark blue and violet

'Arabi Treasure' (Burnett 1962) Intense violet blue with large beards

'Bedtime Story' (Ritchie 1982) Violet with lighter standards

'Charm Song' (Brown 1968) Lovely ruffled flaring violet

'Indigo Flight' (Naylor 1988) Dark blue self

'Jay Kenneth' (Goett 1963) Purple violet with blue beards

'Marty' (Jones 1977) Lavender with bright orange beards

'Spring Wine' (Peck 1976) Deep maroon red

'Svelte' (Hager 1970) Deep blue self

'Temple Meads' (Bartlett 1992) Deep purple falls with lighter standards

'Treasure' (Sturtevant 1922) Violet purple

'Voila' (Gatty 1972) Deep reddish violet with blue beards

Plicata

'Arctic Fancy' (Brown 1964) An excellent violet on white

'Bold Print' (Gatty 1981) White and purple plicata

'Cheers' (Hager 1975) White with violet markings on the falls

'Doll Type' (Hager 1963) Delicate violet on white plicata

'Early Edition'* (Keppel 1968) White with heavy purple markings

'Light Laughter' (Scopes 1984) Copper on primrose plicata

'Nice 'n' Nifty' (Ensminger 1982) Violet standards above white falls edged with violet

'Peggy Chambers' (Taylor 1976) Violet standards with violet plicata markings on the white falls

'Pot Luck' (Hager 1976) Deep mulberry plicata

'Rare Edition' (Gatty 1980) Very superior, wide flowers of mulberry purple on intense white petals

'Raspberry Acres' (Greenlee 1968) Maroon on white

'Sandy Capers' (Warburton 1966) Pinkish brown standards and white falls heavily marked with the same colour

Variegata pattern

'Apache Warrior' (Brown 1971) Golden brown with reddish brown on the falls

'Bronzaire' (Bartlett 1991) Honey-coloured lightly ruffled flowers with paler standards

'Gracchus' (T.S. Ware 1884) Not the brightest flower but exquisitely lovely with pale yellow standards and white falls heavily veined with maroon

'Honorabile' (Lemon 1840) Yellow standards and brown falls on this ancient iris

'Oklahoma Bandit' (Nichols 1979) Ruffled flowers of rich gold and maroon

'Sunny Dawn' (Jones 1988) Bright yellow with orange-splashed falls and red beards

BORDER BEARDED
White

'Audacious' (Hager 1981) White with red beards

'Just Jennifer' (Taylor 1983) Strong-growing white with yellow beard

Yellow

'Curlew' (Taylor 1967) A neat bright yellow with white flare on the falls, a superb plant

'Gold Intensity' (Austin 1954) Yellow with orange beards

'Honey Glazed' (Niswonger 1982) Yellow falls and cream standards

'Marmalade Skies' (Niswonger 1978) Ruffled apricot with orange beards

'Meadow Court' (Neel 1965) Ruffled yellow with maroon spot on falls

'Moonlight'* (Dykes 1923) Clear yellow and can flower in autumn

Pink

'Apricot Skies' (Brook 1996) apricot pinks with orange beards

'Happy Song' (Hamblen 1977) Pink standards and beards and white falls

'Marmalade Skies' (Niswonger 1978) Apricot orange flowers

'Peaches 'n' Topping'* (Niswonger 1980) White

standards and peach falls. Has the potential to
rebloom

'Peach Petals' (Niswonger 1986) White standards and
pink falls with orange beards – the colour of peach
flowers, not fruit

'Pink Lamb' (Blaycock 1984) Pretty ruffled pink with
red beards

'Saucy Peach' (Muhlestein 1959) Peach pink with
orange beards

Blends

'Brown Lasso' (Buckles 1975) Butterscotch standards
with violet falls bordered brown. This is one of the
best iris of all time, flaring falls and a good grower,
absolutely superb in every way

'Cotati' (Foster 1979) Ruffled flowers of interesting
violet shades, the falls deeper than the standards

Pale blue

'Impetuous' (Boushay 1980) Ruffled pale blue with
white beards

'Sounder' (Lankow 1979) Pale blue standards and
paler falls

'Zeeland' (Scopes 1984) Pale blue with deeper falls

Dark blue and violet

'Ouija' (Scopes 1974) Deep, pure red

'Thundercloud' (Keppel 1972) Deep purple-blue with
orange beards

'Timmie Too' (Wolff 1961) Deep violet self

Plicata

'Harlequinade' (Scopes 1972) Not quite a true
plicata but similar in shades of copper, yellow and
white

'Stepping Little' (Kuesel 1973) Dark violet on pure
white

Variegata pattern

'Cherry Falls' (Douglas 1949) Not the most modern,
but bright flowers of yellow and cherry red

'Whoop 'em Up' (Brady 1973) The most brilliant
variegata of lovely form – my favourite

MINIATURE TALL BEARDED
White and yellow

'Amethyst Sunset' (Welch 1972) Yellow standards

and amethyst falls

'Chickee' (Dunderman 1980) Yellow veined with gold

'Dancing Gold' (Brizendine 1971) Gold standards
with white falls rimmed with yellow

'Louise Hopper' (Hager 1980) Pale yellow

'Nambe' (Williamson 1946) Deep yellow, sometimes
with mauve flush on the falls

'Painted Rose' (Roberts 1964) Yellow with pink in the
centre of falls

'Spanish Coins' (Witt 1976) Bright yellow with golden
beards

'Topsy Turvy' (Welch 1963) Gold standards and white
falls with orange beards

Variegata pattern

'Bumblebee Deelite' (Norrick 1986) Super little flowers on slender stems, very aptly named

'Grandpa's Girl' (Fisher 1983) Yellow standards and
red/violet falls with a yellow edge

'Lodestar' (Hall 1925) A very bright variegata that
must have been decades ahead of its time when
introduced

'Lucky Charm' (Fisher 1986) Golden standards over
deep red falls

'Smarty Pants' (White 1949) Yellow with red-striped
falls

Pink

'Carolyn Rose' (Dunderman 1971) Pink standards and
cream falls with lilac edging

'Lively Rose' (Fisher 1985) As the name suggests

'New Idea' (Hager 1970) Deep rose pink with yellow
beards

'Puppy Love' (Hager 1980) Pink with orange beards

'Slim Jim' (Williams 1978) Soft violet and white

Light blue

'Hazy Skies' (Williams 1978) Pale greyish blue

'Joette' (Williams 1977) Lavender blue with yellow
beards

Deep blue, purple and violet

'Chian Wine' (Guild 1976) Purple with orange beard

'Little Paul' (Fisher 1983) Violet self with orange beard

'Shrinking Violet' (Hager 1965) Striking violet flowers
of graceful habit

'Tid-Bit' (Sturtevant 1925) Dainty light violet

'Blue Pools' has the deep thumbprint that marks many dwarf iris.

'Velvet Bouquet' (Varner 1983) Two shades of purple

Plicata
'Carolyn Rose' (Dunderman 1970) Pink on white plicata
'Desert Quail' (Roberts 1958) Yellow on white plicata
'Doll Ribbons' (Dunderman 1978) White marked with violet
'Dotted Doll' (Fry 1987) Lavender standards, white falls and lavender edging
'Lady Belle' (Varner 1986) Purple on white plicata
'White Canary' (Roberts 1972) Pale blue plicata
'Widget' (Williamson 1943) Blue and white plicata

Browns and blends
'Black Lady'* (Rawdon 1979) A creepy space-age combination of orange and brown standards, black falls, yellow beards and green horns, and it can remont in exceptional conditions
'Disco Jewel' (Guild 1978) Reddish brown with lilac markings

DWARF BEARDED
(MDB= Miniature Dwarf Bearded)
White
'Angel's Kiss' (Willott 1975) White with yellow hafts and white beards
'Betty Wood' (Varner 1978) Creamy white with pale violet beards
'Bibury' (Taylor 1975) Ruffled creamy white, an excellent plant for garden display
'Blue Pools' (Jones 1972) White with blue thumbprints on the falls
'Bright White' (Welch 1958) Good pure white MDB
'Carilla' (Taylor 1965) Cream with blue beards
'Cotton Blossom' (Jones 1969) The colour of cotton blossom – greenish cream
'Daisy Fresh' (Willmott 1988) White MDB with yellow markings
'Doll Dear' (Blodgett 1979) Cream with pale blue centre to the flower
'Favorite Angel' (B. Jones 1990) Ruffled creamy white self
'Frosted Angel' (Blyth 1984) White with blue beards and flush on falls

'Stockholm' has perky horizontal falls that make the most of the contrast between the primrose falls and the pale blue beard.

'**Green Halo**' (Greenlee 1955) Pale creamy green with darker marks on the falls

'**Green Spot**' (Cook 1951) A classic cultivar of white with green spots on the falls

'**Ice Chip**' (Niswonger 1986) Pure white with pale blue spot

'**Joanna Taylor**' (Taylor 1971) White MDB with deep blue, veined spot on the falls

'**Kentucky Bluegrass**' (Jones 1970) Pale creamy green with blue beards

'**Lilli-White**' (Welch 1957) A wavy-edged white with pure white beards

'**Little Pearl**' (Boswell 1984) Ivory and cream shades MDB

'**Low Snow**' (Ritchie 1984) White with pale blue marks around the beards

'**Luscious One**' (Palmer 1978) Pale yellow and cream with green thumbprint on the falls

'**Mrs Nate Rudolph**' (Briscoe 1972) Rather tall stems of grey flowers shaded with gold

'**Music Caper**' (Roberts 1974) Ruffled white flowers with pale yellow patches on the falls and white beards

'**Nylon Ruffles**' (Doriot 1961) Lovely flaring ruffled cream flowers with yellow markings on the falls and a notably fine scent

'Oliver' (Nichols 1971) Cream with orange beards surrounded with brown

'Pale Suede' (Greenlee 1971) Grey shades

'Queen's Ivory' (Naylor 1988) Cream with blue beards

'Snow Elf' (Brown 1958) Ruffled white with darker lines around beard

'Westar' (Jones 1984) White with deep blue beard

Yellow

'Angelic' (Palmer 1974) Cream standards and yellow falls

'Baby Blessed'* (Zurbrigg 1979) Vigorous yellow with pale flare and beards on falls. Can remont well in warm areas

'Baria' (Cook 1951) Fragrant pale yellow

'Bee Wings' (A. Brown 1959) Lemon MDB yellow with brown markings on the falls

'Brassie' (Warburton 1957) Bright yellow with greenish falls

'Brass Tacks' (Keppel 1977) Deep orange with violet beards

'Broad Grin' (Lankow 1986) Interesting blend of gold, pink and pale yellow

'Buttercup Charm' (A. Brown 1970) Yellow MDB with orange spot on the falls

'Dancing Eyes' (Sindt 1968) Pale yellow with brown 'eyes' on the falls

'Dash Away' (Waite 1981) White standards over yellow on large plants

'Dawn Favour' (Soper 1960) Lemon with pale blue beards

'Easy Strolling' (Boushay 1979) Bicolored yellow with blue beard

'Forest Light' (Taylor 1982) Lemon yellow and cream with dark brown patch on falls

'Frosty Crown' (Willott 1986) White over deep yellow falls

'Galleon Gold' (Schreiner 1977) Golden yellow with blue beards

'Golden Dewdrops' (Palmer 1975) Pure deep yellow

'Golden Starlet' (Plough 1971) Yellow, made more beautiful by the deeper colour in the centre of the flower, with pale blue beards

'Honington' (Taylor 1980) Creamy deep yellow with ruffling

'Inscription' (Boushay 1978) Pale yellow with purple thumbprint on the falls

'Joyful' (Gatty 1977) Yellow with orange at the centre of the flower and pale blue beards

'Kayo' (Niswonger 1979) Bright flowers on quite a tall plant in bright yellow with bright blue beards

'Laced Lemonade' (Warburton 1969) Two tones of yellow and lacy edges

'Lemon Flare' (Muhlstein 1953) Lots of large pale yellow flowers

'Magic Flute' (Beattie 1962) Golden yellow self

'Mary McIlroy' (Taylor 1984) Ruffled deep yellow with white beards

'Melon Honey' (Roberts 1972) Orange/amber with pale flare around the beards

'Mister Roberts' (Willott 1978) Large yellow flowers

'Ohio Belle' (Willott 1977) Pale yellow with deeper mark around the beards

'Path of Gold' (Hodson 1943) Reliable old yellow MDB

'Pet' (Hager 1982) Peach and orange

'Pigmy Gold' (Douglas 1953) Small yellow with long flowering season

'Saltwood' (Taylor 1971) Yellow with lighter standards and edge to falls

'Sarah Taylor' (Taylor 1968) Pretty primrose with blue beards

'Show Me Yellow' (Anderson 1990) Canary yellow with deeper beards

'Snow Troll' (Goett 1963) Pale blue and dull yellow

'Stockholm' (Warburton 1974) Yellow with violet beards

'Sun Doll' (B. Jones 1986) Bright yellow with nice scent and buds like yellow roses

'Surprise Orange' (Collins 1975) Gold MDB with deeper beards

'Sweet Kate' (Scopes 1985) Pale yellow with blue beards

'Wizard of Id' (Dyer 1980) Lovely old gold with purple flushes and beards

'Zipper' (Sindt 1979) Bright yellow MDB with blue beards

Variegata pattern

'Aztec Star' (Niswonger 1981) Pale yellow standards and falls with red colour on falls and yellow beards

'Barbushka' (Boushay 1980) Gold and maroon with blue-tipped beards

'Byword' (Boushay 1975) Pale yellow and brown

'Eyebright' (Taylor 1977) Deep yellow with maroon on falls and light patch below beards

'Fire One' (Plough 1978) Bright little flower in lemon and red

'Golden Ruby' (Niswonger 1986) Flared yellow and crimson with blue beards

'Gold 'n' Rust' (Small 1979) Bright yellow marked with brown on falls

'Gypsy Boy'* (Blodgett 1987) Gold standards over olive brown falls. It is thought to remont

'Splash of Red' (Niswonger 1986) Pale yellow with red blotch on the falls and orange beards

'Watercolor' (Roberts 1968) Yellow with chestnut brown falls rimmed with yellow

'Wow' (Brown 1969) Well-named bright flower of yellow and maroon

Pale blue

'Alpine Lake' (Willott 1981) Pale blue MDB with deeper blue spot on the falls

'April Ballet' (C. Palmer 1973) Light blue MDB with violet spot on the falls

'Austrian Sky' (Darby 1959) Pale blue with darker markings

'Blue Bumble' (Willott 1977) Light blue with deep spot on the falls

'Blue Denim' (Warburton 1958) Blue self with white beards

'Blue Hendred' (Watkins 1969) Masses of flowers

'Blue Moss' (Jones 1972) Mid blue with brownish green marking on the falls

'Boo' (Markham 1971) White standards and pale blue falls marked with violet spots and white beards

'Delicate Air' (Warburton 1961) Soft greenish blue

'Derry Down' (Scopes 1979) Soft lavender blue

'Encanto' (Brown 1974) Greeny blue with light beard

'Enchanted Blue' (Palmer 1973) Dark blue veins over pale blue

'Greenstuff' (Farrington 1986) Curious green and lavender blend with orange-tipped beard

'Irish Doll' (Brown 1962) MDB with white standards and blue falls

'Jeremy Brian' (Price 1975) Pale sparkling blue

'Joyous Isle' (Dyer 1981) Light blue standards over brassy green falls and deep blue beards

'Katy Petts' (Taylor 1978) Large, with characteristic

purple spot on falls

'Keyhaven' (Taylor 1971) Pale blue with white beards

'Myra's Child' (Green-Lee 1971) Neat pale blue

'Ornament' (Hager 1971) Pale blue with purple patch on the ruffled falls

'Puppet' (Hager 1968) Lavender blue with brown markings and beards on the falls

'Sleepy Time' (Schreiner 1987) Light blue MDB with deeper marking around the white beards

'Small Sky' (Muhlestein 1963) Light ruffled blue with yellow beard

'Small Wonder' (Douglas 1953) Pure soft blue with pale beard

'Starry Eyed' (Gatty 1974) White standards and deep blue falls with white rim

'Thousand Lakes' (Brook 1996) Pale blue standards with falls marked with creamy green and with blue beards

'Tinkerbell' (Douglas 1954) Blue with deeper centre in the flower

'Tirra Lirra' (Scopes 1985) Quite tall ruffled blue

Dark blue and violet

'Adrienne Taylor' (Taylor 1963) Mid blue with purple flush on falls

'Amaranth Gem' (Muhlestein 1962) Deep crimson with violet on falls

'Arnold Velvet' (Humphrey 1971) Deep blue with contrasting white beard

'Banbury Ruffles' (Reath 1970) Deep blue with purple spot

'Boo' (Markham 1971) Purple amoena colouring with white standards

'Brannigan' (Taylor 1966) Violet with slightly darker falls

'Bright Moment' (Hager 1982) Amoena pattern with white standards and white-edged violet falls

'Button Box' (Schreiner 1988) Rosy purple with deeper spots on the falls

'Clay's Caper' (Hager 1975) Dull purple with violet beards

'Court Magician' (Nichols 1985) Dark violet with white flash on the falls

'Darkover' (Scopes 1983) Maroon with blue beards

'Dark Spark' (Sindt 1967) Dark with light beards

'Demon' (Hager 1971) Very dark maroon with

'Little Black Belt' has remarkable colouring for any iris, but is especially lovely in a dwarf.

blue beards

'Derring-Do' (Greenlee 1962) Purple with blue beard

'Double Lament' (Taylor 1969) Violet with deep central mark on the falls

'Fuzzy' (Westfall 1971) Deep purple with large, light beards

'Grapelet'* (Aitken 1989) Purple-violet MDB

'Ingenuity' (Palmer 1982) Lavender and violet ruffled flowers with orange and white beard

'Jack O'Hearts' (Douglas 1953) Violet with lilac beards

'Jersey Lilli' (Dennis 1958) Deep blue and purple with a white beard

'Jewel Bright' (Scopes 1983) Ruffled purple and maroon

'Little Black Belt' (Niswonger 1978) Almost black flowers enhanced with pale blue beards

'Little Blackfoot' (Reinhardt 1966) Small dark flowers

'Little Shadow' (Douglas 1953) Deep violet self

'Loudmouth' (Rich 1970) An arilbred with violet flowers with a large black signal on the falls – rather special and exotic

'Merseyside' (Farrington 1982) Purple with blue beards

'Michael Paul' (Jones 1979) Ruffled flowers of deep purple

'Pixie Plum' (Hamblen 1970) Deep purple and maroon

'Queen's Pawn' (Jones 1975) Deep maroon with mauve beards

'Raspberry Jam' (Niswonger 1981) Very floriferous plum purple

'Ruby Contrast' (Brown 1970) Maroon with lovely blue beard, a striking little flower

'Ruby Locket' (Niswonger 1987) Purple with large maroon patch on the falls and blue beards

'Ruth Knowles' (Knowles by M. Tubbs 1992) Purple with blue beards

'Smell the Roses' (Byers 1988) Violet blue with deeper spot and good scent

'Tarheel Elf' (Niswonger 1982) Dark purple ruffled flowers with blue beards

'Tease' (Hager 1975) Deep red and purple ruffled flowers

'Toots'* (Williams 1977) Wine red with yellow beard, it is said to remont

'Westwell' (Taylor 1978) Deep violet with white flare on falls

Plicata

'Clap Hands' (Hager 1974) Brown on yellow plicata

'Concord Touch' (Willott 1974) White with narrow violet rim

'Dale Dennis' (Dennis 1955) Lilac plicata markings over white on the falls

'First Step' (Willott 1983) White with deep violet

'Little Dogie' (Roberts 1958) Purple on white with white beards

'Menton' (Farrington 1988) Purple on white with purple beards

'Peppermint Twist' (Schreiner 1977) White, edged with rosy purple

'Pixie Flirt' (Willmott 1989) MDB, maroon plicata on white

'Scribe' (Taylor 1975) Blue plicata

'Skip Stitch' (Rawdon 1977) Ruffled purple on white

'Tiny Freckles' (Farrington 1986) Pale lilac and cream MDB, edged with brown speckling

'Whisky' (Farrington 1986) White MDB, veined and edged with violet

Pink

'Betsey Boo' (Warburton 1975) Pink with reddish beards and greyish marks on the falls

'Gigglepot' (Blyth 1980) Buff pink with bright tangerine beards

'Oriental Blush' (Wilmott 1980) Pale buff pink with blue beards

'Peach Eyes' (Blyth 1986) Pale pink with brown thumbprint and lavender beards

'Regards' (Hager 1966) Lavender pink with deeper, maroon falls

'Vim' (Schreiner 1973) Deep mauve pink and lavender

Blends, reds and browns

'Abracadabra' (Hager 1976) Blend of brown and purple

'Centrepiece' (Jones 1961) Pale green standards and falls with purple patch on falls

'Exotic Shadow' (Rawdon 1979) Light blue standards above brown falls

'Gingerbread Man' (Jones 1968) Brown with striking purple beards

'Hocus Pocus' (Hager 1974) Brown and lavender with violet beards

'Hoodwink' (Boushay 1983) Mauve and brown with yellow beards

'Indian Pow Pow' (Brown 1971) Two shades of brown with blue beards

'Jade Mist' (Dyer 1977) Pale green shades with blue beards

'Jasper Gem' (Welch 1983) Brownish red shades MDB

'Jolly Fellow' (Brown 1972) Odd blends of green and brown with pale blue beards

'Libation' (Hager 1974) Purple-red MDB with yellow beards

'Little Chestnut' (Brizendine 1970) Neat bright brown with darker falls

'Little Dandy' (Riley 1975) Light caramel with maroon speckling on falls

'Little Rosie Wings' (Douglas 1957) Deep red with darker falls

'Prince' (Brown 1975) Honey brown with blue beards

'Taupkin' (Wood 1969) Blend of green and grey

'Tomingo' (Roberts 1966) Pure ruby red

'Welebos' (Seedon 1977) Blue, khaki and yellow – nicer than it sounds

Black

'Dark Vader' (Miller 1987) Deep violet black with blue beard

SIBERIAN IRIS
Blue and purple

'Anglesey' (H. Foster 1986) Ruffled violet blue with violet lacing

'Anne Dasch' (Varner 1977) Light purplish blue with deeper edges

'Annemarie Troeger' (Tamberg 1980) Mid blue with white patch at the top of the falls

'Beaumaris' (H. Foster 1988) White Cambridge blue with white edge to falls

'Berliner Runde' (Tamberg 1990) Mid blue with greyish cast

'Berlin Sky' (Tamberg 1993) Light blue, darkening at the centre of the flower

'**Blue Mere**' (Hutchinson 1959) Purple-blue

'**Brynmawr**' (H. Foster 1989) Deep wine purple with golden signal on falls

'**Caesar**' (Morgan 1930) Elegant older style purple-blue

'**Cambridge**' (Brummitt 1964) Classic and popular light blue with yellow fall markings

'**Dark Circle**' (McEwen 1976) Ruffled deep violet

'**Dreaming Spires**' (Brummitt 1964) Lavender standards over deep purple falls

'**Emperor**' (Barr 1916) Dark purple blue

'**Eric the Red**'* (Whitney 1947) Wine purple that can rebloom

'**Friendly Welcome**' (Varner 1977) Mid blue

'**Germantet One**' (Tamberg 1993) Dark blue

'**Glaslyn**' (H. Foster 1990) Ruffled in two shades of blue

'**Hoar Edge**' (Hewitt 1990) Deep violet with white edge to the falls

'**Isla Serle**' (H. Foster 1991) Ruffled flowers in pale violet and deep blue

'**Kingfisher**' (Dykes 1923) Mid blue

'**Lady of Quality**' (McEwen 1982) Violet and pale blue with thin white edge to the falls

'**Llangors**' (H. Foster 1989) Purple with gold and white signal on the falls

'**Llyn Brianne**' (H. Foster 1989) Mid blue with deeper violet markings on the falls and gold signal

'**Oban**' (M. Foster 1989) Royal blue with silver edges

'**Navy Brass**' (McEwen 1973) Classy flowers of navy blue with golden marks on the falls

'**Orville Fay**' (McEwen 1969) Blue self

'**Papillon**' (Dykes 1923) Ancient but elegant blue and white veined flowers

'**Perry's Blue**' (Perry 1912) Mid sky-blue

'**Pirate Prince**' (Varner 1977) Deep purple

'**Polly Dodge**' (McEwen 1968) Deep reddish purple

'**Pontypool**' (H. Foster 1990) Purplish blue with thin white edge to the falls and white signals on the falls

'**Purpeller**' (Tamberg 1980) Red violet-blue

'**Purple Cloak**' (Hutchinson 1963) Lighter purple-blue over deeper falls

'**Purple Mere**' (Hutchinson 1959) Deep purple-blue

'**Reddy Maid**' (McEwen 1978) Wine red with white flares on the falls

'**Ruffled Velvet**' (McEwen 1973) Deep reddish-purple

'**Ruffles Plus**' (McEwen 1982) Very ruffled deep violet

'**Savoir Faire**' (DuBoise 1974) Bright violet enhanced by yellow signal marks

'**Sea Shadows**' (Brummitt 1964) Turquoise blue

'**Shirley Pope**' (McEwen 1979) Intensely dark purple with white signal to give an almost black and white flower

'**Showdown**' (Varner 1975) Reddish purple

'**Silver Edge**' (McEwen 1973) Ruffled mid blue with silver edge to the falls

'**Soft Blue**' (McEwen 1979) Ruffled flowers of pale blue and white veins

'**Swank**' (Hager 1968) Deep blue

'**Teal Velvet**' (McEwen 1981) Very dark purple

'**Violet Mere**' (Hutchinson 1963) Violet

'**Welcome Return**'* (McEwen 1976) Ruffled violet blue with white-edged falls. Often produces a succession of flowers after the main display

White and yellow

'**Anniversary**' (Brummitt 1965) White with yellow hafts

'**Butter and Sugar**'* (McEwen 1976) White standards over yellow falls. This can also produce later flower spikes

'**Creme Chantilly**' (McEwen 1981) Pale cream that fades to white

'**Dreaming Yellow**' (McEwen 1969) White standards over ruffled cream falls

'**Forncett Moon**' (Metcalf 1993) White with yellow signal patch

'**Fourfold White**' (McEwen 1969) White with yellow at the centre of the flower

'**Golden Crimping**' (McEwen 1985) Cream with yellow edge to the falls

'**Harpswell Happiness**' (McEwen 1983) Blend of cream and yellow

'**Limeheart**' (Brummitt 1968) White with greenish hafts

'**Mikiko**' (Tamberg 1993) White

'**Rimouski**' (Preston 1937) Small creamy white flowers

'**White Queen**' Reliable old white

'**White Swirl**' (Cassebeer 1957) Famous white with flaring falls

'**Wisley White**' (RHS Gardens Wisley 1940) White with yellow markings

Mauve, lilac and pink

'Dance Ballerina Dance' (Varner 1982) Ruffled white with pink and violet markings

'Fourfold Lavender' (McEwen 1982) Ruffled lavender with pale edges to falls

'Lavender Bounty' (McEwen 1983) Lavender pink

'Mrs Rowe' (Perry 1916) Mauve blend

'Sparkling Rose' (Hager 1967) Mauve with blue flash

SPURIAS
Yellow and white

'Archie Owen' (Hager 1970) Bright yellow

'Dawn Candle' (Ferguson 1965) White, yellow and orange

'Elixir' (Hager 1963) Orange-yellow

'Golden Lady' (Combs 1957) Large pale yellow ruffled flowers

'Good Nature' (Ferguson 1958) Lemon yellow

'Imperial Sun' (McCown 1984) Pale yellow and golden

'Lydia Jane' (Walker 1964) Ruffled white with yellow

'Norton Sunlight' (Coe 1969) Gold, with blue edge to falls and standards

'Shelford Giant' (Foster 1913) Tall creamy white with yellow

'Sierra Nevada' (Walker 1973) White with yellow signal

'Sunny Day' (Sass 1931) Deep yellow

'Sunny Side' (Craig 1951) White and yellow

'White Heron' (Milliken 1948) Large white self

Purple and blue (usually with yellow flares on the falls)

'Belise' (Simonet 1964) Well-branched blue with white-veined falls

'Blue Zephyr' (Washington 1943) Late-flowering, light blue

'Farolito' (Hager 1965) Pale lavender with orange on falls

'Happy Choice' (Niswonger 1976) Pale blue standards over pale yellow, blue-edged falls

'Lord Wolsey' (Barr 1899) Deep purple and white

'Media Luz' (Hager 1967) Lavender and cream

'Missouri Gal' (Niswonger 1976) Pale blue standards above blue-edged yellow falls

'Neophyte' (Hager 1963) Deep violet and orange striking flower

'Port of Call' (Hager 1965) Deep, violet blue with pale yellow on falls

'Protégé' (Hager 1966) Medium blue with white veins on the falls

'Ruth Cabeen Nies' (Nies-Walker 1949) Blue-violet with yellow patch on the falls

'Suspense' (Hager 1966) Light purple with cream veins on the falls

'Vintage Year' (Niswonger 1979) Purple with yellow signal on the falls

'Violet Zephyr' Well-branched violet

Brown and yellow (often with violet or purple)

'Adobe Sunset' (McCown 1976) Deep orange bordered with brown

'Barbara's Kiss' (McCown 1981) Violet, yellow and brown

'Betty Cooper' (McCown 1981) Violet, brown, yellow and orange

'Connoisseur' (Hager 1965) Beige and copper with lilac style crests

'Driftwood' (Walker 1956) Chocolate brown with yellow

'Essay' (Hager 1963) Violet, brown and yellow

'Janice Chesnick' (McCown 1983) Gold with brown-ish edges

'Redwood Falls' (Ferguson 1969) Maroon standards over yellow and brown falls

'Redwood Supreme' (Niswonger 1976) Dark brown and orange

PACIFIC COAST HYBRIDS
Short = less than 30cm (1ft)
Medium = 30–45cm (1–1½ft)
Tall = more than 45cm (1½ft)

'Amethyst Crystal' (Earnshaw-Whittles 1981) Tall violet blue

'Arnold Sunrise' (Humphrey 1975) Short white and orange

'Banbury Beauty' (Brummitt 1960) Tall lavender

'Banbury Fair' (Brummitt 1969) Short white and lavender

'Banbury Melody' (Brummitt 1973) Short deep pink with cream

'Banbury Velvet' (Brummitt 1969) Short violet

'Big Money' (Ghio 1982) Short yellow

'Big Wheel' (Ghio 1981) Short raspberry pink with deep centre to the flower

'Blue Ballerina' (Knowles 1971) white standards

Spurias are useful in midsummer when the TBs are fading.

above pale blue falls marked with black veins and a purple flash

'Broadleigh Carolyn' (Broadleigh Gardens 1993) Short purple and blue

'Broadleigh Joyce' (Broadleigh Gardens) Short lilac and purple

'Deepening Shadows' (Ghio 1984) Medium deep purple

'Drive You Wild' (Ghio 1985) Short red violet marked with gold

'Encircle' (Ghio 1980) Short white with pale blue plicata markings

'Fine Line' (Witt 1977) Tall Calsibe of yellow and cinnamon pink

'Going West' (Ghio 1984) Short brown

'Golden Waves' (Witt 1979) Tall Calsibe with yellow, freckled flowers

'Goring Ace' (Maynard 1990) Short crimson on gold

'Ivor Knowles' (Knowles 1991) Short blue and white bi-tone

'Katinka' (Scopes 1988) Medium lilac and mauve

'Mission Santa Cruz' (Ghio 1982) Short magenta

'No Name' (Brummitt 1968) Short yellow with deeper falls

'Pinewood Amethyst' (Wise 1991) Short amethyst

'Pinewood Charmer' (Wise 1994) Short yellow and pink blend

'Pinewood Poppet' (Wise 1994) Short pretty purple and white

'Pinewood Sunshine' (Wise 1994) Short yellow with paler edge to falls

'Pajaro Dunes' (Ghio 1984) Short pale brown

'Popinjay' (Scopes 1988) Medium lilac maroon and gold

'Purple Dream' (Scopes 1983) Medium mauve-purple with yellow signal on the falls

'Quintana' (Corlew 1980) Short yellow and brown

'Rio Del Mar' (Ghio 1979) Short light blue

'Roaring Camp' (Ghio 1984) Short gold and brown

'Short Order' (Ghio 1982) Short golden yellow and brown

'Simply Wild' (Ghio 1980) Very short distinctive buff and pink flowers which carry a striking black flash on the falls

'Sugar Candy' (Brummitt 1966) Short fawn and maroon flowers

WHERE TO SEE IRIS

National Collections in the UK

AWARD-WINNING (BEARDED) IRIS

Christine Barker, Myddelton House, Bulls Cross, Enfield, Middlesex, EN2 9HG
Tel. (01992) 713838

A collection of 90 cultivars set in the historic garden created by the plantsman E. A. Bowles. Open Feb–Oct Monday–Friday (except Bank Holidays) 10.00–15.30, also last Sunday in every month 14.00–17.00. Best season late spring to early summer.

IRIS ENSATA

Dr J. Smart, Marwood Hill Gardens, Marwood, Barnstaple, Devon, EX31 4EB
Tel. (01271) 42528

A collection of 200 cultivars of Japanese iris. Open dawn to dusk daily except Christmas and New Year period. Best season early to midsummer.

IRIS SIBIRICA
(AWARD-WINNING CULTIVARS)

K. W. Davis, Lingen Nursery, Lingen, Bucknell, Shropshire, SY7 0DY
Tel. (01544) 267720

A composite collection of more than 60 Siberian cultivars based on award schemes, held in a number of gardens. Visits by appointment only. Best season midsummer.

IRIS SERIES SPURIAE

Belsay Hall, Belsay, Newcastle-upon-Tyne, NE20 0DX
Tel. (01661) 881636

The 20 species and subspecies can be seen by appointment.

IRIS UNGUICULARIS AND IRIS LAZICA

Ann Ala, Hall Farm, Weatheroak Hill, Nr Alvechurch, Birmingham, B48 7EG
Tel. (01564) 822131

In winter the garden is colourful with 25 varieties and cultivars. Visits by appointment only.

IRIS UNGUICULARIS

Mr R. Nutt, Great Barfield, Bradenham, High Wycombe, Buckinghamshire, HP4 4HD
Tel. (01494) 563741

The garden is open according to details given in the *Gardens of England and Wales Open for Charity* yellow book published each year, and by appointment. Best season early spring.

IRIS SPECIES

Department of Botany, Plant Science Laboratories, University of Reading, Whiteknights, PO Box 221, Reading, Berkshire, RG6 6AS
Tel. (01734) 318163

In addition to 170 cultivars the collection comprises more than 80 species. Visits by appointment only.

Most botanic gardens grow a wide range of species, especially the more unusual types. The trial grounds at the Royal Horticultural Society Gardens at Wisley are an excellent place to see a wide range of cultivars on trial, and there is an iris garden at The Gardens of the Rose, Royal National Rose Society, Chiswell Green, St Albans, Herts AL2 3NR.

Spuria 'Russian White' is an elegant plant.

WHERE TO BUY IRIS

Many of these nurseries have display fields or gardens which are an ideal place to see iris before buying.

UK

David Austin Roses Ltd,
Bowling Green Lane, Albrighton, Wolverhampton,
West Midlands, WV7 3HB
Tel. (01902) 373931
Wide range, especially bearded

Avon Bulbs,
Burnt House Farm, Mid-Lambrook, South Petherton,
Somerset, TA13 5HE
Tel. (01460) 242177
Iris species

Rupert Bowlby,
Gatton, Reigate, Surrey, RH2 0TA
Tel. (01737) 642221
Unusual species

Broadleigh Gardens,
Barr House, Bishops Hull, Taunton,
Somerset, TA4 1AE
Tel. (01823) 286231
Smaller iris, especially PCI

Cambridge Bulbs,
40 Whittlesford Road, Newton,
Cambridge,
CB2 5PH
Unusual species

P. & J. Christian,
PO Box 468, Wrexham, Clwyd, LL13 9XR
Tel. (01978) 366399
Unusual species

Croftway Nursery,
Yapton Road, Barnham, Bognor Regis,
West Sussex, PO22 0BH
Tel. (01243) 552121
Bearded iris

Kim W. Davis,
Lingen Alpine Nursery, Lingen,
Nr Bucknell, Shropshire, SY7 0DY
Tel. (01544) 267720
Iris species and PCIs

Four Seasons,
Hillhouse Farm, Cheney's Lane,
Forncett St Mary, Norwich, NR16 1JT
Tel. (01508) 488344
Wide range

Goldbrook Plants,
Hoxne, Eye, Suffolk, IP21 5AN
Tel. (01379) 668770
Siberian and water iris

Holden Clough Nursery,
Holden, Bolton-by-Bowland,
Clitheroe, Lancashire, BB7 4PF
Tel. (01200) 447615
PCIs and Siberians

V. H. Humphrey,
Westlees Farm, Logmore Lane ,
Westcott, Dorking, Surrey, RH4 3JN
Tel. (01306) 889827
Huge range of modern iris

W. E. Th. Ingwersen Ltd,
Birch Farm Nursery, Gravetye,
East Grinstead, Sussex, RH19 4LE
Tel. (01342) 810236
Small species

Iris Garden,
Roan Cottage, Dukes Kiln Drive,
Gerrards Cross, Bucks, SL9 7MD
Tel. (01753) 884308
Bearded and others

Kelways Nurseries Ltd,
Langport, Somerset, TA10 9SL
Tel. (01458) 250521
Especially bearded

Norman Payne,
84 Whatley Avenue,
Merton Park, London SW20 9NU
Tel. (0181) 540 4794
Japanese iris

Potterton & Martin,
The Cottage Nursery, Moortown Road,
Nettleton, Caistor, Lincolnshire, LN7 6HX
Tel. (01472) 851792
Species and aril iris

Stapeley Water Gardens Ltd,
London Road, Stapeley, Nantwich,
Cheshire, CW5 7LH
Tel. (01270) 623868
Water iris

Van Tubergen,
Bressingham, Diss,
Norfolk, IP22 2AB
Tel. (01379) 888282
Unusual and bulbous iris

Wychwood Carp Farm,
Farnham Road, Odiham,
Basingstoke, Hampshire, RG25 1HS
Tel. (01256) 702800
Water iris

Zephyrwude Irises,
48 Blacker Lane, Crigglestone,
Wakefield, West Yorkshire, WF4 3EN,
Tel. (01924) 252101
Huge range of smaller bearded iris

FRANCE
Cayeux Nursery,
Poilly-lez-Gien,
45500 Gien,
Wide range

HOLLAND
Kawana,
Wynegembaan,
B-2520 Ranst
General list

AUSTRALIA
Rainbow Ridge Nursery,
Taylor Road, Dural,
New South Wales 2158
General list including John Taylor introductions

Tempo Two,
PO Box 60A, Pearcedale,
Victoria
Bearded iris including Barry Blyth introductions

USA & CANADA
Aitken's Salmon Green Garden,
PO Box 367, Potter Valley,
California 95469
Wide range

Cooley's Gardens,
PO Box 126, 11553 Silverton Road, NE,
Silverton,
Oregon 97381
Bearded iris

'Maui Moonlight' is a bright Intermediate Bearded iris.

Cooper's Garden,
2345 Decatur Avenue North,
Golden Valley, Maine 55427
Species iris

Crystal Palace Perennials,
PO Box 154,
St John, Indiana 46573
Aquatic iris

Eartheart Gardens,
RR 1, Box 847, South Harpswell,
Maine 04079
Siberian iris

Ensata Gardens,
9823 East Michigan Avenue,
Galesbury, Michigan 49053
Japanese iris

MoonShine Gardens,
PO Box 367, Potter Valley,
California 95469
Bearded iris

Pleasure Iris Gardens,
425 East Luna Azul Dr,
Chaparral, New Mexico 88021
Wide range

Pope's Perennials,
39 Highland Avenue,
Gorham,
Maine 04038-1701
Wide range

Portable Acres,
2087 Curtis Dr,
Penngrove, California 94951
Pacific Coast hybrids and species

Rialto Gardens,
1146 W Rialto, Fresno,
California 93705
Bearded iris

Schreiner's Iris Gardens,
3629 Quinaby Road,
Salem,
Oregon 97303
Bearded iris

IRIS SOCIETIES

The British Iris Society,
Cy Bartlett,
The Old Mill House,
Shurton, Stogursey,
Bridgwater, Somerset, TA5 1QG, England
Tel. 01278 733485

The American Iris Society,
Marilyn Harlow,
Membership Secretary,
PO Box 8455, San Jose,
California 95155, USA

Aril Society International,
c/o Mr and Mrs H. Shockey,
4611 Rio Grande Lane,
NW Albuquerque,
New Mexico 87107, USA

Canadian Iris Society,
c/o Mrs A. Richardson,
R R 2 Hannon, Ontario,
Canada

Danish Iris and Lily Society,
(Dansk Iris øg Liljeklub),
Lars Pedersen,
Klovermaksvej 9, Hylke,
8660 Skanderborg, Denmark

Iris Society of Australia,
Mrs H. Pryor, PO Box 11,
Gordon, NSW 2072,
Australia

Japan Iris Society,
Oide-cho 9-31,
Nishinomiya 662,
Japan

New Zealand Iris Society,
c/o Mr H. Collins,
6 Pye's Pa Road,
R D 3 Tauranga,
New Zealand

Societa Italiana dell' Iris,
c/o The Secretary,
Palazzo Strozzi,
Firenze, Italy

Société Française des Iris et Plantes Bulbeuse,
c/o Mme A. M. Chesnai,
19 Rue du Dr Kuryemme,
78350 Jouy-en-Josas,
France

Western Australia Iris Society,
Mrs M Hayes, 43,
Ivanhoe Street,
Morley 6162,
Western Australia,
Australia

Iris Society of South Africa,
The Secretary,
PO Box 2924,
Edenvale,
South Africa 1610

PLATE VIII

I. 'Crystal Halo'
Japanese iris

I. 'Brownstone'
Spuria

I. 'Miss Coquette'
Japanese iris

I. 'Golden Waves'
Calsibe

All plants shown at approximately ⅓ size

I. 'Kalamazoo'
Japanese iris

I. 'Janice Chesnik'
Spuria

I. foetidissima citrina

I. 'Shelford Giant'
Spuria

I. 'Gerald Darby'

I. 'Missouri Gal'
Spuria

AWARD-WINNING IRIS

'Sunny Day' – an award-winning spuria iris. It is the aim of most hybridizers that their plants should be honoured with an award.

It is difficult to choose iris for the garden from the many thousands that are currently available, whether from the horticultural trade, from enthusiasts or from societies. However, a number of award schemes have been developed to recognize the best iris available. All these schemes have their limitations – for example, the organizer cannot always guarantee that the trials are comprehensive, and judging criteria may not always be exactly those that signify a good garden plant. Despite this, award schemes offer a good rule of thumb for plant selection and do have the merit that if they are awarded in your area they may be a good guide to the plants that will do well in your own garden.

AWARD OF GARDEN MERIT

The most important garden award in the UK, which is quoted as a standard of excellence in other countries also, is the Award of Garden Merit (AGM) bestowed upon plants by the Royal Horticultural Society. AGMs are given to plants that fulfil certain criteria: excellence of use for ordinary garden decoration, good constitution, availability in the trade, freedom from particular pest and disease problems, ability to grow without highly specialized care (other than that required by the genus as a whole) and varietal stability. Although the AGM has been awarded to plants for many decades the RHS reinstituted the award in 1992, and from that time every existing AGM has been or will be reviewed by the Society or associated specialist societies. The new AGM is given after controlled trial, observation in a growing environment or discussion by committee. Those given before 1992 have been rescinded, and all awarded after that date will be reviewed regularly.

Iris species and primary hybrids

I. albicans
I. aucheri
I. bucharica
I. chrysographes
I. confusa
I. cristata
I. crocea
I. delavayi
I. douglasiana
I. ensata
I. florentina
I. foetidissima
I. foetidissima
  'Variegata'
I. forrestii
I. × fulvala
I. 'Gerald Darby'
I. germanica
I. graminea
I. histrioides 'Major'
I. 'Holden Clough'
I. hoogiana
I. japonica
I. japonica 'Variegata'
I. kerneriana
I. lactea
I. lacustris
I. laevigata
I. laevigata
  'Variegata'
I. latifolia
I. lazica
I. lutescens
I. magnifica
I. milesii
I. missouriensis
I. orientalis
I. pallida ssp. *cengialtii*
I. pallida ssp. *pallida*
I. pallida 'Variegata'
I. pseudacorus
I. pseudacorus
  'Variegatus'

I. reticulata
I. sanguinea
I. setosa
I. sibirica
I. sintenisii
I. unguicularis
I. variegata
I. versicolor
I. wilsonii
I. winogradowii

Pacific Coast hybrids

'Agnes James'
'Arnold Sunrise'
'Banbury Melody'
'Big Money'
'Blue Ballerina'
'Broadleigh Carolyn'
'Danbury Beauty'
'Danbury Gem'
'Danbury Velvet'
'Golden Waves'
  (Calsibe)
'Lavender Royal'
'Lincoln Imp'
'Little Tilgates'
'No Name'
'Phillida'
'Pojaro Dunes'
'Ring O'Roses'
'Rio del Mar'
'Roman Emperor'
'Short Order'

Bearded iris
ID = Intermediate or dwarf

'Adrienne Taylor' IB
'Amigo' TB
'Annikins' ID
'Arctic Fancy' ID
'Bibury' ID
'Blue-Eyed Brunette' TB

'Blue Luster' TB
'Bromyard' ID
'Bronzaire' ID
'Brown Lasso' ID
'Buckden Pike' TB
'Cannington Skies' TB
'Chiltern Gold' ID
'Cliffs of Dover' TB
'Dancer's Veil' TB
'Dark Rosaleen' ID
'Designer's Choice' TB
'Double Lament' ID
'Dovedale' TB
'Dusky Dancer' TB
'Early Light' TB
'Edale' TB
'Eyebright' ID
'Eye Magic' ID
'Fierce Fire' ID
'Gay Parasol' TB
'Green Spot' ID
'Happy Mood' ID
'Ice Dancer' TB
'Jane Phillips' TB
'Jeremy Brian' ID
'Katie-Koo' ID
'Lime Grove' ID
'Mary Frances' TB
'Mary McIlroy' ID
'Maui Moonlight' ID
'Melon Honey' ID
'Miss Carla' ID
'Ouija' ID
'Olympic Torch' TB
'Orange Dawn' TB
'Pale Shades' ID
'Paradise' TB
'Paradise Bird' TB
'Pascoe' TB
'Peggy Chambers' ID
'Purple Landscape' ID
'Raspberry Blush' ID
'Roman Emperor' TB
'Rose Violet' TB
'Royal Contrast' ID

'Saltwood' ID
'Sarah Taylor' ID
'Scintilla' ID
'Shepherd's Delight' TB
'Snowy Owl' TB
'Soaring Kite' TB
'Song of Norway' TB
'Stepping Out' TB
'Sun Miracle' TB
'Sunny Smile' ID
'Superstition' TB
'Sweet Kate' ID
'Tangerine Sunrise' TB
'Tarot' ID
'Tintinara' TB
'Tirra Lirra' ID
'Titan's Glory' TB
'Vanity' TB
'Vinho Verde' ID
'Violet Icing' TB
'Warleggan' TB
'Wensleydale' TB
'Wharfedale' TB
'Whiteladies' ID
'Wirral Gold' ID

Siberian and spuria iris

'Anniversary' Siberian
'Belise' Spuria
'Cambridge' Siberian
'Dreaming Spires'
  Siberian
'Orville Fay' Siberian
'Ruffled Velvet' Siberian
'Sea Shadows' Siberian
'Shelford Giant' Spuria
'Sunny Day' Spuria
'Wisley White' Siberian

Others

I. 'Professor Blaauw'
  (Dutch iris)

THE DYKES MEDAL

This is the premier award given by the American and British Iris Societies. In the year that it receives an AGM or Award of Garden Commendation (AGC), an iris must be sent to a minimum of five trial gardens where it must be grown for three years (these may include the gardens where trialling led to the AGC if the plant is divided and replanted to allow judging of a three-year-old plant). After three years the plant will be judged, and the Dykes Medal may be awarded.

British Dykes Medal Winners
(where a year is omitted no award was given)

Year	Cultivar	Raiser
1927	'Margot Holmes'	A. Perry
1929	'Joyance'	K. Dykes
1930	'G. P. Baker'	A. Perry
1931	'Gudrun'	K. Dykes
1934	'Golden Hind'	H. Chadburn
1935	'Sahara'	G. Pilkington
1940	'White City'	O. Murrell
1941	'Mabel Chadburn'	H. Chadburn
1948	'Maisie Lowe'	J. L. Gibson
1949	'Blue Ensign'	H. R. Meyer
1952	'Seathwaite'	H. Randall
1953	'Arabi Pasha'	G. Anley
1955	'Benton Cordelia'	C. Morris
1957	'Golden Alps'	L. Brummitt
1958	'Tarn Hows'	H. Randall
1959	'Headlines'	L. Brummitt
1960	'Kangchenjunga'	H. Miller
1961	'Patterdale'	H. Randall
1962	'Arcady'	H. Fothergill
1963	'Dancer's Veil'	P. Hutchinson
1964	'Primrose Drift'	L. Brummitt
1965	'Mary Todd'	H. Randall
1966	'Ancient Egypt'	H. Fothergill
1967	'Blue-Eyed Brunette'	C. Hall
1969	'Golden Forest'	P. Hutchison
1970	'Constance West'	A. Howe
1971	'Cambridge'	M. Drummitt
1972	'Shepherd's Delight'	H. Fothergill
1973	'Muriel Neville'	H. Fothergill
1975	'Tyrian Robe'	C. Hall
1976	'No Name'	M. Brummitt

1977	'Annabel Jane'	B. Dodsworth
1978	'Cotsgold'	J. D. Taylor
1979	'Anniversary'	M. Brummitt
1980	'Kildonian'	B. Dodsworth
1981	'Jill Rosalind'	B. Dodsworth
1982	'Dibury'	J. Taylor
1983	'Dovedale'	B. Dodsworth
1984	'Bewick Swan'	B. Dodsworth
1985	'Roman Emperor'	B. Dodsworth
1987	'Buckden Pike'	B. Dodsworth
1988	'Wensleydale'	B. Dodsworth
1989	'Early Light'	N. Scopes
1990	'High Peak'	B. Dodsworth
1991	'Wharfedale'	B. Dodsworth
1994	'Orinoco Flow'	B. Dodsworth

American Dykes Medal Winner
(where a year is omitted no award was given)

Year	Cultivar	Raiser
1927	'San Francisco'	W. Mohr
1929	'Dauntless'	C. Connell
1932	'Rameses'	H. Sass
1933	'Coralie'	W. Ayres
1935	'Sierra Blue'	E. Essig
1936	'Mary Geddes'	T. Washington
1937	'Missouri'	J. Grinter
1938	'Copper Lustre'	J. Kirkland
1939	'Rosy Wings'	M. Gage
1940	'Wabash'	E. Williamson
1941	'The Red Douglas'	J. Sass
1942	'Great Lakes'	L. Cousins
1943	'Prairie Sunset'	H. Sass
1944	'Spun Gold'	H. Glutzbeck
1945	'Elmohr'	P. Loomis
1947	'Chivalry'	J. Wills
1948	'Ola Kala'	J. Sass
1949	'Helen McGregor'	R. Graves
1950	'Blue Rhythm'	A. Whiting
1951	'Cherie'	D. Hall
1952	'Argus Pheasant'	F. DeForest
1953	'Truly Yours'	O. Fay
1954	'Mary Randall'	O. Fay
1955	'Sable Night'	P. Cook
1956	'First Violet'	F DeForest
1957	'Violet Harmony'	F. Lowry
1958	'Blue Sapphire'	Schreiner
1959	'Swan Ballet'	T. Muhlestein

Dykes Medal winner 'Edith Wolford'.

1961	'Eleanor's Pride'	E. Watkins
1962	'Whole Cloth'	P. Cook
1963	'Amethyst Flame'	Schreiner
1964	'Allegiance'	P. Cook
1965	'Pacific Panorama'	N. Sexton
1966	'Rippling Waters'	O. Fay
1967	'Winter Olympics'	O. Brown
1968	'Stepping Out'	Schreiner
1970	'Skywatch'	C. Benson
1971	'Debby Rairdon'	L. Kuntz
1972	'Babbling Brook'	K. Keppel
1973	'New Moon'	N. Sexton
1974	'Shipshape'	S. Babson
1975	'Pink Taffeta'	N. Rudolph
1976	'Kilt Lilt'	J. Gibson

1977	'Dream Lover'	E .Tams
1978	'Bride's Halo'	H. Mohr
1979	'Mary Frances'	L. Gaulter
1980	'Mystique'	J. Ghio
1981	'Brown Lasso'	Duckles/Niswonger
1982	'Vanity'	B. Hager
1983	'Ruffled Ballet'	E. Roderick
1984	'Victoria Falls'	Schreiner
1985	'Beverly Sills'	B. Hager
1986	'Song of Norway'	W. Luihn
1988	'Titan's Glory'	Schreiner
1990	'Jesse's Song'	B. Williamson
1991	'Everything Plus'	D. Niswonger
1992	'Dusky Challenger'	Schreiner
1993	'Edith Wolford'	B. Hager
1994	'Silverado'	Schreiner
1995	'Honky Tonk Blues'	Schreiner

WHERE TO PLACE IRIS

A large number of irises can be succcessfully planted in many different parts of the garden. An asset of the thousands of hybrids that have been raised is that they often combine the attributes of different species, and selection of the most vigorous plants has meant that most modern hybrids are able to thrive in a wide range of conditions.

This list of garden situations gives specific plant recommendations but is not definitive because of the wide variations in climate, soils and other variables. Plants that require greenhouse or specialized treatment are not included and are featured in the chapter on iris for specialists (*see page 68*).

SUNNY ROCK GARDEN

With a well-drained soil and planting pockets between rocks that can be adapted to suit the individual needs of plants, a rock garden can be the perfect place for many of the smaller iris.

Small bearded iris These include the small species such as *I. pumila* and *I. chamaeiris*, the Miniature Dwarf Bearded iris (flowering in mid- to late spring), the slightly bigger species such as *I. lutescens* and *I. aphylla* and the Standard Dwarf Bearded iris (flowering in late spring). They require watering after flowering to produce new increases.

Associated plants should not be so vigorous that they swamp the rhizomes of the iris, though arabis and aubrieta can be trimmed back hard immediately after flowering to keep them neat and give the iris rhizomes room to breathe. Mossy and encrusted saxifrages make neat flowering mats with small flowers that complement the iris. Invasive plants with underground stolons such as *Campanula porscharskyana* should be avoided.

Regelia and Oncocyclus iris In protected sites a few of these iris may survive outside, especially if protected from winter rain. They require heavy feeding in spring and may interfere with other alpines so are best grown in isolation. *I. hoogiana* and *I. susianus* are worth trying (flowering in late spring).

Iris unguicularis This tough, hardy iris will thrive in a parched sunny pocket if the untidy foliage can be tolerated.

Bulbous iris Where height is required the tall Dutch, English and Spanish iris make a show of colour in late spring and early summer as the majority of alpine plants are looking past their best. The dwarf *I. reticulata* and others of the subgenus Hermodactyloides flourish on the rock garden and bring their bright blooms to the garden scene in early spring. All will grow through a mat of foliage but their leaves are prominent after flowering, which may detract from other plants. These iris are best planted in small pockets, in clumps where the mass of flowers is most effective rather than scattered through other plants. They can be successful under dwarf deciduous shrubs which will later hide their foliage.

Juno iris This is the ideal place for the Juno iris that flourish outside, such as *I. bucharica* and *I. magnifica* (flowering in mid- and late spring). Although the plants will grow through foliage of other plants, which may provide some early frost protection, they are a tasty treat for slugs and snails and so are best kept clear of other plants and surrounded by a dressing of gravel around the neck.

Snake's head iris *Hermodactylus tuberosus* benefits from this situation but the leaves are very obtrusive and the flowers not showy. It often looks best when growing through a dwarf spiky or deciduous shrub such as *Convolvulus cneorum* or *Corokia*.

PEAT BANK

The peat bank is an ideal site for the cultivation of dwarf rhododendrons, cassiopes, primulas and meconopsis if the soil is acidic and in part shade. This situation suits many of the prettiest iris. Because such a garden feature is usually raised above natural soil level it is a practical way to grow lime-hating plants on alkaline soils.

Evansia iris The predominantly Asian evansias are well suited to such a situation, particularly if it is sheltered from cold winds and frost. Where large feature plants are required *I. confusa* and *I. wattii* would be attractive, though these species are both rather tender. *I. japonica* is hardier and lower-growing. At the front of beds, where they would creep over peat blocks and be most at home, plant *I. lacustris, I cristata* and *I. gracilipes*.

Iris graminea Although this species does not require such choice soil it will thrive here if not too shaded and bring interest and scent in late spring.

Iris kerneriana Most of the spurias are too large for this situation but this slender species will add grace and colour in spring.

Iris ruthenica This flowers from late spring to midsummer and is neat and clump-forming. It will thrive in the drier parts of the peat garden.

Iris setosa This tolerant iris will grow almost anywhere, but the shorter forms such as *I. s.* ssp. *canadensis* and *I. s.var. arctica* are ideal.

Iris verna This is a plant from woodland habitats that, while not common in Britain, would do very well in this position.

SUNNY GARDEN BORDER

The sunny garden border can be exceedingly variable. Even if moist in spring it can be dry in summer because of the water requirements of other plants, while hedges, fences and even other plants can affect light. When combining iris for effect be adventurous, but in addition to considering form, texture, colour and flowering times, don't forget to allow for the needs of the iris — there will be one that fulfils your requirements and will grow happily.

Bearded iris In sunny borders these iris, in all their heights and forms, are perfect to give colour from mid-spring until midsummer. They must not be swamped by other plants, particularly after flowering and in winter. Because they benefit from regular division they can be moved as borders develop.

Evansia iris *I. milesii* and *I. tectorum* are especially suitable and give an unusual look to borders.

Siberian iris If the soil is moderately moist all the Siberian iris, including *I. sibirica, I. sanguinea, I clarkei, I. forrestii* and all the hybrids will thrive. Their robust growth and ability to thrive without attention suit permanent planting.

Iris setosa All forms of this species thrive in sun.

Spuria iris All the spuria iris, species and hybrids, will grow if the soil is not too poor. They are slow to establish but long-lived.

Bulbous iris The Dutch, English and Spanish iris can be used to bring quick colour to borders and are cheap enough to be used as bedding bulbs.

Juno iris The most robust Juno iris such as *I. bucharica* and *I. magnifica* may grow well at the front of a mixed border.

SHADY GARDEN BORDER

Not all shady borders are dry but in those that are the only iris that will survive is *I. foetidissima*. Where the shade is not too severe, and other plants such as heuchera, hosta, ferns, epimediums and tiarella will grow, the choice of iris is wide.

Evansia iris *I. tectorum* and *I. japonica* will grow but may not flower as freely as in sun. They must not be crowded out by more vigorous plants. *I. lacustris* and *I. cristata* will grow if given protection from slugs and smothered if the soil is acid.

Pacific Coast Iris If the soil is acid and the shade not too dense, many will thrive. Although slow to establish these iris are long-lived and reliable.

Siberian iris In light shade these often perform well, though flowering may be less than on plants grown in full sun.

Iris foetidissima The extraordinarily tough stinking iris will grow beautifully in moderate shade and survive even deep shade.

Iris graminea The small flowers and leafy clumps fit in well with other shade-loving plants.

Iris setosa Another situation where this tough though short-lived iris will grow.

TROUGHS

Gardeners who grow alpines or other small plants in sinks and troughs can choose any of the smallest bearded iris (MTBs) if the soil is well-drained and neutral or alkaline. If it is acid they can also grow the tiny Evansias such as *I. cristata*. The easier Juno iris (troughs could be moved to protection in winter if the other planting is unaffected) and *I. reticulata* and related small bulbous iris are also suitable, though the foliage of the latter is unsightly in late spring.

HEAVY SOILS

Heavy soils are less of a problem for herbaceous iris than the bulbous iris, which frequently perish because clay soils are often wet in winter and warm up less quickly in spring. If improved with gravel, coarse sand and humus, heavy soils can support a wide range of plants. These cold, often wet soils encourage slugs and snails, which must be controlled.

Bearded iris All the bearded iris grow well in heavy soils if planted in sun, and often grow better than in poor, sandy soils that benefit from good drainage.

Evansia iris The hardiest Evansia iris such as *I. milesii* and *I. tectorum* should grow well.

Siberian iris All the Siberian iris will grow in heavy soils and appreciate the more constant moisture levels.

Water iris The Japanese iris derived from *I. ensata* will grow in heavy soil as long as it is moist, as will all the other water iris including *I. laevigata*, *I. pseudacorus* and *I. versicolor*.

Spuria iris The spuria iris prefer the moisture and fertility associated with heavy soils and will often grow vigorously without any attention in such soils.

POOR, SANDY SOILS

Free-draining soils suit many of the iris from arid parts of the world as well as some of the commoner garden plants and bulbous iris. However, even the xerophytic Oncocyclus iris require a substantial amount of nutrition and very sandy soils may result in plants living for many years but never gaining the vigour to flower and grow well. With the exception of *I. unguicularis*, all iris will grow better if a poor, sandy soil is improved with garden compost or well-rotted manure. Apart from the bearded iris, which need to have their rhizomes exposed to the air, they will benefit from a spring mulch of the same material every year. It should be not be applied in autumn because much of the plant food will be leached out of the soil by winter rains.

Bearded iris The taller sorts require good soil to grow well, so the dwarf and intermediate hybrids and species are best in these conditions.

Pacific Coast Iris In semi-shade these dwarf iris will grow, though they will not flower well in very poor soils.

Iris unguicularis Plant this in the least hospitable soils, leave it alone and it will be a mass of blooms in winter.

Bulbous iris All the bulbous iris from dwarf to cut flower types will grow for at least one season, but will not flower well the second if too starved or parched.

Juno iris The easiest species such as *I. bucharica* should be well suited if fed when in growth.

MOIST AND WET SOILS

The only iris that can be relied upon to grow permanently in wet conditions (with the plant crowns under water) are *I. laevigata* and *I. pseudacorus*. Others that tolerate or prefer moist soils at or near the water line are the Siberian irises, *I. ensata*, *I. versicolor* and the Louisiana iris such as *I. fulva* (if given shelter and sun).

NATURALIZING IN GRASS

Only the most robust iris can be naturalized in grass. Because it is not possible to mow over most iris as is the treatment for most flower meadows (in midsummer and mid-autumn) large clumps are the most easily dealt with. It is important to control any perennial weeds before adding flowers to turf, and cut grass (hay) should be raked up and removed after cutting to deplete the fertility of the soil (this discourages coarse grasses and favours flowering perennials). This subject is under-exploited but some iris could be used effectively at the transition of the cultivated garden and the flower meadow. In particular the tall spurias would be excellent, and look very striking. At pond margins *I. pseudacorus* will grow happily in grass and with careful attention during establishment Siberian iris would look beautiful.

POTS

The fact that many iris are sold in pots at nurseries and garden centres proves that almost any iris will grow in a pot. However, the rhizomatous bearded iris are less suited than others because they quickly run to the edge

The Siberian iris 'Timpcals', one of the many hundreds of cultivars now available to gardeners.

of the pot and need repotting. The dwarfer, slower-spreading types are better. The Japanese water iris are traditionally grown in pots, a system that suits gardeners without ponds, and the Evansias are also good for this type of cultivation. *I. confusa* and *I. wattii*, which are not reliably hardy, can be grown in pots and protected in winter. Those iris not suited to temperate conditions such as the Oncocyclus and most of the Junos can be grown in pots under glass, and the dwarf reticulata iris planted in shallow pans and pots will brighten the house in early spring.

LOW-MAINTENANCE GARDENS

I hesitate to suggest any iris to gardeners who want to do the very minimum for their plants apart from the cheap bulbous iris, which are planted and then regarded as finished. However, the Siberian and Spuria iris in particular thrive with little attention as long as they are planted correctly. The Pacific Coast Iris also reward disturbance with a taciturn response so could be regarded as low maintenance, though they are not plants for the uncaring gardener. Most tall bearded iris require little attention and division only after three years, and it is to be hoped that after three seasons of magical flowers even the most lackadaisical gardener will have developed sufficient enthusiasm for this.

GLOSSARY

Aggregate (or complex) A group of closely related species or hybrids that are difficult to distinguish from each other. An example is the large number of hybrids between *I. pallida* and *I. variegata* that have been variously described as species in the past.

Amoena An iris with white or very pale standards and deeper-coloured falls. Reverse amoenas show the opposite coloration. Blue and purple are the most common and best established colours in this colour pattern.

Anther The pollen-bearing organ, held on a long stalk (filament) under the style arm of the iris flower. The iris flower has three anthers (in common with all *Iridaceae*) but these are widely separated in most. Each anther opens by two slits to release pollen. In some hybrids that show male sterility these anthers are thin and claw-shaped, an indication that they will produce little or no pollen. If these plants are used in hybridizing they should be used as the female parent.

Anthesis The period when the flower is open, from bud-burst to wilting.

Apogon Those iris that do not have a beard or crest on the falls (or less usually, standards), such as Pacific Coast Iris (Series Californicae) and Siberian iris (Series Sibiricae).

Aril A fleshy appendage on the seeds of some plants that is palatable to ants and other insects. It probably helps seed distribution as the insects carry away the seed and aril before consuming the aril, leaving the seed unharmed. In the iris genus this structure occurs on plants in the sections Hexapogon, Regelia, Pseudoregelia and Oncocyclus.

Arilbred An iris hybrid that has an aril iris (usually Regelia or Oncocyclus iris) in its ancestry. They are often also called Oncobreds. Large flowers, subtle colouring and a silky appearance to the petals are typical of arilbred iris. A number of different terms have been introduced, with shorter cultivars usually called arilmeds and dwarf hybrids sometimes known as Oncopumilas.

Arilmed A short bearded iris cultivar with an aril iris in its ancestry.

Backcross Crossing a hybrid back with one of its ancestors in order to enhance a desirable characterestic.

Beard The bushy strip of hairs on the falls (and standards in the Section Hexapogon) of iris flowers. It probably acts as a guide to insects in conjunction with veining and haft markings on the falls; it may give better grip to large pollinating insects or force their body to be lifted up as they clamber into the flower. This may ensure that the insect's back comes into contact with the stigma and anther, effecting successful pollination.

Bicolor An iris that has standards and falls of two different colours. If there are more than two colours in indistinct regions this is a blend.

Bitone An iris that has standards and falls of two different shades of the same colour. Because the two colours could be present on both standards and falls, this is a more general term than amoena. Though amoenas are bitones, not all bitones are amoenas.

Blade The flat broad surface of a leaf or any petal.

Blend Those colour patterns that are too complex or indistinct to classify elsewhere.

Bract A leaf on the flowering stem that has a flower or flower stem growing from the point where it is attached to the stem.

Bulb An underground, shortened stem (basal plate) with fleshy leaves (scales) that store food so that the plant can survive periods of adverse conditions.

Calcicole A plant that prefers soils with a pH of more than 7 (neutral), usually containing calcium (alkaline).

Calcifuge A plant that dislikes lime and prefers an acid soil with a pH lower than 7 (neutral).

Calsibe (or Cal/Sib) Any hybrid between plants of the two different series Californicae and Sibiricae.

Chromosome The structure in a plant (or animal) cell nucleus that contains the genetic information in areas called genes. The chromosomes are strands of genes that contain DNA (Deoxyribosenucleic acid). In most organisms there are two sets of identical or very similar chromosomes. This is called diploid. Because sexual reproduction requires the uniting of genetic information from two parents, the sex cells (pollen = male and egg cell = female) have just one set of chromosomes and are called haploid. By chance, some iris have twice the usual complement of chromosomes (4). These 'tetraploids' produce sex cells with two sets of chromosomes and if hybridized with diploids they may not give fertile seeds or may produce triploid offspring with three sets of chromosomes. These may be healthy garden plants but are often a dead end for plant breeders because they are sterile.

Clone A set of genetically identical individuals propagated by vegetative means. The sexual reproduction of offspring inevitably involves mixing of genetic material from the two parents (except in apomicts such as *Taraxacum* [dandelion] where seed is set without fertilization). Clonal material has the advantage that it is predictable and identical. Seed-raised plants should not bear the cultivar name of their parent except to state that they are seedlings of this cultivar.

Closed Referring to the standards of bearded hybrids which are curved and touch or overlap at the top.

Corm An underground storage organ which is a method of surviving adverse conditions in a dormant state. It differs from a bulb in that the food is stored in a solid mass of stem, not fleshy leaves (scales). A new corm is produced annually, usually above the old.

Crest The jagged, serrated ridge of tissue on the falls of Evansia (crested) iris such as *I. tectorum*. The two petaloid, upright parts at the end of the style arm are also called crests or style crests.

Cross A hybrid or to hybridize.

Cultivar A composite word derived from, and meaning, cultivated variety. It is preferred to variety to describe a plant because it differentiates those that originate in cultivation from plants with the botanical rank of *varietas* found in the wild. Naturally occurring varieties are written in Latin (*Iris pallida* var. *illyrica*) while cultivars are written with a capital letter within quote marks (*Iris pallida* 'Aureovariegata'). A cultivar is often a hybrid, but hybrids can also occur naturally and are often given Latin names with an × before the hybrid name (*I.* × *pseudopumilioides*, which is a hybrid of *I. pumila* and *I. aphylla*). A cultivar may also be a spontaneous colour variation (sport) or a variegated or dwarf plant that originated without hybridizing.

Dehisce The opening of the anthers to release pollen or the seed pod to disperse seeds.

Diamond-dusted Used to describe petals which look as though they have gold dust on or in them.

Diploid Having two sets (2n) of chromosomes in the usual vegetative state (the sex cells will have half the number and be haploid).

Disc The larger, rounded part of the falls, excluding the haft. It is also called the blade.

Domed Of the standards, meaning that they are rounded and curved so that they touch or overlap at the top of the flower.

Edo The old name for Tokyo, Japan, which is used for the older kinds of Japanese water iris.

Embryo The result of successful fertilization after pollination. This potential plant will grow after germination of the seed and be sustained by food reserves within the seed during its early stages of development.

Endemic A plant that is native to a specific area and not found elsewhere.

Eupogon The bearded or pogon iris.

Falls The three outer or lower petals (tepals) of the iris flower. In bud these are the outer petals that surround the other flower parts and as the flower opens the falls unfurl and become horizontal or hang vertically to reveal the standards. They are often ornamented with beards or crests and usually show more contrasting markings than the standards.

Fan The leaves of a single growing point or shoot of an iris, usually emerging from the rhizome at ground level.

Fertilization The combining of the male and female haploid sex cells (gametes) to produce a (usually) diploid cell that will in a healthy seed develop into an embryo capable of germination. Fertilization occurs after pollination but is dependent upon factors other than the mechanical transfer of pollen.

Filament The 'stalk' that holds the anther in a flower.

Flared Describes the position of falls or standards that are held away from the vertical to give a wider flower shape.

Flounce A feature that is seen in some space-age iris where the end of the beard on the fall of bearded iris lifts away from the petal surface as a series of small petals.

Frilled Fine ruffling and often serration of the petal edges, particularly the falls.

Gene A position on the chromosome that controls a character or group of characters.

Genus (plural genera) A group of plants that have a number of characteristics in common. The plants in the same genus will have a greater similarity than other plants in the family to which the genus belongs. Plants of the same species have even more features in common. The genus *Iris* is divided into subgenera and these form the basis of proposals to split the genus into a number of different genera including Juno (currently Subgenus Scorpiris), Iridodictyum (currently Subgenus Hermodactyloides) and Xiphium (currently Subgenus Xiphium).

Haft The part of the fall nearest the centre of the flower. Often it is marked with contrasting colour in stripes, but it may also be narrow and stalk-like.

Halo A pale area around a darker zone on the falls in some iris flowers.

Haploid A cell that contains a single set of chromosomes. Haploid cells are almost exclusively involved in sexual reproduction.

Herbaceous A plant that survives winter (or other adverse conditions) by retreating underground and remaining dormant as small buds, without the food reserves of bulbs or corms (though some may have fleshy roots). Most herbaceous plants are not woody, but some shrubby plants will act as though herbaceous in extreme conditions.

Hexaploid An iris with six sets of chromosomes, usually produced after doubling the chromosome count of a triploid to introduce fertility.

Higo Japanese iris developed in 1860 for pot culture.

Horn A petaloid protuberance at the end of the beard

on modern bearded iris. The possession of this feature makes the cultivar a 'space-age' iris.

Hybrid The result of combining two genetically different and taxonomically distinct plants through sexual reproduction. Hybrids can occur in the wild but most are produced in cultivation as an attempt to combine desirable characteristics from the two parents. A primary hybrid has two species as its parents and often has a predictable appearance. More complex hybrids between other hybrids are less easy to predict.

Inflorescence The part of the stem or plant body that carries and is dedicated to the production of flowers. In most iris the inflorescence is the upper part of the aerial stem that carries and includes the flowers and bracts.

Internode The section of stem between nodes (the point where leaves arise). New shoots arise from the nodes of stems (rhizomes in bearded iris).

Ise A group of Japanese iris developed in the Ise-Matsuzuka district of Honshu in about 1800.

Lace A feature of some iris flowers that gives a delicate, obscured outline to the edge of the petals due to a large number of minute indentations that distort but do not puncture the petal tissue.

Lamina Another word for the greater part of the leaf or petal surface (also known as the blade).

Lateral A sideshoot on a flower stem (or growth stem)

Lilliput Any Standard Dwarf Bearded iris (SDB) or Miniature Dwarf Bearded iris (MTB) less than 25cm (8in) in height at flowering time.

Line cross A method of hybridizing where a seedling is crossed with itself or closely related plants. It is used when a plant shows desirable characteristics that could be emphasized through line crossing but lost if a wider gene pool were introduced by including other parents. Prolonged line-crossing may result in loss of vigour or other defects (inbreeding) and the occasional introduction of other parents helps to retain the health of the stock.

Luminata A colour pattern in bearded iris when a blended fall has a paler centre or flare in the centre.

Membranous Thin and transparent, used to describe bracts, spathes or even parts of petals.

Mirror The white or pale patch around the beard of some cultivars. Also called a blaze.

Monocotyledon A major division of the plant kingdom comprising flowering plants that produce a single seed leaf when they germinate. Other basic characteristics are flower parts in multiples of three (or just one or absent), parallel veins in grass-like leaves and a root system without tap roots. Many are bulbs and only comparatively few are woody. They are contrasted with dicotyledons which have two seed leaves, usually broad leaves with netted veins, and flower parts in multiples of four or five.

Mutation A spontaneous change in the physical appearance and (often) genetic characteristics of a plant through asexual means. A mutation can be advantageous and result in new colours and variegated foliage, but can also be damaging and cause undesirable features.

Natural hybrid A cross between two species that occurs in the wild.

Naturalized Describes an introduced plant that has either escaped into the wild from cultivation or was deliberately introduced to the wild and has been able to sustain or increase its population without benefit of cultivation.

Nectary An organ that produces nectar in order to attract and feed pollinating insects or protective insects such as ants. Most nectaries are located at the base of the flower.

Neglecta An iris with pale blue standards and dark blue or purple falls.

Offset A young plant that grows at the base or side of the main plant. It may be a small bulb (bulblet), corm (cormlet) or rhizome.

The spuria iris 'Media Luz' is valued by gardeners because, like all spurias, it provides the last display of summer.

Out cross The introduction of new genetic material into a breeding programme by crossing a plant with another, unrelated plant. This is also called a wide cross. One advantage of out crossing is that the resultant seedlings may show hybrid vigour. However, it has the disadvantage that the results are extremely unpredictable.

Ovary The female part of the flower (below in an iris flower) that contains the ovules (potential seeds) and will grow into a seed pod (capsule in iris) if pollination and fertilization are successful.

Ovules The unfertilized female sex cells that become seeds once fertilized by the male sex cells in the pollen.

Pedicel The stem of a single flower (below the ovary and above the bract) – not to be confused with the perianth tube which often looks like a stem.

Peduncle The main flower stem from which the individual pedicels carry the flowers.

Perianth The outer part of a flower, usually the protective sepals and the showy petals but not including the sexually functional stamens and ovary.

Perianth tube The tubular part of the flower that separates the rest of the flower from the ovary. In species such as *I. unguicularis* it is the only 'stalk' that the flowers seem to possess and picking the flowers severs the flower from the ovary.

pH A measure of the concentration of hydrogen ions in an aqueous solution. The pH is measured on a scale that runs from 0 to 14. Gardeners know it as a measure of soil acidity or alkalinity. A reading of 7 is neutral; smaller values show an acid soil while higher readings are alkaline, and likely to have larger amounts of lime or chalk (calcium) in the soil. The pH scale is logarithmic and a pH of 8 is ten times more alkaline than a pH of 7, so differences of just one point are significant. Although some plants (such as rhododendrons) require an acid soil and react badly to calcium (largely because they cannot control its uptake) the majority of iris are not particular about soil pH, except that most of the Subgenus Iris prefer an alkaline soil and many Pacific Coast Iris and Siberian iris prefer acid soils.

Plicata An iris flower pattern that has a pale ground colour edged or stitched with a deeper colour that typically follows the patterning of the veins in the petals. The standards may show varying degrees of colouring. The most usual colouring is white or cream with blue or purple markings, though any colour can be included.

Pod parent The female parent that will be fertilized with pollen from another plant and will bear the seed pod. The opposite is the pollen parent.

Pogon A bearded iris.

Pollen The male haploid sex cells produced by flowers from the anthers. Pollen may not be shed as soon as the flower is open, and the flower may be sexually female with a receptive stigma before pollen is released. Iris pollen is comparatively large and sticky and is designed to be carried by insects to other flowers.

Pollination The transfer of pollen from the anther of one flower to the female part (stigma) of another flower (cross pollination) or the same flower (self pollination). In nature, cross pollination is advantageous because it creates greater genetic diversity in a population, which may endow it with a greater ability to adapt to new conditions, and prevents genetic homogeneity, which may leave a population susceptible to attack from disease or pests.

Polyploidy Having more than the usual two sets of chromosomes in the cell nucleus, such as tetraploid and triploid.

Primary hybrid A hybrid between two species. Natural hybrids occur in the wild, but hybridization of some species may only be possible in cultivation where two species that would otherwise not come into contact are grown together.

Reblooming iris An alternative term for remontant (*see below*).

Regeliocyclus Hybrid iris produced by crossing Regelia and Oncocyclus iris. Originally the term referred to crosses between *I. korolkowii* and Oncocyclus iris but has widened to cover any species within the groups. The hybrids were intended to combine the comparative ease of culture of the Regelia iris with the odd flower shapes of the Oncocyclus iris. In theory, if the mother plant was an Oncocyclus iris the hybrid should be called an Oncoregelia. Breeding work was initiated by the Dutch bulb company of Van Tubergen and most hybrids have mythical names such as 'Ancilla', 'Thor' and 'Theseus'.

Remontant Any iris that follows the usual period of bloom with flowers later in the season. Most interest is shown in remontant bearded iris and Siberian iris but many other iris have been known to remont, even if only sporadically.

Reticulate Meaning netted, this can refer to the veining of leaves, but in iris it describes the skin of the bulbs of *I. reticulata* and related species.

Rhizome A thickened, often fleshy, horizontal stem that grows at or below the surface of the soil. In iris the leaves grow vertically from the upper parts and the roots grow from the lower surface. Bearded iris usually require planting with the rhizome on the surface where sun can reach and 'ripen' it, but other iris with less fleshy rhizomes are less particular in this respect.

Rice grain The tiny bulblets produced by some bulbous iris after flowering. Though these are useful for propagation, because of their small size they may take several years before reaching flowering size and are therefore considered undesirable in garden use.

Ruffling Distinct waviness to the edge of iris petals. Bubble ruffling is more pronounced, with irregular distortion caused by extra petal tissue.

Self This may describe either a flower that is essentially one colour, with no patterning, or the process of pollinating a flower with its own pollen (selfing).

Sepal The outer perianth segments that may look like petals but are more usually green and protective. Iris flowers have sepals that have been adapted into 'petals' (the falls) to attract pollinators instead of protecting the flower bud, a function carried out by the bracts and spathes.

Signal A showy area of contrasting (often darker) colour around the beard area (or base of) the falls.

Spathes (spathe valves) The small leaves enclosing the flower buds which may be green and fleshy or dry and papery when the flower opens.

Species A smaller taxonomic group than a plant family or genus. A species should be visually distinct and stable when reproduced sexually (meaning that it comes true when grown from seed). A species may vary in its characters over its geographic range, making precise taxonomy difficult. The term 'species' is sometimes used to refer to 'unusual' plants, often in an attempt to give them added distinction, but when applied to cultivars it is incorrect.

Stamen The male part of the flower, consisting of the filament and the anther. In most iris it is held above the fall and below the style arm.

Standard The inner or upper petals in an iris flower. When in bud the standards are surrounded by the falls, but once the flower is open the standards are usually held erect. In *I. danfordiae* the standards are almost absent and in the Juno iris the standards are held horizontally and are much smaller than the falls. Standards usually have less marking than falls but in the section Hexapogon they also possess beards.

Sterile Incapable of reproduction by sexual means perhaps because the plant does not produce functioning pollen or fertile ovules. In cultivation, plants can be sterile because they are represented by a single clone that is self-sterile and needs to be pollinated by another individual of the same species. Sterility may be caused by polyploidy.

Stigma (stigmatic flap) The part of the female organs of the flower that receives pollen. The stigma secretes a sugary solution that not only helps the pollen grains become attached but also stimulates them to germinate and begin the fertilization of the ovules.

Stolons Extended horizontal stems that are used by the plant as a means of exploiting new soil and for reproduction.

Stratification The exposure of sown seeds to cold temperatures in winter, or artificially in a refrigerator, in order to stimulate germination.

Style The female part of the flower between the ovary and the stigma. The pollen grains germinate on the stigma and produce a pollen tube, through which the male sex cells migrate the length of the style into the ovary to reach the ovules.

Style branches (arms) In iris the style is divided into three petal-like branches that are often showy, and protect the anthers from rain. They terminate in the style crests and stigmatic flap.

Substance A term used to describe the petals of a flower – in particular the firmness and thickness of the petals. Good substance is particularly important in an iris that flowers when wet or windy weather can be expected. It is also necessary to help a flower stand up to hot weather, when flowers of poor substance would wilt prematurely.

Symmetry When hybridizing, the aim of the breeder should be to produce flowers that have a natural and pleasing balance or symmetry. The term also refers to the configuration of a flower. From above, an iris flower shows radial symmetry (actinomorphic), meaning that a line (or mirror) could be positioned in a number of places (running through the centre of the flower) to divide the flower exactly in half. Viewed from the side, as most iris are seen, the flowers show bilateral symmetry with a single line of symmetry.

Synonym Another name for a plant that is not the officially recognized name at the time, though it may be well known.

Tailored Describes a flower that is not ruffled or flared and has a crisp, neat outline and appearance.

Taxon (plural taxa) An unspecified unit of naming (taxonomy).

Tepals The name given to the 'petals' of a flower when the true petals (inner perianth segments) are almost indistinguishable from the outer perianth segments (sepals). The term is particularly used for monocotyledon and bulbous plant groups such as crocus, lilies and tulips where all six tepals are almost identical. In iris, although the sepals are petal-like, they are different enough from the petals ('standards') to be called falls.

Tetraploid A plant that has four sets of chromosomes. This is double the usual amount found in most other living organisms. A tetraploid iris may be larger in all its parts, with a more robust habit, thicker leaves and more intensely coloured flowers than its diploid counterpart. This is interpreted by some as coarseness. Tetraploidy can be artificially induced by exposing embryos and other plant parts to colchicine, a substance that causes the sex cell to remain diploid. The results are very erratic, but once a plant is tetraploid it is likely to remain stable and is not a freak or mutation. Tetraploids can be crossed with other tetraploids to give fertile off-spring and with diploids, but the offspring will be triploid and sterile.

Thumb print The distinctive darker marking on the falls of many short bearded iris.

Triploid A triploid has three sets of chromosomes, $1^1/_2$ times the usual complement. Triploid plants are sterile and unable to set seed. This is a benefit in bedding plants that would otherwise have to be dead-headed, and is not a disadvantage in iris except to hybridizers.

Tunic The outer layer (or skin) of bulbs.

Variegata A colour pattern in bearded iris that owes its origin to I. variegata. Typically the standards are a shade of yellow and the falls will be marked, to a varying degree, with maroon on the same colour ground.

Variegated Leaves that have areas of the normally green surface marked with a paler (usually yellow, cream or white) colour. Most variegated iris have linear striping, though this is not necessary for the application of the term.

Variety A taxonomic unit below species and sub-species.

Vector An organism (usually aphid) that carries and spreads plant diseases (usually viral). The gardener can be a vector by carrying diseased plants from one garden to another.

Vegetative reproduction Increasing the plant by division, cuttings or any method that does not include the formation of sex cells, fertilization and the resulting mixing of genetic material. Vegetative reproduction is needed to maintain and increase stocks of cultivars. It may also be called clonal reproduction.

APPENDIX H
BIBLIOGRAPHY

Bulletins and Yearbooks of the American Iris Society and The British Iris Society.

Cassidy, G.E. and Linnegar, S.
Growing Irises 1982, reprinted 1985, pb 1986, revised pb 1987, Christopher Helm, Bromley, Kent.

Dykes, W. R.
The Genus Iris Cambridge 1913, reprinted Dover Publications Ltd, New York 1974.
A Handbook of Garden Irises London 1924.

Fenner, Robin A.
A Genius Undeclared: The Life, Works and Times of William J. Caparne 1994.

Hager, Ben.
The Iris: the Rainbow Flower. Photographs by Josh Westrich. Thames & Hudson, London, 1989.

Innes, Clive.
The World of Iridaceae Ashingtonia, Sussex 1985.

Kohlen, Fritz.
Iris Christopher Helm, London, 1987.

Lynch, R. Irwin.
The Book of the Iris The Bodley Head, London, 1903.

Mathew, Brian.
The Iris Batsford, London, 1981, 1989.

McEwen, Currier.
The Japanese Iris University Press of New England, Hanover, New Hampshire, 1990.
The Siberian Iris Timber Press, Oregon, 1996.

Price, Molly.
The Iris Book Dover Publications, London, 1966.

Randall, Harry.
Irises Batsford, London, 1969.

The Species Group of the British Iris Society.
A Guide to Species Iris – Their Identification and Cultivation Cambridge University Press, 1996.

Spender, R. E. and Pesel, L. F.
Iris Culture for Amateurs Country Life, London, 1937.

INDEX

Italic page numbers refer to picture captions. Cultivars are listed in Appendix A, pp. 112-31

PICTURE ACKNOWLEDGEMENTS

Karl Adamson 9, 24-5, 40-1, 51, 58-9, 90-1, 110-11, 138-9; John Fielding 15, 20, 64, 66, 67, 72, 74, 75, 76, 117; Geoff Stebbings 11, 17, 19, 27, 28, 29, 30, 31, 32, 33, 34, 36, 37, 42, 63, 71, 82, 83, 85, 86, 88, 98, 100, 102, 103, 108, 109, 114, 143; Justyn Willsmore 1, 2, 3, 6, 45, 48, 53, 55, 56, 60, 62, 80, 84, 93, 94-5, 96, 97, 106, 119, 120, 123, 124, 127, 130-1, 133, 134, 136, 140, 147, 152